HOW YOUR
MIND CAN HEAL
YOUR BODY

HOW YOUR MIND CAN HEAL YOUR BODY

DAVID R. HAMILTON PhD

HAY HOUSE

Australia • Canada • Hong Kong • India
South Africa • United Kingdom • United States

First published and distributed in the United Kingdom by:
Hay House UK Ltd, 292B Kensal Rd, London W10 5BE.
Tel.: (44) 20 8962 1230; Fax: (44) 20 8962 1239. www.hayhouse.co.uk

Published and distributed in the United States of America by:
Hay House, Inc., PO Box 5100, Carlsbad, CA 92018-5100.
Tel.: (1) 760 431 7695 or (800) 654 5126;
Fax: (1) 760 431 6948 or (800) 650 5115. www.hayhouse.com

Published and distributed in Australia by:
Hay House Australia Ltd, 18/36 Ralph St, Alexandria NSW 2015.
Tel.: (61) 2 9669 4299; Fax: (61) 2 9669 4144. www.hayhouse.com.au

Published and distributed in the Republic of South Africa by:
Hay House SA (Pty), Ltd, PO Box 990, Witkoppen 2068.
Tel./Fax: (27) 11 467 8904. www.hayhouse.co.za

Published and distributed in India by:
Hay House Publishers India, Muskaan Complex, Plot No.3, B-2,
Vasant Kunj, New Delhi – 110 070. Tel.: (91) 11 4176 1620;
Fax: (91) 11 4176 1630. www.hayhouse.co.in

Distributed in Canada by:
Raincoast, 9050 Shaughnessy St, Vancouver, BC V6P 6E5.
Tel.: (1) 604 323 7100; Fax: (1) 604 323 2600

A catalogue record for this book is available from the British Library.

ISBN 978-1-84850-023-5

Printed in the UK by CPI William Clowes Beccles NR34 7TL

To Ryan, Jake and Ellie.
You have brought huge amounts of joy to our family.

Nothing splendid has ever been achieved except by those who dared to believe that something inside of them was superior to circumstances.

Bruce Barton

Contents

Acknowledgements   ix

Introduction   xi

PART I: THE MIND CAN HEAL THE BODY   1

1   The Power of Positive Thinking   3

2   The Power of Believing   19

3   Drugs Work Because We Believe in Them   31

4   The Power of Plasticity   43

5   The Mind Can Heal the Body   51

6   The Power of Visualization   63

7   To Stress or Not to Stress   81

8   How to Visualize   91

9   The Power of Affirmations   107

PART II: TRUE STORIES   115

Introduction   117

10   Cancer   119

11   Heart   139

12   Regeneration   147

13   Pain, Chronic Fatigue and ME   155

14 Viruses, Allergies and Autoimmune Conditions   163
15 Weight Loss   179

PART III: IN CLOSING   183
16 The Power of Love   185

Appendix I: Quantum Field Healing (QFH)   199
Appendix II: Visualizations   211
Appendix III: DNA Visualizations   269
References   273

Acknowledgements

First, I'd like to thank my partner Elizabeth Caproni for her constant love and encouragement. Through Elizabeth I have come to believe in myself, and only from this space have I been able to write and speak at the level that I do.

From my earliest memories, my mum and dad have encouraged me to do what I want to do and to believe that I can. To Mum and Dad: this is me doing it! Thank you.

I wish to say a huge thanks to all the people who shared their personal stories in this book and to those who shared stories that did not make the final version. I believe that it's the telling of our stories that inspires other people. To those of you who shared your stories, whether they made the final version or not, by having the courage to do so, you have inspired many people to recognize that they also have the ability to heal themselves. Words cannot convey just how important a gift this is.

I would like to thank Kevin Doherty for the great job of editing this book and Lizzie Hutchins for expert guidance. And with this being my third book with Hay House, I would like to thank all the staff of Hay House UK, past and present, for their warmth and for helping me to feel such a part of the Hay House family.

I'd also like to thank my friend Kevin Waite for reading (twice) the first draft of this book, for making some important suggestions and also for creating some really great visualizations, all of which helped to bring this book into its final state.

I'd also like to thank my friend Bryce Redford for encouragement, inspiration and motivation.

I have sought clarification from experts in the field for some important points in this book. I would like to say thank you in particular to Barbara Andersen, Fabrizio Benedetti, Lyn Freeman and Stephanie Wai-Shan Louie for this and also for sending me important research information or pointing me towards relevant pieces that I was not aware of.

I spend a lot of my writing time in coffee shops and even refer to my most-visited coffee shops as my offices. So last but not least I would like to say thanks to the staff at Starbucks and Caffè Nero in Windsor, UK, for creating the perfect atmosphere for me to write.

Introduction

This is a book about using the mind to heal the body. After I wrote my first book, *It's the Thought that Counts*, which described the mind–body connection (and the mind–world connection), people began asking me how to use it to heal themselves. At talks I found myself explaining the how, and at workshops I found myself teaching it. At one of my workshops a lady asked if I was planning to write about it. I started writing this book the following day.

This book gives practical tools that you can use to heal a whole variety of medical conditions. About ten years ago it would be true to say that there was little medical evidence that the mind could heal the body, although there was plenty of evidence pointing towards it; but research published every other week now is building a considerably strong case that our previous assumptions and beliefs – that the mind could not heal the body – are just plain wrong.

Since 2006, visualization has shown positive results in stroke and spinal injury rehabilitation, as well as improving the movement of Parkinson's disease patients. Patients just use their minds to imagine moving normally and the moment they do this, the arm or leg that they imagine moving is stimulated at a microscopic level and the brain area that governs the arm or leg is also stimulated. The result is that over time their movement improves. In stroke cases, some damaged brain areas even begin to regenerate.

The placebo effect has shown us for years that the power of belief can influence the course of a whole range of medical conditions, including asthma, hay fever, infections, pain, Parkinson's disease, depression, congestive heart failure, angina, cholesterol levels, blood pressure, arthritis, chronic fatigue syndrome, athletic performance, weight loss, stomach ulcers and insomnia, and even that it could alter immune and growth hormone levels. And recent research has shown that when a person takes a placebo and believes it to be a real medicine, chemical changes occur in the brain on account of their belief. Now we know for certain – fact – that thoughts, emotions and beliefs are not just subjective ideas in the mind but cause real chemical and physical changes in the brain and throughout the body.

I have made some sizeable leaps in this book in suggesting that almost any illness can be healed using the mind, or at least that improvements can be made. I am aware that this is a big claim to make but I feel that when people's health is at stake, and indeed their lives, we can't always wait for science to catch up and publish research, maybe ten years later, showing that what many believe to be true – that the mind can heal the body – actually is true for that specific illness. People don't always have that long.

It would be more of a mistake for me to write that the mind can't heal the body, at least until the day science discovers that it can. We are barely scratching the surface in our understanding of real human potential. Einstein said, 'We still do not know one thousandth of one per cent of what nature has revealed to us.' I believe we need to entertain the real possibility that much of what we have not yet proven includes the ability of the mind to heal the body of almost anything.

Some might say that I'm giving people false hope, but I think that is a rather negative stance to take. The poet John Lydgate wrote, 'You can please some of the people all of the time and all of the people some of the time, but you can't please all of the people all of the time.' I'd rather give people hope and see them turn that into wellness than avoid inspiring them with possibilities because of the risk that some may not get the results.

I remember when I was a scientist in the pharmaceutical industry that I enjoyed looking at the plants in the office I shared with about 20 others. There must have been about 30 different plants, which helped to create a nice atmosphere. Many of them were small plants and they sat on the windowsill, which meant that they were the first things you saw when you entered the office in the morning. It was a pleasing sight.

One day, after I had been in that office for over a year, someone carelessly knocked one of the plants off the windowsill and it almost landed on their foot. It didn't, but it was classified as a 'near miss'. The next day a memo came around the whole department saying that from that day forward, no plants were to be allowed on the windowsill, in case they fell off and injured someone, and they never were for the remainder of my time there.

There was no need to ban small plants from the windowsill – a note to remind everyone to be more careful would have sufficed. I think that we can focus too much on the negatives at times and, especially with goals, we often don't shoot for the stars just in case it doesn't work out for us.

With this book, I have aimed for the stars. I believe that the majority of people will find something helpful in it, but I know that I can't please everyone. If you don't get results, please understand that my sincere motivation here is to help and I do really believe that we all have reservoirs of untapped potential within us.

I have always been a motivational type of person. When I was growing up I'd always be helping people to shoot for their goals and believe in themselves. In my twenties I became an athletics coach. Mostly there would be good, and often great, results. But occasionally people (observers) would level the criticism that I was giving people false hope, that it was best just to tell them to aim lower or to be 'realistic'. But what is realistic? It is someone's opinion. It is not fact.

But I have always understood where the critics were coming from, even though I didn't agree with them. I felt pain when I saw how sad a young triple jumper whom I coached was when he didn't jump as far as he wanted to in the 1999 UK National Junior League Athletics Final, especially when I'd instilled the belief in him that he could win the gold medal. But I think that without the belief, the chances of a gold medal were almost zero. With the belief, he really was capable of winning it.

Actually, with one of his jumps, which was a foul because the tip of his toe went one millimetre over the plasticine, he would have won the gold medal by over a foot. But I felt so sad for him because I could see that he was sorely disappointed that he hadn't performed as well as he wanted to. But without the belief, I am certain he would never even have made the final, let alone have been anywhere near the kind of jumper he was.

And so it is with using the mind to heal our bodies. I believe that when we aim high, even shoot for the stars with the hope that we can heal ourselves completely, then great things are possible. If we don't even try, then we will never know what was possible.

Mark Twain wrote, 'Dance like nobody's watching; love like you've never been hurt. Sing like nobody's listening; live like it's heaven on earth.'

And using the mind to heal is not new. People have been using their minds to heal themselves for thousands of years. Vedic teachings over 3000 years old, for instance, refer to the use of the mind for healing through meditation.

So, from the space of my belief that the mind can impact almost any condition, I have included an A–Z list of medical conditions, illnesses and diseases at the end of the book and suggested one or more visualizations that could be used to heal or positively affect each one.

My research into the power of the mind over the past 26 years (I read my first book on the topic, *The Magic Power of the Mind* by Walter M. Germain, when I was 12) has shown me that people intuitively know how to heal themselves. We know that we need to become calm and rid ourselves of stress. We also know that we need to develop a positive attitude. But we also need to know the right practical visualization principles.

As confirmation of this, I've collected several stories from people all around the world who have healed themselves of serious illnesses like cancer and diabetes, and not-so-serious conditions like hay fever and pain. As I read through them I was astonished to notice a striking similarity. The people used the same principles, which they just seemed to intuitively know, and these were the principles that I had also been teaching and that I also seemed to intuitively know. The first part of the book reveals these principles and you can see them in action in the second part.

The book is in three parts. The first part outlines research in the rapidly emerging field of mind–body science. I have included evidence for the power of positive thinking and the placebo effect, the most up-to-date research into how our thoughts and emotions cause micro-changes in the brain, and cutting-edge research into using the mind to heal the body.

Part II of the book contains people's stories of healing. These kind people have shared how they used their mind to heal themselves of various diseases. They have described the images they used and how often they visualized. Their hope is that their personal journeys may inspire other people to believe that they can be healed too, as well as provide them with some practical information on how to go about it.

Part III of the book is the shortest section, but in many ways the most powerful, and talks about the power of love. I have always been a believer that love heals.

The book also has three appendices. The first is a healing technique that I call 'Quantum Field Healing' (QFH), the second is a list of medical conditions and visualizations for their healing, and the third is two DNA visualizations.

Throughout the book I recommend that if you decide to use visualization you should continue any treatment that you are currently receiving. What I'm saying is that visualization should be used *as well*. My premise for this is that when we are receiving medication, we must think. So we will have thoughts. This book provides direction for those thoughts and suggests what you could think *about* to aid your recovery.

I hope you enjoy the book and that you can take something positive from it.

Warm wishes.

David Hamilton
November 2008

PART I

THE MIND CAN
HEAL THE BODY

The Power of Positive Thinking

A pessimist sees the difficulty in every opportunity; an optimist sees the opportunity in every difficulty.
Winston Churchill

Optimists live longer than pessimists! That's the conclusion of a 30-year study involving 447 people that was conducted by scientists at the Mayo Clinic. They found that optimists had around a 50% lower risk of early death than pessimists and wrote that '...mind and body are linked and attitude has an impact on the final outcome – death'. A startling statistic! Optimists were also found to have fewer physical and emotional health problems, less pain and increased energy, and they generally felt more peaceful, happier and calmer than the pessimists.

A 2004 study published in the journal *Archives of General Psychiatry* found a similar thing. It concluded that there is a '...protective relationship between ... optimism and all-cause mortality in old age'. Optimism protects you from illness.

The scientists studied the responses given by 999 Dutch men and women between the ages of 65 and 85 to a range of statements, including:

'I often feel that life is full of promises,'
'I still have positive expectations concerning my future,'
'There are many moments of happiness in my life,'
'I do not make any more future plans,'
'Happy laughter often occurs,'
'I still have many goals to strive for,'

and:

'Most of the time I am in good spirits.'

The results were startling. Those who showed high levels of optimism, who would perhaps respond affirmatively to the first question, had a 45% lower risk of death from any cause and a 77% lower risk of death from heart disease than those who reported high levels of pessimism.

Another study examined the autobiographies of 180 Catholic nuns that were written when the nuns first entered a convent. Scientists examined the autobiographies 60 years later and discovered that the nuns who wrote more positively when they first entered the convent lived much longer than their colleagues whose writing was more negative.

One of the reasons that a positive attitude is so important is because it boosts our immune systems and therefore our ability to fight illness. In a 2006 study conducted at Carnegie Mellon University, scientists studied the effects of common cold and influenza viruses on people with different attitudes. One hundred and ninety-three healthy volunteers were interviewed to determine the levels of positive or negative feelings that they felt in their lives. Then they were exposed to either of the viruses using nasal drops. It turned out that positive people were much more resistant to the viruses than negative people.

As we go through our lives, our attitudes affect how we react to viruses, bacteria and other pathogens. A positive, optimistic outlook on life is ultimately best for our overall health and longevity.

We also deal with life situations differently depending upon our attitude to them. A positive attitude helps us to cope with challenges and even see them as opportunities, which ultimately benefits our health.

A University of Chicago study examined the attitude and health of 200 telecommunications executives who had been affected by corporate downsizing. It found that the executives who saw the downsizing as an opportunity for growth were healthier than those who saw it as a threat. Of those with the positive attitude, less than one-third developed an illness during or shortly after the downsizing. But of those with a negative attitude, over 90% became ill. In other words, looking at the same event as positive or negative has a hugely different effect upon health.

Some of the best-studied effects of attitude show that it powerfully affects the heart. One such study, involving 586 people and conducted by scientists at Johns Hopkins University, found that a positive attitude was the best prevention against heart disease.

In 2003, scientists at Duke University Medical Center, on examining 866 heart patients, discovered that the patients who routinely felt more positive emotions (e.g. happiness, joy and optimism) had about a 20% greater chance of being alive 11 years later than those who experienced more negative emotions.

And in a 2007 study, Harvard scientists studied the effects of 'emotional vitality', which was defined as 'a sense of positive energy, an ability to regulate emotions and behaviour, and a feeling of engagement in life'. The study involved 6265 volunteers and found that those who had high levels of emotional vitality were 19% less likely to develop coronary heart disease than those with lower levels.

HARD MARRIAGE, HARD HEART

The above title is taken from a scientific review paper that discussed a 2006 study by scientists at the University of Utah which had found that the attitudes of married couples profoundly impacted their hearts.

The scientists videotaped 150 married couples discussing marital topics and categorized them according to how they related to each other. They found that the couples who were most supportive of each another had healthier hearts. And the couples who were most hostile towards each other had more hardening of their arteries. Hard marriage, hard heart!

Being supportive of another person is much better for health than holding anger and bitterness and constantly criticizing them.

In some research, hostility is defined as evading a question and as irritation and direct and indirect challenges to a person asking a question. Other research defines it as an attitude of cynical beliefs and lack of trust in other people. Yet others define it as being aggressive and challenging. In one 25-year study that used these types of definition as a criterion to determine hostility levels, the people who were most hostile had five times more incidents of coronary heart disease than those who were least hostile and more trusting of people, accepting and gentle.

The connection between attitude and the heart is so reliable that a 30-year study published in 2003 in the *Journal of the American Medical Association* concluded that '...hostility is one of the most reliable indicators of coronary heart disease risk.'

Scientists can quite accurately calculate a person's risk of heart disease by examining their diet and lifestyle – what kinds of foods they eat, how much exercise they get, whether they smoke or drink lots of alcohol. People with a high fat and cholesterol diet, who don't exercise much and who smoke and drink lots of alcohol are usually most at risk. But scientists can just as accurately calculate the risk based upon attitude – whether people have a positive or negative attitude or how hostile they are towards others. The good news is that just as you can change your diet and lifestyle, you can change your attitude. It's up to you.

Of course circumstances in life might be so testing that it is inevitable that we become 'hardened' to some extent, but we still have a choice, no matter what. I am deeply inspired by the story of Viktor Frankl, a survivor of the Nazi concentration camp in Auschwitz. In his 9 million-copy best-selling book, *Man's Search for Meaning*, he writes,

> *We who lived in concentration camps can remember the men who walked through huts comforting others, giving away their last slice of bread. They may have been few in number, but they offer sufficient proof that everything can be taken from a man but one thing: the last of the human freedoms – to choose one's attitude in any given set of circumstances, to choose one's own way.*

Frankl's words are a message of hope that no matter what, our attitude is our choice. If we search deep within ourselves, we can always make the highest choice, the one from the softest heart, the one that helps other people to find comfort and happiness; and, in so doing, the one that makes us healthier.

SATISFACTION

A study of 22,461 people by scientists from the University of Kuopio in Finland found that the people who were most satisfied with their lives lived longer. They defined life satisfaction as 'an interest in life, happiness and a general ease of living'. Reporting in the *American Journal of Epidemiology* in 2000, they found that the men who were most dissatisfied with life were more than three times as likely to die of disease than those who were most satisfied.

It's not so much what happens to us in life that determines our health and happiness. It's what we do with what happens that matters most. If you live in a nice house but you see someone with a nicer house, do you feel dissatisfied that your house is not good enough or do you give more thought to what you love about your own home and the people who share it with you?

It is said that the grass is always greener, but if you notice your own grass and don't pay so much attention to other grasses, then you will experience more happiness and better health in life. It's what *you* focus on that matters most. It's *your* attitude that counts.

TO COMPLAIN OR NOT TO COMPLAIN

How often do you complain? In his inspiring book *A Complaint Free World*, Will Bowen encourages us to take up the challenge to go 21 days without complaining. That means to refrain from complaining, criticizing or unfairly judging. He encourages us to wear a purple wristband and to change it to the other wrist every time we complain.

It's an eye-opener. Most people initially have to move it more than 20 times a day. It's great for making you aware of just how you behave. But after a short time, people find it quite easy to go four or five days without making a single complaint. That's a huge difference and, as far as I am concerned, a great boost to their health.

Complaining about things and criticizing people has become a way of life for so many of us that we don't even notice how often we do it. It's a habit. And we rarely complain about the truth of things, only how they seem to us. The same thing may mean something completely different to someone else. For instance, say a delivery you were expecting didn't arrive. You complain that this has ruined your day, setting back your entire schedule. You stress yourself, creating untold negative effects on your body. Someone else with a late delivery might decide that there's something else they can be getting on with and (from personal experience) might find the delay turns out to be for the best. Is the delay actually a good or a bad thing? That's up to you. But what you decide matters for your health.

Complaining even affects the people around us. We rarely notice this, but we're like tuning forks. When you hit the fork, other things nearby resonate with it. This is also what happens when we consistently complain around people – we trigger their complaints too. All of a sudden they too are inspired to find fault with life and the world. Complaining becomes a bacterium that we carry around with us, infecting most people that we encounter.

Our thoughts and attitudes inspire our actions, and our actions create our world. So our thoughts and attitudes create our world. What kind of world do you choose? This is Will Bowen's sentiment in his book. If we stop complaining then we can get to work on creating a better world. And we are doing something positive for the health of our bodies at the same time.

Instead of complaining, try to focus on what you're grateful for. Gratitude begets gratitude. The more things you focus on that you are grateful for, the more things you notice and experience that you can be grateful for. And it's good for your heart.

MONEY BUYS HAPPINESS WHEN YOU SPEND IT ON OTHERS

This was the title of a press release issued on 20 March 2008 by the University of British Columbia in Canada. It describes research showing that people who give money away are happier than those who spend it all on themselves.

The research was conducted by scientists from the University of British Columbia and published in 2008 in the journal *Science*. The results showed that people who spent some of their money 'pro-socially', that is, they spent it on gifts for others or on charitable donations rather than on themselves, were happier.

The research involved 632 people who were asked to rate their general happiness and give a breakdown of their monthly income and spending (including bills, gifts for others, gifts for themselves and donations to charities). The authors reported that, 'Regardless of how much income each person made, those who spent money on others reported greater happiness, while those who spent more on themselves did not.'

The happiest people were the ones who gave money away. This lies contrary to what most people think – that we need to keep all of our money for ourselves 'in case', and that the more we accumulate, the happier we will be. But it needn't be large sums that we give away.

To test this theory, the scientists gave 46 volunteers either $5 or $20 and asked them to spend it by 5 p.m. that day. Half were asked to spend the money on themselves and the other half were asked to spend it on others. The people who spent the money on others reported feeling happier at the end of the day than those who spent it on themselves. The scientists said, 'These findings suggest that very minor alterations in spending allocations – as little as $5 – may be enough to produce real gains in happiness on a given day.'

Why not decide to give something away today, to whomever you wish and in whatever way you wish?

Many other studies have found that, even though our income and disposable income are higher than they were for our grandparents 50 years ago, we are not any happier. In fact, some polls have found that people nowadays are less happy than people were 50 years ago.

The British Columbia research shows that the level of income isn't as important as what we do with our income. Earning a small salary but showing generosity with it leads to greater happiness than earning millions and spending it all on yourself. Money is not the issue. You can be rich and be happy and you can be poor and be happy. Happiness lies in what you do with what you have. It's down to you!

Indeed, in one aspect of the research, the scientists measured the levels of happiness of 16 employees at a Boston company after they had received profit-sharing bonuses of between $3000 and $8000. The researchers found that happiness was independent of the size of the bonus, but a product of what the recipients did with it. The employees who spent more of it on presents for others and gifts to charity were happier than those who spent it all on themselves.

BEING POSITIVE ABOUT GETTING OLDER

Attitude affects how fast we age. In fact, positive people live longer! That's the conclusion of some research conducted by scientists at Yale University who studied the responses of 660 people to a series of questions about attitude such as 'As you get older, you are less useful. Agree or disagree?' Those who generally disagreed with these types of statements, and therefore had the most positive attitudes about ageing, lived about seven and a half years longer than those who agreed and therefore had the most negative attitudes about ageing.

And just as attitude affects the heart, the Yale scientists even concluded that attitude was more influential than blood pressure, cholesterol levels, smoking, body weight and exercise levels in how long a person lived.

And a 2006 University of Texas study that examined 2564 Mexican Americans over the age of 65 found that positive emotions reduced blood pressure.

In 2004, scientists from the University of Texas even found that frailty was linked with attitude. They studied 1558 older people from the Mexican-American community and to determine levels of frailty they measured weight loss, exhaustion, walking speed and grip strength. Over time, they found that the people with the most positive attitudes were less likely to become frail.

And in a similar result to the satisfaction study reported earlier, a 2006 study into satisfaction found that people over the age of 80 lived longer if they were satisfied with their lives. Publishing in the *Journal of Gerontology*, scientists from the University of Jyväskylä in Finland examined 320 volunteers who filled out a 'Life Satisfaction' questionnaire. They found that those who were most satisfied had half the risk of death over the next ten years of those who were least satisfied.

Essentially, if you have a positive attitude and keep your mind and body active, you stay healthier for longer and when you do get sick you recover faster. Your mental and physical abilities also stay with you longer. That's the conclusion of much of the research currently looking at the relationship between attitude and the ageing process. We don't need to age as fast as we think we do.

Many people cling to the idea that the brain and body decline with age and use it to explain why they forget some things, why they sometimes can't think clearly and why they feel stiff when they get up. OK, the brain and body do change. But how fast they change is something that we have an impact upon.

DEVELOPING A YOUNGER BRAIN

A recent study by scientists from Posit Science Corporation, a company specializing in brain training, showed that age-related mental decline is actually reversible. Lack of use is the main cause of mental and physical decline. 'Use it or lose it' is an applicable term. If you stop using a muscle, it atrophies and becomes weaker. If you keep using it, it becomes stronger. And even if you have lost muscle through not using it, an exercise regime will restore some, or a lot, of its function. The same is true with mental functions. If we use our brain, even when we are older, it works better.

For the study, the scientists designed a training programme that improved neural plasticity, which is the ability of the brain to grow. As you'll see later in the book, the brain is not a hard-wired lump of matter, as was once believed, but something that is constantly changing in response to our experiences.

Publishing in *Proceedings of the National Academy of Sciences, USA*, the scientists reported that elderly adults gained a substantial improvement in memory after doing the training. The study involved volunteers between the ages of 60 and 87 taking part in an eight-to-ten-week auditory memory programme that involved listening to sounds for one hour a day, five days a week. At the end of the programme their memories had improved so much that they were performing like adults aged 40–60 instead of adults aged 60–87. Their mental abilities had improved by around 20 years!

Scientists from Harvard conducted a novel experiment in 1989. They took volunteers over the age of 70 to a retreat centre and asked them to act as though it was 1959 for a week. The environment in the centre was a recreation of 1959. Music from 1959 was played, there were magazines from 1959, the volunteers wore 1950s clothing and the TV even showed taped shows from the 1950s. The volunteers also had to converse with each other as if it was 1959, discussing topics and current affairs of the time.

At the start the scientists took a host of physiological measurements, including height, finger length, strength, mental cognition and eyesight. After ten days in the centre, they took those measurements again and discovered that the volunteers had got physiologically younger by several years just by acting as though they were younger. They grew taller, their fingers grew longer, they had improved mental functions and their eyesight had improved. Some of the volunteers had become mentally and physiologically younger by 25 years.

This shows that how we use our brain and how often we use it really matters. When we are younger we are constantly engaged in mental activities. As we go through our adult lives we use our brains less and less. In the early stages of our professional lives we are still highly active, but over time we gradually become less mentally active, just as we gradually become less physically active. But we don't need to. We just need to find other things to do. Many of the people who have lived healthy lives way into their nineties have been mentally active right up until their final days.

Recent research in neuroscience has found that one of the best ways to exercise our brains as adults is to learn a new language. We don't need to speak it fluently or even visit the country whose language we are learning (although we may be motivated to once we can speak a little of it), we only need to use our brains to learn the language. Research has shown that doing so can actually reduce the risk of Alzheimer's. A study published in the

Journal of the American Medical Association found that, 'On average, a person reporting frequent cognitive activity ... was 47% less likely to develop Alzheimer's disease than a person with infrequent activity.'

Many adults believe so much that the brain has to significantly decline with age that they enter into a self-reinforcing spiral – like a negative placebo effect – that alters how they behave. They start to behave like elderly people instead of remaining young at heart. But part of this attitude comes from looking at people around them and how they behave. Some of our friends and colleagues may act older, but in other places other people of the same age act younger. How we act should reflect how we feel, not how we think we're supposed to.

We have come to believe in ageing so much that how we think we are supposed to act is deeply imprinted on our psyche. Some authors have pointed out, however, that ageing is cultural. We age at the rate we believe we're supposed to, due to misunderstanding about ageing, prejudices and folklore. In the audio programme *Magical Mind, Magical Body*, Deepak Chopra MD said, 'One of the things that is becoming very clear about the ageing process is that what we consider normal ageing may be a premature cognitive commitment...We, as a species, get committed to a certain reality of ageing.'

An interesting study published in the *Journal of Personality and Social Psychology* showed this. It involved people who were given a list of words with which they were asked to make up sentences. But there were actually two lists. Some of the people had a few extra words added to theirs: 'old', 'grey', 'wrinkle', 'bingo' and 'lonely' – words that are associated with being old. It was called a 'priming' experiment, because people were primed with specific words.

After each person finished their session they had to walk out of the room and down the corridor to reach the exit. One of the scientists was sitting outside the testing room and inconspicuously timed how long it took each person to walk down the corridor to a mark that was placed on the floor.

The people who used the normal set of words took 7.30 seconds on average to reach the mark. The people who were primed with 'old', 'grey', 'wrinkle', 'bingo' and 'lonely' took 8.28 seconds – 13.4% longer. They also walked more slowly, like an older person would, and closer examination would probably have revealed hunched shoulders and maybe one or two people rubbing aching body parts from having sat on a chair for so long while they did the test.

One of the things that this study shows is that a degree of ageing is all in the mind. So act how you feel, not how you think you're supposed to.

The comedian Billy Connolly had me in fits of laughter once. He said that he knew he was getting older when he started to get up from his seat and caught himself making the sound 'Ooooohhh.' We sometimes do this out of habit, or just because others do it. We unconsciously pick up on their actions and behave the way we're 'supposed' to. I noticed one of my nephews do it once when he was four years old and a few of the adults around him had just got up from their seats. I had to give him the positive reinforcement that he was really fit (much fitter than the 'old people') because he could spring up from his seat without making any noise. He never did it again.

In another priming experiment, conducted by scientists from North Carolina State University and published in 2004 in the journal *Psychology and Aging*, 153 people were asked to do memory tests after being primed with certain words. Some were primed with the words 'confused', 'cranky', 'feeble' and 'senile' and others with the words 'accomplished', 'active', 'dignified' and 'distinguished'. When they then did memory tests, older adults primed with the 'old' words fared much worse than the ones primed with the more positive words. The scientists wrote that '...if older people are treated like they are competent, productive members of society, then they perform that way too'.

It's not just our own attitudes and how we treat ourselves that are important, but also how we treat other people. If you treat someone like an old infirm person, as well as it probably annoying them when you speak to them as if they're a child, it can gradually erode their spirit and cause them to start believing that how you treat them is how they should be.

It is my opinion that if people believe that they should still be fit and active in their nineties and if, when we are younger, we treat older people as holders of wisdom, life experience and stories, then there will be many more people in society who are mentally and physically active in their eighties and nineties than we currently see. It's really up to us.

Attitude is everything, they say. I think it really is. If we learn to see the positive side of things then we will live longer, healthier, happier lives. A good way to do this is to stop complaining and start to be grateful.

In the next chapter we will see how what we believe can be so powerful that it can affect our ability to heal illness.

The Power of Believing

*The outer conditions of a person's life will always be found
to reflect their inner beliefs.*

James Allen

What if scientists discovered a new drug that could cure or
improve the symptoms of most known diseases – just one pill!
Wouldn't it make headline news all around the world and become
the greatest-selling drug of all time? Such a thing already exists.
Let me introduce to you: the placebo!

A placebo is a dummy drug that is made to look just like a real
drug. It is used in medical trials so that the drug can be tested
against a control. Being a control, it is not supposed to heal – but
it does, because patients believe that it's a real drug. Their mind
heals them.

*The placebo effect has evolved from being thought of as a
nuisance in clinical pharmacological research to a biological
phenomenon worthy of scientific investigation in its own right.*

These are the words of Fabrizio Benedetti, a neuroscience professor at the University of Turin School of Medicine, a world authority on the placebo effect and a member of the Placebo Study Group of the Mind/Brain/Behaviour initiative at Harvard University.

Since the advent of brain-imaging technology, there has been a surge of interest in the placebo effect. Research now shows that when we believe that we are taking a drug but it's really a placebo, the brain lights up as if we really were taking the drug and produces its own natural chemicals.

This has recently been shown with Parkinson's disease. The symptoms of Parkinson's disease arise from impaired production of a substance called dopamine in part of the brain. This affects movement. Research has shown that Parkinson's patients given a placebo but told that it is an anti-Parkinson's drug are able to move better. Brain scans have even shown that the brain is activated in the area that controls movement and dopamine is actually produced. The improved movement is not just a 'psychological' thing. It is a physical release of dopamine in the brain.

CHEMICALS IN THE BRAIN

The production of chemicals in the brain when a person takes a placebo was first proven in 1978 when scientists at the University of California at San Francisco showed that placebo analgesia (when a person gets pain relief from a placebo) occurs because the brain produces its own natural analgesics (painkillers). It was found that these were opiates, like morphine, but that they were the body's own natural versions of morphine, which are referred to as *endogenous* opiates. More modern research is beginning to show that the same kind of thing happens when placebos are given for any condition – the brain produces a natural drug that's tailor-made to combat the illness.

There are thousands of natural substances in the brain and body. In the words of Dawson Church, author of *The Genie in Your Genes*,

> *Each of us holds the keys to a pharmacy containing a dazzling array of healing compounds: our own brain… Our brains are themselves generating drugs similar to those that the doctor is prescribing for us.*

In a 2005 scientific paper published in the *Journal of Neuroscience* Fabrizio Benedetti wrote, '…placebo effects seen with different treatments are more likely to track closely with the active treatment to which they are experimentally paired.'

In other words, if a person is given a drug to treat a condition and then it is secretly swapped for a placebo, the chemicals produced are believed to be natural versions of the drug that was originally used. If it is a painkilling drug, the brain produces natural painkillers. Similarly, studies on depression suggest that the brain produces natural antidepressants.

Brain scans have now shown that taking a placebo in place of the antidepressant fluoxetine (Prozac), for instance, affects most of the same brain areas as the actual drug.

The brain always produces its *own* drugs. This is mind over matter at the molecular level.

No longer can the placebo effect be dismissed as just a figment of people's imagination – just 'all in the mind'. When you believe something, chemicals are produced in your brain and they carry out powerful roles that give you exactly what you believe should happen.

Chemicals are produced *because* of a state of mind.

AS YOU BELIEVE

The placebo effect is often quoted at 35%, meaning that it works 35% of the time. But this is a very broad generalisation. It actually varies greatly depending upon the illness, the nature of the medical trial and even the personality of the doctors giving the medicine – and of course the desire of the patient to get better and how much they believe that they will get better. It has been known to vary from as low as 10% to as high as 100% in some studies. The higher figures indicate that the capacity for healing is within us. In some placebo studies, that ability has been tapped into more than it has in others.

A lot of placebo research has focused on pain. In one Canadian study that used heat pain, more than 70% of people had relief from their pain after they took a placebo. And MRI brain scans showed a reduction in activity in regions of the brain that are pain-responsive.

Placebo effects are very common and usually high with heart medicines. Many scientists believe that this is due to the strong brain–heart link. In 2007 a drug company reported results of a trial for a new drug for congestive heart failure. Tests showed that the drug improved the condition of 66% of patients, which is very good. But the placebo improved 51% of patients.

In a 1988 trial of the drug acyclovir as a possible treatment for chronic fatigue syndrome (CFS) conducted by scientists at the National Institute of Allergy and Infectious Diseases in the USA, 46% of people improved on the drug and 42% on the placebo. In a 1996 study trialling the steroid hydrocortisone as a possible treatment for CFS, 50% of people improved on the placebo. One woman in her thirties with severe CFS who was 'very significantly impaired', had 'no energy, couldn't work and spent most of her time at home' showed a remarkable recovery after receiving placebos.

Results like these don't mean than the disease is not real, as some people believe, but that we have the ability to develop a state of mind that can heal it.

In a 1997 study of drugs to treat benign enlargement of the prostate gland, more than half of the men on the study had a significant reduction of their symptoms after receiving placebos.

Research has even shown that the same substance can act as both a placebo and a nocebo (the nocebo effect is the opposite of the placebo effect, where a patient develops negative symptoms). In a 1969 paper published in *Psychosomatic Medicine*, 40 asthmatics were given an inhaler containing a placebo (water vapour) but were told that it contained allergens that would cause bronchoconstriction (constriction of the airways). Nineteen of them (48%) then suffered considerable constriction of their airways, with 12 of the group experiencing full-blown asthma attacks. When they were then given another inhaler and told that it would relieve their symptoms, it did, even though it also contained a placebo.

One person in the study was told that the inhaler contained pollen. She then swiftly developed hay fever as well as airway constriction. In a second experiment she was told that the inhaler just contained allergens but no pollen. This time she only developed asthma symptoms. In a third experiment she was again told the inhaler contained pollen and once again she developed hay fever as well as asthma.

PERFORMANCE-ENHANCING PLACEBOS

A 2007 placebo study described an experiment that simulated an athletics competition involving non-professional athletes who had regularly been given morphine in training (for the study). But on the day of competition the morphine was secretly swapped for a placebo. When they competed, the athletes' performances were at the same level as would have occurred had they actually taken morphine. In other words, athletes can run just as well naturally as they can when taking performance-enhancing drugs. The body naturally produces its own drugs, although they are not drugs in the anabolic steroids sense but natural substances that help us to perform at a high level.

A 2007 study conducted at Harvard University even found that people who get the same level of exercise receive different benefits from it depending on whether they believe it's good exercise or not.

The study involved 84 hotel-room maids whose job actually provided enough exercise to exceed the US Surgeon General's recommendation for daily exercise. However, the women didn't know this and most didn't see themselves as physically active. When the Harvard scientists surveyed them, they learned that 56 of the women didn't believe that they got any exercise at all. So they split the women into two groups. With one group, the scientists went through with the women all of the activities that they did during the day, from lugging heavy equipment around, vacuuming and changing bedsheets to general cleaning, and explained how many calories each activity burned. Then they told the women that their daily activities exceeded the Surgeon General's recommendations. They didn't tell the other group anything.

After a month, the scientists took physical measurements of the women. The group who now knew that they were getting good exercise had lost weight and there was a decrease in their waist-to-hip ratio, body mass index and body fat percentage and a 10% reduction in their blood pressure. It's a powerful thing, the mind!

The things that you believe even affect your academic performance. A 2006 study published in the journal *Science* examined the mathematics scores of 220 female students who had read one of two different fake research reports. Half read one report and the other half read the other one. In one it was claimed that scientists had discovered genes on the Y chromosome (that only men have) that gave men a 5% advantage over females in mathematics. The other fake paper claimed that men had a 5% advantage only because of the way teachers stereotyped girls and boys at an early age.

When the students were tested, the group who believed that the difference was just stereotyping, and therefore that they were just as good at mathematics as men were, did much better than those who thought that they had a genetic disadvantage.

THE POWER OF POSITIVE CONSULTATION

The placebo effect is often seen as a nuisance in medical trials. Therefore some companies try to remove it in an attempt to get a more accurate picture of how well the drug works. But things don't always go to plan.

In a typical trial, patients are given either a drug or a placebo. The ones who improve on placebo are called 'placebo responders' and are then removed from the trial. A new trial then begins that doesn't have any known placebo responders. But some studies have shown that if, say, 35% of people improve on placebo in the first trial, then in the second one, even though the placebo responders have been removed, a new 35% of patients still respond to the placebo.

This is a total enigma for many companies who set up the trials. But the reason for this result in these trials lies in the only factor that hasn't changed between the two studies – the doctors! They still say the same things and communicate with the same enthusiasm from one study to the next. What they say, how they say it, their enthusiasm for the treatment and how they relate to the people receiving it matters a lot.

For example, in a 1954 study, patients with bleeding ulcers were given water injections but told either that the injections would cure them or that they were being given experimental injections of undetermined effectiveness. Of the patients who were told that the injections would cure them, 70% showed excellent improvement, but of the group who were told that it was an experimental injection, only 25% improved.

In another study, Fabrizio Benedetti tested the effects of a hidden placebo on arm pain. When a placebo was secretly given through a saline drip, the pain level didn't change. But when the placebo injection was given in full view of the patients and they were told, 'I am going to give you a painkiller. Your pain will subside after some minutes. Be calm and comfortable and report your pain sensation during the next minutes,' the pain diminished.

In a 1978 study involving dental injections, patients were given either an 'oversell' message about a placebo tablet they received before an injection in the mouth where the dentists made the drug sound really great or an 'undersell' message where the dentists made out that the drug might or might not work. The patients who had the oversell message had much less pain when they had their injection, as well as less anxiety and fear, than the patients who were given the undersell message.

And in a 1987 *British Medical Journal* paper titled 'General practice consultations: is there any point in being positive?' 200 patients were given either a positive consultation or a negative one (for minor ailments). In the positive consultations, the patients were told what was wrong and that they would be better in a few days. In the negative consultations, the doctor told the patients that they weren't certain what was wrong. Two weeks later, 53% of all the patients had got better – but 64% of those who had a positive consultation reported that they were better compared with only 39% of the negative consultation patients. The 'power of positive consultation' was almost twice as good as the power of a negative one.

Knowing how enthusiastic to be in conveying a message can be a challenge for today's doctors. On the one hand, they know that what they say counts, but on the other hand they have to be responsible in conveying the truth about what the drugs have been proven to do, including their limits. But what they say clearly matters, as does how they say it. Current research clearly shows that empathy, warmth and authority, as well as enthusiasm and confidence, have a considerable effect. More research is needed to permit the doctors more freedom in what they can and can't say, as well as in what is the most effective way to say something. But it's up to you what you believe. The power lies within you.

THE POWER OF OPTIMISM

Although these results point to the power of the doctor's personality, the personality of the patient also affects how they receive the message and therefore how well the placebo works for them.

Between 2005 and 2007, scientists at the University of Toledo in Ohio compared the responses of optimists and pessimists to placebos. Over a series of experiments, they gave the optimists and pessimists a tablet (placebo) and told them that it would make them feel unwell. The pessimists responded more and felt more unwell than the optimists. Then the scientists gave optimists and pessimists a placebo sleep treatment and told them that it would make them sleep better. This time, the optimists responded more and slept better than the pessimists.

Optimists are more likely to benefit from something that is going to make them better, while pessimists are more likely to respond to something that is supposed to make them worse. The key to healing lies within us.

CONDITIONING – BOOSTING THE POWER OF THE PLACEBO

We can boost the power of the placebo. It is called conditioning. In a typical conditioning experiment, scientists give a patient a real drug for a couple of days and then secretly swap it for a placebo the next day. Of course, the patient doesn't suspect anything, so when they receive their 'medicine' (actually the placebo) they expect to get the usual level of relief that they've been getting during the past few days when they were taking the actual drug. And they do. They have been 'conditioned' to believe that each injection or tablet will work, just as Pavlov's dogs were conditioned to salivate when they heard a bell ring.

Studies suggest that the longer conditioning is carried out, the more powerful the effect; the deeper into the body's systems the mind can penetrate, the more powerful the placebo becomes. In some conditioning experiments the placebo effect has been boosted to 100%.

In one experiment, scientists gave volunteers a flavoured drink containing a chemical called 'cyclosporin A' that suppressed the immune system. Each time the volunteers took the drink, their immune systems weakened. After several days the scientists swapped the drink for one that didn't have any 'cyclosporin A' in it, but the volunteers still developed weakened immune systems. If, on the first day, the scientists had given the patient a drink and told them that it would weaken their immune system, it wouldn't have as much of an effect. The placebo effect would have been less.

Similarly, in one experiment conducted by Benedetti where volunteers were given a placebo and were told that it was a drug that would reduce pain, it reduced pain levels. But when the scientists told the volunteers that it would increase growth hormone levels it had no effect.

To alter growth hormone levels, the scientists needed to boost the power of the placebo. They conditioned subjects with a substance known as 'sumatriptan', which is known to boost growth hormone levels. After a few days of taking sumatriptan, which resulted in increased growth hormone levels, the patients secretly received a placebo instead. Yet their growth hormone levels still increased.

On the first day the placebo had no effect, but, through conditioning, the mind had associated taking sumatriptan with changed hormone levels, even though the subjects weren't consciously aware of the changes.

The brain contains trillions of neural circuits that are linked to every part of the body. We condition our neural circuits to fire over and over again, so that when we take a pill or have an injection, even though it is a placebo, the same circuits fire as when we took the drug because our unconscious awareness associates the pill or injection with immune or hormonal changes, as the last two studies showed.

If we tried to consciously affect our immune systems or growth hormone levels (without any knowledge of how to do it), we wouldn't have much success. Conditioning boosts the power of placebos or the power of the mind. It allows us to change systems in the body that we wouldn't ordinarily be able to. It shows that we have considerable power to heal ourselves using our minds. We just need to tap into that power.

Later in the book we will learn that we can alter the body's systems another way and thus boost the power of the mind through repetitive visualization of a healing process.

Drugs Work Because
We Believe in Them

Believe none of what you hear and half of what you see.
Benjamin Franklin

Some drugs never make it to the marketplace because trials show that they are no better than placebos. In some cases their effectiveness is low, but in other cases their effectiveness is high. It just so happens that the placebo effect is high too. Thus a drug that might be quite good is deemed ineffective. But completely missed in these examples is the power of the placebo – the power of the minds of the people who receive the drugs in the trials.

This is often the case with antidepressant medications. Some of the world's best-selling antidepressant drugs have been deemed ineffective because new evidence has shown that most of their power is due to the placebo effect.

In a 2008 meta-analysis (a summary of many studies) of fluoxetine (Prozac), venlafaxine (Effexor), nefazodone (Serzone), and paroxetine (Seroxat), covering 35 clinical trials involving 5133 patients, the placebo effect was shown to account for 81%

of the effect of the drugs. The only significant difference between the drug and placebo existed for severely depressed patients. With such a high placebo effect it is impossible to prove that the drugs actually work. They probably do, but the studies show that we have a much greater ability to heal ourselves than we'd ordinarily think. The fact that millions of people all over the world have benefited from one or more of these drugs demonstrates the immense power of the human mind.

It might be that one of the ways that antidepressant placebos work is that they give people hope. Thus a placebo can do the same job. The patient feels some relief at the knowledge that something might work and this positive expectation is enough to trump some of the depressive feelings, particularly when the medication is taken every day. In a sense, it is like being given a positive expectation of hope every day. But hope comes from within. It is something that we have according to what we believe. Thus the power to heal lies not just in hope, but in our ability to have hope.

We can put our hope or faith in anything or anyone and it can heal us. But the key to harnessing the power of the mind is to recognize that it is what we focus upon that matters, what we think and believe. And this comes from within us.

We unconsciously place hope or faith in things all the time, things that have meaning for us. But note, once again, that it is the *meaning* that we give these things that causes healing, not the things themselves. The power lies in each of us.

THE MEANING EFFECT

In his excellent book *Meaning, Medicine and the 'Placebo Effect'*, anthropology professor Daniel Moerman, another member of Harvard's Placebo Study Group, calls many placebo effects 'meaning responses'. He calls them this because it's the meaning that the patient gives the treatment that heals them. In other words, much of the power to heal lies in our own perception of a medicine or treatment.

In his book, Professor Moerman writes, 'Meaning responses follow from the interaction with the context in which healing occurs – with the "power" of the laser in surgery, or with the red colour of the pill that contains stimulating medicine. Sometimes, a bandage on a cut finger works better if it has a picture of Snoopy on it.'

There's no medical reason why a cartoon on a plaster heals a cut faster on a child, yet it does. The cartoon has meaning for the child and it is the child's thoughts that then speed up the healing of the wound.

If a person is treated for an illness with a large machine that shoots lightning bolts out of it, then it will probably work better than a tablet, even if the machine and the tablet are both placebos. It's not the machine or tablet that heals, but our perception of it. Hence placebos work better if they smell medicinal, have a technical-sounding name or if they are painful or invasive.

In 'Placebos and Nocebos: The Cultural Construction of Belief', C.G. Helman writes,

> The doctor's office, hospital ward, holy shrine or house of a traditional healer can be compared to a theatre set complete with scenery, props, costumes and script. This script, derived from the culture itself … tells them how to behave, how to experience the event and what to expect from it. It helps to validate the healer, and the power of their methods of healing.

Much power to heal ultimately lies within us, in our ability to choose how we look at things and what meaning we give to them.

FEELING THE BLUES

Our thoughts about the colour of tablets affect how well they work. Scientists at the University of Cincinnati tested blue and pink stimulants and sedatives on 57 students; both 'drugs' were actually placebos, although this was unknown to the students.

Blue 'sedatives' were found to be 66% effective but pink ones were only 26% effective. The colour blue proved to be 2.5 times better than pink for creating a relaxed feeling. Generally, blue is a calming colour. But if blue had a different meaning in another culture you would expect the results to be different. This is indeed the case.

Daniel Moerman describes some interesting research in *Meaning, Medicine and the 'Placebo Effect'*. He quotes two Italian studies that examined blue placebo sleeping tablets. They worked well for women but not for men. In men, the blue placebos actually worked as stimulants. Moerman explains that blue is the colour of the Virgin Mary's cloak, so in Italy, blue is associated with peace. At least it is for women. But the power of this symbol is overruled in most men. Blue is the colour of the Italian football strip and football is a very big deal in Italy, especially for men.

I had the good fortune of being in Italy during the 2006 World Cup (that Italy won) and I can testify to this. I was in Lucca, a town in Tuscany, during some of Italy's matches. Every winning game was followed by a celebration involving a lot of the town, with local men waving their blue football tops while driving around on motorcycles, singing and beeping their horns. Moerman points out that rather than being a calming colour, blue most likely 'means success, powerful movement, strength and grace on the field, and, generally, great excitement'. At least for men it does, hence blue sleeping tablets don't work as well for Italian men as they do for Italian women because of what the colour means to them.

WHERE YOU LIVE MATTERS

Our beliefs are influenced by our culture, thus the placebo effect varies depending on where we live. In a US study of migraine treatments, 33.6% of patients who received placebo injections had relief and 22.3% of patients who had placebo tablets had relief. Placebo injections in the USA were 1.5 times better than placebo tablets. In Europe, the picture is different. In a European trial, 27.1% of patients who took tablets received pain relief, but 25.1% of patients who received injections had pain relief. In Europe, tablets work better for migraines than injections do.

Moerman points out that 'getting a "shot"' is much more common in the US, so people believe in it more; hence a placebo injection is better there. But in the UK, we 'pop pills', hence a placebo tablet works better here.

This type of cultural effect is common with other drugs too. A trial of Tagamet done in France found it to be 76% effective. The placebo was 59% effective. But in Brazil, the drug was 60% effective and the placebo only 10%. Amazingly, the placebo worked as well in France as the actual drug did in Brazil, a demonstration of the power of our minds to affect whether a medicine works or not.

FOR BETTER OR WORSE – IT'S IN THE MIND

Tagamet used to be the best drug for treating stomach ulcers, at least until Zantac came along in the 1980s. A number of trials had shown that Tagamet was around 70–75% effective. But once Zantac came along, which was marketed as being much better, patients' (and doctors') opinions about Tagamet wavered. It was no longer the 'best' drug. The next set of Tagamet trials found its effectiveness to be only 64%. Had Tagamet's chemical formula changed? Had people's biochemistry radically altered in the time between the two sets of trials? No. All that had changed were their beliefs *about* Tagamet. Interestingly, Zantac then took over as the main anti-ulcer drug, showing around 75% effectiveness, which is not really very different from the originally reported power of Tagamet.

Our minds have been shown to affect aspirin too. A 1981 study involving 835 women, which was conducted at the University of Keele in the UK, found that having a brand name on the tablet made a big difference to how effective the aspirin was.

The study used two types of aspirin tablets – one labelled with a well-known brand name and the other as 'analgesic'. And there were also two types of placebo tablets, labelled in the same way – either with the well-known brand name or as 'analgesic'. The women were separated into four groups so that they would receive only one type of tablet.

The results showed, amazingly, that the branded aspirin tablets worked better than the unbranded ones, yet it was the same drug. And the branded placebos reduced pain much more than unbranded ones, yet they were the same placebos. Both aspirin and placebo tablets worked better if they were branded. And incredibly, the unbranded aspirin tablet wasn't that much better than the branded placebo.

I have personally seen this type of thing happen with paracetamol tablets. Branded tablets (Panadol in the UK), which are shaped and designed differently from the cheaper, mass-market plain tablets that are sold in supermarkets, seem to work better. When I asked some people their thoughts, it turned out that it was the sound of the name, the brand, the price, the appearance and the packaging of the tablets that gave them faith in Panadol. The mass-market tablets, they said, looked cheap and less powerful, and because of this perception they were, indeed (according to my small analysis), less effective, even though it was the same drug.

Pharmaceutical companies often choose names for drugs that enhance their perceived effect. In a 2006 paper published in *Advances in Psychiatric Treatment*, psychiatrist Aaron K. Vallance suggested that the name 'Viagra' actually enhanced the effect of the drug. It is similar-sounding to the words 'vigour' and 'Niagara', which creates a perception of vigorousness and power. There is no doubt that the name makes a difference. If it was called 'Flopsy', I doubt it would work so well!

Herbert Benson, Harvard medical professor and author of the bestseller *Timeless Healing*, studied angina drugs that were well known and effective in the 1940s and 1950s, helping 70–90% of people who took them. When they were later retested in higher-quality trials they were found to be much less effective. From then on, they stopped working so well for people, even though they had worked previously. Benson suggested that it was mostly because the doctors prescribing them didn't believe in them as much as they previously did. Therefore they were unlikely to be as enthusiastic as they had been when they initially prescribed them.

In *Meaning, Medicine and the 'Placebo Effect'*, Daniel Moerman refers to these results, writing, 'Sceptics can heal 30% to 40% of their patients with inert medication, while enthusiasts can heal 70% to 90%, with the same drugs.'

There is sometimes little difference between two drugs for the same condition. There is a difference in test-tube trials. Drugs are very powerful. As a scientist in the pharmaceutical industry, I used to study them. I still get excited when studying the chemistry of how a drug interacts with the body's systems. Designing and developing drugs is a painstaking and highly skilled process that requires exceptional skill in manipulating the chemical structure of molecules.

But test tubes don't involve human consciousness. Once a person ingests a drug, that person's thoughts *about* the drug become all-important. The person is either going to believe that it will work or that it might not. But what they believe will affect how well the drug works.

I would like to see this factor taken more into account in medicine. Many doctors do take it into account, but it is not universally taught in medical schools as something that they should actively use in their treatments. In many schools, more emphasis is put on the ethical considerations about giving placebos than on their ability to heal. Some family doctors and doctors in hospital wards prescribe placebos when they can see no medical reason for the person's complaints. Once the person receives their placebo, their symptoms frequently reduce.

Placebos heal. That is a fact! But the real power comes from inside us. Placebos are symbols to which we attach our thoughts of hope or relief. The thoughts are ours.

YOU MUST TAKE ALL OF YOUR PLACEBOS

For some illnesses, four tablets work better than two. Many studies have also shown that four placebos are better than two placebos. In 1999, scientists from the University of Amsterdam summarized the combined results of 79 separate studies of anti-ulcer drugs involving 3325 patients. They collected the data together for all the trials where patients took placebos four times a day (1821 patients) and found that the ulcer had healed in 44.2% of the patients after four weeks. They also pooled the data of the trials where patients took placebos twice a day (1504 patients) and the healing rate was only 36.2% after four weeks. The study conclusively proved that four placebos were better than two.

Studies have shown that drugs don't work as well if a patient doesn't take the full course of medication that their doctor prescribes. This is common sense. You should take your medication when you are supposed to and always continue to the end of the course of treatment. But studies have shown that placebos don't work as well either if you don't stay the course.

In a trial involving the cholesterol-lowering drug clofibrate, 1103 men were given the drug and 2789 had the placebo. The survival rates were recorded five years later. For the men who received the drug, the rate was 80%; for those on the placebo it was 79.1%.

Looking more closely at the data, the researchers discovered that the survival rates actually depended upon whether the men stuck to their course of medication or not. They were said to be 'good adherers' if they took 80% of their medication. After five years on the drug, 85% of the good adherers were alive, but only 75.4% of the poor adherers were still living. This is common sense and is what you would expect to see. However, looking at the men who received placebos, 84.9% of the good adherers were alive after five years and 71.7% of the poor adherers were alive. Even though they received placebos, not taking all that they were supposed to had a significant effect. For this particular condition, it was a death sentence.

The same type of thing has been shown with antibiotics. A 1983 *Journal of Pediatrics* study reported that people who took their full course of tablets had less fever or fewer infections than those who didn't, regardless of whether the tablets were real drugs or placebos. Of the good adherers, 82% were free of infections or fever, while this was only 47% for the poor adherers. In the placebo group, 68% of the good adherers remained symptom-free but only 36% of the poor adherers were so. Infections and fevers returned in twice as many people who didn't take all their placebos as those who did.

Sometimes circumstances take over our lives – we get lazy, we think we'll be OK now that the condition is pretty much cleared up – and we don't complete the course. But nagging doubts about what we 'should' have done occasionally enter our minds. It is these thoughts that cause the relapses.

SHAM SURGERY

Studies have shown that, for some conditions, just the knowledge that we've had an operation can heal us, even if we haven't actually had one but just think we have. In one study a group of patients were given 'internal mammary artery ligation' surgery for angina, in which arteries were tied off to divert blood supply to the heart. Another group were given what is known as 'sham' surgery, which is fake surgery. They still had an operation but the arteries weren't tied.

After the surgery in which the arteries were tied off, 67% of patients reported substantial improvement – they had much less pain, required less medication and were able to exercise for longer without an angina attack. But amazingly, 83% of patients who received the sham surgery experienced the same level of improvement. It was a reasonably small study – 21 patients received real surgery and 12 received sham surgery – but the effect was still clear: for the majority of people, knowing that they were getting surgery was at least as good as actually getting it.

Eventually, after this study and a few others, the surgical technique was discontinued. By then more than 100,000 people had experienced it. And the reason for its discontinuation? Some surgeons didn't believe it was doing any good. Yet it had made an enormous positive difference to their patients – in many cases, simply because *they* believed in it.

Just seeing a scar after an operation activates the placebo effect. In a sham surgery for arthritis, surgeons merely made an incision in the knee but patients recovered most of their movement and were able to walk pain-free as much as people who had actual surgery. Studies have shown that, for some conditions, regardless of whether a surgery is real or not, if you believe that it is (and why wouldn't you?) and are optimistic about it, you will receive the same benefit as if you have actually had surgery. Once again, the power lies within you.

IT'S WHAT YOU KNOW

Such is the power of your thoughts about surgery or an injection that medicines are most powerful when you know you're getting them. If a medicine is hidden, or even if you are asleep when you get it (so you don't know about it), it doesn't work as well as when you do know you're receiving it. One study of Alzheimer's patients found that they often don't get the full benefit of drugs for other conditions (e.g. high blood pressure), because they can't remember taking the medicine.

In a 1994 experiment involving a powerful painkiller for cancer pain (naproxen) the drug worked much better for patients who were given information about the experiment. The patients were either given the drug and it was secretly swapped for the placebo after one day, or they received the placebo and it was secretly swapped for the drug. The key to the experiment was that half of them were told that this might happen and the other half weren't.

The study showed that naproxen worked better than the placebo. But both naproxen and the placebo worked substantially better for the patients who knew what was going on. Having information boosted the power of both the drug and the placebo.

And amazingly, in the group who knew about the experiment, the placebo worked even better than the drug did in the patients who didn't know about it.

In other words, as unbelievable as it sounds, a placebo works better than a drug for some conditions if you are handed the placebo but the drug is administered secretly. In Benedetti's words, 'The existence of the placebo effect suggests that we must broaden our conception of the limits of ... human capability.'

Human consciousness has the ability to make a poor medicine work much better, or an inert substance act like a powerful medicine, or sham surgery work like real surgery. The mind really can heal the body. In the next chapter we are going to learn how our brain actually changes as we think: even further evidence that thoughts can heal.

The Power of Plasticity

To think is to practice brain chemistry.
Deepak Chopra

Your brain is growing as you read these words. Scientists call the phenomenon 'neural plasticity'. Everything you see, hear, touch, taste and smell changes your brain and every thought causes microscopic changes in its structure. In a sense, thoughts leave physical traces in the brain in much the same way as we leave footsteps in the sand.

As you think, millions of brain cells (neurons) reach out and connect with each other, moulding the actual substance of the brain just as an artist moulds her clay. The connections between brain cells are called neural connections. Think of the brain as a giant 3-D map containing towns with networks of roads linking them. And new roads are constantly being added to the map as some towns expand.

In a similar way, your brain contains maps and these also expand. For instance, if you used your right hand for a few hours without using your left, the 'map' for your right hand would expand as several new roads (neural connections) were forged in it. In this way, as we go through life our brain maps are in a continual state of expansion and contraction.

Take a well-known study of symphony orchestra musicians, for example. Publishing in *NeuroImage* in 2002, scientists from the Magnetic Resonance and Image Analysis Research Centre at the University of Liverpool showed that years of being a musician had expanded an area of the brain known as Broca's area, which is an area associated with language and musical abilities. When they compared this area of the brain with people who weren't musicians, it was much bigger in the musicians.

Similarly, studies of blind people who learn Braille found that as they practise, the brain maps governing the tips of their index fingers expand.

To extend the map analogy, you could imagine individual neurons as trees. Neurons have branches and these reach out to connect with the branches of other neurons. Each town, then, contains trees instead of houses and the roads are branches that connect trees with one another.

THOUGHTS CHANGE THE BRAIN

As I've pointed out, it's not just your physical experiences, which are processed through your five senses, that change your brain. Your thoughts shape it too.

A 2007 scientific study of mathematicians, for instance, published in the *American Journal of Neuroradiology*, showed that the area of the brain that controlled mathematical thinking was biggest for those who had been mathematicians longest. With each year spent as a mathematician – thinking, abstracting and analyzing as a mathematician does – more new branches were added to the 'mathematical map'.

A recent study of London taxi drivers found the same thing. Brain maps had expanded through years of learning and memorizing routes. Learning is more than just your brain processing what you see, hear, touch, taste and smell; it involves what you think about what you see, hear, touch, taste and smell. And these thoughts change your brain. Studying, therefore, changes the brain.

Indeed, a 2006 study published in the *Journal of Neuroscience* found brain map changes when students were studying for their exams. Scientists at the University of Regensburg in Germany followed 38 medical students while they studied for their medical exams and discovered that the areas of the brain that process memory and abstract information grew thicker.

So our experiences *and* our thinking change the brain. The brain is not a static lump of organic matter that delivers genetically programmed instructions to the body, as many of us have come to believe. It is a constantly changing network of neurons and connections. And we are the cause of the changes. Norman Doidge, MD, author of *The Brain That Changes Itself*, writes, 'The idea that the brain is like a muscle that grows with exercise is not just a metaphor.' Just like a muscle, the brain grows thicker as we use it.

As we grow new connections in any one area of the brain, their density pushes neurons apart in the same way that if two adjacent trees were to grow thousands of new branches, the space between them would become denser and the trunks would be pushed apart. In this way, the brain becomes thicker as we repeat the same thought, ponder the same ideas or dream the same dreams over and over again.

It comes as no surprise to learn, then, that meditation changes the brain. A study of meditators using the Buddhist 'Insight' meditation was conducted at Massachusetts General Hospital in 2005. It showed that the meditation had increased the thickness of the prefrontal cortex of the brain – the area that controls concentration, free will and compassion.

Thus, when you visualize healing your body, which we shall learn to do later in the book, the first thing that occurs is that you actually change the microscopic structure of your brain. Visualization is not just a subjective thing, an inert mish-mash of mental pictures that are just there to make you feel good, but a process that causes real chemical and structural changes in the brain. With visualization, almost immediately, mind changes matter.

USE IT OR LOSE IT – A LEOPARD *CAN* CHANGE ITS SPOTS

If you repetitively flexed your right hand over several days, the brain map for your right hand would expand because lots more neural connections would have formed in it. But if you stopped doing this and then switched to flexing your left hand, the map for your right hand would shrink because you were no longer using your right hand and the map for your left hand would grow instead.

As Norman Doidge has pointed out, the brain is like a muscle. The more you use a muscle, the thicker it gets. If you stop using it, then it atrophies and gets smaller. Thus, any time you change your way of thinking, many connections that correspond to your old way dissolve and connections that correspond to your new way of thinking begin to grow.

So let's say you've always been complaining about things. You will have built up brain maps that process your negative thoughts and emotions. But after reading this book you decide that you are going to look at things differently. You realize that your thoughts affect your body. You decide to think positively and practise gratitude. Now you grow new maps that process your new way of thinking. Complaint-based maps then begin to shrink. In a surprisingly short space of time (many studies have shown it to be around 21 days – that's why Will Bowen recommends that we go 21 days without complaining) your new positive gratitude map is larger than the negative complaint-based one. At the neurological level, positive thinking and gratitude become a habit. These new ways are now wired into your brain and you really are a different person.

We needn't think that we or our loved ones can't change our ways. All we need to do is make the effort to change our minds. Our brains respond to the changes and, in time, as they develop new maps, we don't need to make as much effort any more. The new behaviour is wired and has become a habit.

TALKING IT THROUGH

There is no longer any doubt that psychotherapy can result in detectable changes in the brain.

These are the words of Nobel Prize winner Eric Kandel. They refer to the growing body of evidence that talk therapies cause neuroplastic change in the brain (another way of saying that brain maps change). In the presence of a good therapist, or friend, talking about our problems actually changes the brain.

MRI studies of talk therapies have shown that neurons in the prefrontal cortex light up (are activated) and activity in the area that processes painful emotions reduces. Talk therapies help us to view a memory from a new perspective so that we no longer feel pain when we think about something that previously caused us emotional distress.

In biological terms, energy is diverted to the front of the brain and away from the area that stores the emotional pain. Millions of new neural connections are born at the front of the brain and, with less energy to feed them, those connections associated with the trauma begin to dissolve. Such is the emotional intensity of trauma, chronic stress and even depression that some degree of neural damage often occurs. But such is the amazing regenerative capacity of the brain that recent studies have shown that we can even repair the damage.

Childhood trauma is linked with a high number of stress-related illnesses in adulthood. It can cause a flood of stress hormones that kill cells in an area of the brain that stores memories (the hippocampus), literally dissolving it. Some scientists view it as a protective mechanism. Neural circuits are literally 'burned out' to prevent us from remembering and thus reliving the trauma. But recent studies have shown that neurons in the hippocampus can be regenerated. The phenomenon is known as neurogenesis. So not only can we literally rewire our brain, but we can regenerate it. Just ten years ago, such an idea was preposterous to science, but now we know it to be fact. And it's much easier to do and more common than you'd think.

NEUROGENESIS

In studies on adult mice living in enriched environments – having a running wheel, the company of other mice, toys, etc. – it was found that the volume of their hippocampi (plural of hippocampus) increased by 15% compared with mice who didn't live in such environments. Neurogenesis had occurred. And the same is true for humans.

In 1998, scientists at the Salk Laboratories in La Jolla, California, first discovered stem cells of neurons in the human hippocampus, which was evidence of neurogenesis. Neurons were in the process of being formed.

We now know that living an active period of life with physical, mental and social stimulation can regenerate damage to the brain. Research has even shown that when we exercise or experience new things, feel excited, enthusiastic, fascinated, are in awe, experience wonder or even experience spiritual states, then neurogenesis also naturally occurs. Many of these states are associated with strong positive emotions. Thus thoughts and emotions can cause neurogenesis and it's likely that talking things through causes neurogenesis too.

Studies have shown that neurogenesis continues right up through old age, to our very last moments. Scientists at the Salk Laboratories recently injected terminally ill volunteers with a special chemical that allows newly formed neurons to be seen under a microscope. They discovered that neurogenesis occurred in the volunteers' hippocampi right up to their final days, no matter how old they were.

Research has expanded into other areas of the brain, and neurogenesis has so far been discovered in the area that processes smell (olfactory bulb), in an area that processes emotion (septum), in an area that processes movement (striatum) and in the spinal cord. This suggests that we have a much higher potential for regeneration than medical science ever previously imagined. The human body is a walking miracle that has amazing power to heal and to regenerate, and this is influenced by our minds. Thoughts and emotions can cause neurogenesis.

Studies have shown that learning new things as adults can enlarge brain maps and most likely causes neurogenesis. As I pointed out in the first chapter, learning a new language is a great way because it encourages us to use different brain areas. It has been suggested that if a vaccine for Alzheimer's existed, it would be learning a new language as an adult.

Learning to play a musical instrument also changes the brain. Even playing board games, doing crossword or sudoku puzzles, or taking a course at college have a positive effect upon the adult brain, no matter how old we are.

Learning new dances is also excellent, because it involves exercise as well as the mind. Simply replaying the dances and moves we've done for years, however, is not as good because we don't have to think about new things. We benefit from the novelty of new experiences. To maximize the positive effects upon our brains, we need to be continually learning.

So as we go through life, no matter how old we are, if we retain our curiosity for new things and exercise our bodies and minds, we can mentally grow younger.

The Mind Can Heal the Body

**Although the world is full of suffering,
it is also full of the overcoming of it.**
Helen Keller

As part of the brain-changing process, thoughts produce chemicals in the brain. Many are known as neurotransmitters. You may have heard of serotonin and dopamine, which are two well-known neurotransmitters. When we think thoughts, neurotransmitters are released from the branch of one neuron and make their way to the tip of a branch of another. This produces a bolt of electricity and is what is known as a neuron 'firing'. When we repeat a thought several times, an additional chemical (protein) is stimulated and makes its way to the centre of the neuron (the nucleus), where it finds DNA. It then activates (switches on) several genes of DNA, which make the substances (proteins) that produce new branches (connections) between the neurons. In this way, repeating a thought produces new connections between neurons and is how the brain changes with our thoughts and experiences.

The process is rapid. Genes are activated within a few minutes and a single neuron may gain thousands of new branches in a very short time. One of the significant things to note here is that the genes have been activated by *a state of mind* within minutes. This is mind over matter rapidly taking place at the genetic level and has a key role to play in many so-called miraculous healings.

Another type of chemical, known as a neuropeptide, is also produced in the brain. There are many different types and these reflect different states of mind, emotions and attitudes. They interface with neurons by attaching to parts of the surface of the neurons known as receptors. Receptors are basically docking ports. Imagine several spaceships docking onto a space station. The space station would have several docking ports, of different shapes and sizes, to cope with the different spaceships.

It is quite similar on the surface of neurons. Neurons contain thousands of receptors that allow neuropeptides of different shapes and sizes and different electromagnetic (vibrational) qualities to dock. Another way to think of it is like a child's learning toy. Remember the one where the child has a coloured table containing different-shaped holes? It usually has circular, triangular, square and star-shaped holes. On a neuron these would be its different shaped and sized receptors. The child also has a circular block, a triangular one, a square one and a star-shaped one, and these fit into their appropriate holes. In the brain, these shaped blocks would be different neuropeptides and thus each neuropeptide would have its own specific receptor. But unlike the child's toy, neurons actually change their receptors. If a certain neuropeptide is produced over and over again in a certain part of the brain, then neurons in that area develop extra receptors to cope. For instance, if endorphin (a neuropeptide) were produced over and over again, neurons would evolve extra endorphin receptors. If they started out with, say, 100, then they might evolve to have 1000. If production of endorphin reduced, then the neurons would gradually shed these receptors. Thus, as well as the mind affecting the number of connections between brain cells and activating genes, it also changes their surface (skin).

This is how addiction and tolerance to substances works. If a person keeps taking a substance – say, heroin – then neurons would evolve more heroin receptors. Soon, as the brain develops thousands of them, the person requires more of the drug to get the same hit.

Many neuropeptides don't just hang around in the brain. Many are released into the bloodstream and travel throughout the body where they carry out important roles. Thus, in a powerful link between the mind and body, our thoughts and emotions produce neuropeptides and they affect the body. Many neuropeptides are even produced in the body instead and can make their way to the brain. For instance, some immune cells make neuropeptides. In this way, the body affects the mind. Mind affects body – body affects mind! It's a two-way process.

Neuropeptides play an important role in the liver, kidneys, pancreas, gut, colon, reproductive organs and skin. They also influence blood sugar, blood pressure, heart rate, respiration, body temperature, the endocrine system, the immune system, sex drive and even appetite. Thus, the mind affects all of these organs and systems.

So not only does our mind affect our brain, it affects our body at the cellular level.

HOW THE MIND AFFECTS THE BODY

In his excellent book *Evolve Your Brain* Dr Joe Dispenza discusses the likely changes in cells throughout the body when a person changes their thinking. Using the example of a person changing from being impatient to being patient, he describes the probable impact upon cells throughout the body.

Just as neurons evolve how many receptors they have, so cells in our organs and throughout the body do the same thing. Initially, in Dr Dispenza's example, neuropeptides associated with impatience would flood the cells in an organ. The cells would then evolve more receptors for that neuropeptide. When the person became more patient, the flow of impatience neuropeptides would cease and the flow of patience neuropeptides take over. The cells would then cut back on the number of impatience receptors because they would no longer be needed and would evolve more patience receptors instead. Thus, as we change our minds, we change our bodies at the cellular level.

Think of the flow of neuropeptides as a coloured dye and the bloodstream as a river. So, as we change our thinking, we change the colour of dye that we drop into the river. Downstream, rocks are coloured by our different thoughts. Now, for this analogy, think of the rocks as cells, although think of them more like large spongy boulders rather than rocks. As we send different-coloured dyes downstream, cells adapt to their changing environment by evolving more or less of that colour of receptor. Change the colour of your thoughts, change your body at the cellular level!

So, when we move from impatience to patience, or from relaxed to calm, or from one thought to another – from a thought of food to a thought of a tree, for instance – we alter the connections between neurons, produce chemicals in the brain and affect cells and systems throughout our body.

Some scientists believe that thoughts only serve to increase or decrease stress and that the link between mind and body is only the link between stress chemicals and cells. I can appreciate how they might arrive at this conclusion, but I do not agree. The mind and brain are not so black and white. Our thoughts are not black and white – stress or no stress, on or off. There are many shades of colour in between. We can produce an infinite number of different thoughts and emotions. The brain and body produce thousands of chemicals and many are constantly finding their way around the body. As we switch from one state of mind to another, even when we are making just a subtle change, we change the tone being produced from the mixture of colours that reflects our thinking. If you are musically inclined, you can even think of your thoughts as producing musical tones instead.

In the impatience–patience example, it is highly unlikely that there is only one neuropeptide involved. For simplicity I have only described the effect of a single neuropeptide. Each state of mind produces a variety of colour (or musical) tones. A subtle shift of perspective produces a subtle shift in tone and this produces a subtle change in cells throughout the body. All throughout the body, cells dance to the tune of the mind. So, when we think of healing from an illness, there is more than just a reduction of stress chemicals interfacing with cells throughout the body. A range of neuropeptides corresponding to our thoughts will make their way out of the brain and flow around the body, painting it in a variety of colour tones or playing different tunes.

THE MIND–DNA INTERFACE

Just as the mind affects genes of DNA in neurons, so it affects genes of DNA in cells all throughout the body. When neuropeptides dock onto their receptors, messages are delivered into the cells. These reach the DNA and genes are either switched on or off or made a little brighter or dimmer.

DNA contains around 25,000 genes. Think of the genes as lightbulbs (I think of them as flashing Christmas-tree lights because multiple genes are involved at the same time). When a gene switches on, a protein is produced. This protein might be something involved in construction, such as in the construction of new cells for tissues, bone, tendon, blood or for the immune system; or it might be an enzyme that will help in the changing of something into something else. For instance, the enzyme pepsin helps to convert the food that we eat into smaller units that the body can use. What is produced might even be a hormone that will deliver a message to another cell. So when genes switch on they produce all that the body needs.

In terms of healing, genes would switch on and proteins would be made that would be used in the construction of new cells, skin, tendon, blood or bone. Genes would also produce proteins that would be involved in the immune response and, if the body had suffered a cut, different ones would be produced to help blood clot around the wound. Some genes would produce proteins that would affect other relevant systems in the body so that the entire organism (your body) would be tipped in the direction of healing.

So, let's say that a person was irritable and hostile. Their brain would produce the appropriate neuropeptides and these would flood throughout the body, finding cells in organs and tissues that they could interface with, ones which had the same 'colour' or 'sound' of receptor.

Wound healing is very sensitive to our mental and emotional state. It is known that hostility and stress slow it down. Neuropeptides of irritation and hostility would interface with cells and deliver messages to DNA. Then genes would be activated and proteins produced. Some genes that are important to the healing process would only be partially activated (or sometimes not at all) – like the dimmer switch only being partially turned on. Other genes would be deactivated or the dimmer switch turned down (growth hormones, for instance, that are important in healing). Thus irritation and hostility would mean that the proteins required for healing would not be produced in as high quantities as they would be in a calm state of mind.

Indeed, in keeping with one of the themes of Chapter 1, scientists at Ohio State University showed that hostility significantly altered healing rate. The study, published in 2005 in *Archives of General Psychiatry* and involving 42 married couples, showed that those who were most hostile healed at only 60% of the rate of those who were least hostile.

And in another 2005 study it was found that stress reduced the levels of growth hormones at the sites of wounds. Growth hormones (which are proteins) are produced when certain genes are switched on; they help healing. The scientists found that mental and emotional stress reduced the levels of growth hormones at wound sites. Thus wounds take longer to heal when we are stressed.

And looking at the actual genes involved, the scientists found that over 100 genes were 'downregulated' during stress, which means that, in the lightbulb analogy, the brightness of around 100 bulbs was dimmed by stress and over 70 were 'upregulated', so 70 bulbs became brighter. The scientists noted that '100 downregulated and 70 upregulated genes' tipped the genetic balance towards the death of cells instead of the birth and growth of cells – and it is birth and growth that are required at wound sites.

If, instead of feeling stress, you felt calm, which might be because of your positive attitude, or maybe your trust in the medical team and belief that everything was going to work out OK, different genes would be upregulated and downregulated, which would speed up healing. More growth hormones would be produced at the site of injury and these would speed up the healing process.

Indeed, in another Ohio State University study, published in 2004 in *Psychoneuroendocrinology*, scientists showed that social support, which leads to a state of calm, speeded up wound healing.

So, all throughout the body, genes are responding to our minds. In *The Genie in Your Genes*, Dawson Church writes, 'Now we're starting to understand that our consciousness conditions our genetic expression, moment by moment.'

So, when we visualize our bodies healing, as we shall learn later in the book, our thoughts affect our genes, aiding the regeneration of a damaged or diseased part of the body. And, as I mentioned, even though the above examples refer to stress or no stress, different thoughts produce different tones. They do not just fit somewhere in the scale between stress and no stress.

The neuropeptides produced by our varied tones of thinking affect a large number of genes. In the last example, 170 genes were affected. Science used to think that it was 'one gene, one function' – that one gene did one thing. But now we know that a mixture of genes is involved in different functions. So, with genes, we know it's not black and white. They subscribe to the 'variety of tones' way of working.

If each gene were a colour or a sound, then different states of mind would produce an infinite variety of tones. This is an area of research that is sure to 'flower' in the next few years.

TRUMPING OUR GENES

Such is the power of our mind to affect our genes, we needn't live in fear of heart disease or cancer if we have a family history of it. A change in attitude and lifestyle could trump many of the 'bad' genes that we might have inherited.

Let's say that a person is born into a family with a history of heart disease, with genes that make their risk of heart disease higher than average. This does not automatically mean that they will develop heart disease. A change in attitude and/or lifestyle will affect numerous genes in the brain and throughout the body.

This may cause the 'bad' genes to be turned down.

So, going with the research reported in Chapter 1, developing a positive attitude, being more optimistic, cutting down on hostility, cutting down on complaining, being more accepting of life and people, focusing on things that you are grateful for, sharing and even developing a warm disposition towards people will all have a beneficial effect.

Lifestyle also affects our genes. A healthy diet, cutting down on toxins and stimulants and having good levels of exercise will all make a positive difference. Living like this means that there's a healthy chance that the heart disease or cancer genes may lie dormant. It's your life, so it's your choice.

Attitude, diet and lifestyle run in families as much as genetics do. The good thing about this is that we have a choice about our attitude, diet and lifestyle. If a person with heart-disease genes adopted the same diet and lifestyle as previous family members who developed the disease, then their genes would likely be similarly activated as in their family members. So the person would be as likely to develop heart disease as their family members were. But in many cases, this occurs mostly because of their diet and lifestyle and not because of their genetics. Genetics, in most cases, play a much smaller role than we had previously believed.

There are, of course, some exceptions. Some people with heart-disease genes and a poor diet and lifestyle never develop heart problems and some people without the genes and with a great diet and lifestyle do; but trumping our genes is true in a very broad sense.

So, if your family has a history of heart problems or cancer, examine your attitude, how you treat people, how you feel, your diet, your exercise levels and how much you drink or smoke, and make any positive changes that are necessary. Consult your doctor and get some good healthy advice.

THE MIND–STEM CELL INTERFACE

The fact that the mind influences genes suggests that the mind influences the growth of stem cells, because stem cells have DNA. Stem cells are cells that morph into any type of cells – like flowers without a head. They have only a stem and thus are able to grow different heads. In this way, a stem cell could become a bone cell, an immune cell, a skin cell, a heart cell, a blood cell or even a neuron. As genes are activated, the stem cells grow into the cells that they are required to become.

You may be familiar with the ethical debates over using embryonic stem cells to treat some diseases. Once transplanted into, say, the liver, embryonic stems cells become liver cells. Transplanted into the heart, the same stem cells would become heart cells instead. Thus transplanting stem cells can encourage the growth of damaged tissue anywhere in the body.

It has long been known that bone-marrow stem cells morph into immune cells, which help us to fight infection. And earlier we learned about neurogenesis. There is evidence to suggest that the stem cells that become neurons begin their lives in the bone marrow too. Recent research has shown that when skin wounds heal, stem cells travel from the bone marrow and morph into skin cells. There is also evidence that stem cells travel from the bone marrow and morph into heart cells, thus regenerating damaged heart muscle.

As we know, neurogenesis is accelerated by novel experiences, powerful emotional states, spiritual experiences and exercise. Therefore it is logical to assume that in these situations the mind is having an effect upon stem cells. It is also known that stress can interfere with neurogenesis. Stress also slows the healing process, which suggests that it might turn down the genes on the stem-cell DNA that are required for it to morph into the cell type required for healing.

Therefore it is highly likely that the mind can either encourage stem cells to morph into new cells or it can interfere with the process. Indeed, in studies of the heart, high levels of stress are known to lower the levels of endothelial progenitor cells (a type of stem cell) that are destined to become heart cells. Thus, since stress can affect stem cells, it is highly likely that many tones of our thoughts, emotions and attitudes also do so.

So, if a person visualizes the healing of a damaged part of their body, I believe that it is certain that they will be having an effect upon the morphing of stem cells into the required cell types for healing.

There is little research in this area but a growing number of scientists believe that some seemingly miraculous healings and spontaneous remissions (where a person recovers overnight) from serious diseases are actually the result of the movement of stem cells from bone marrow and their morphing into cells that regenerate a damaged area.

Indeed, in his excellent book *The Psychobiology of Gene Expression*, award-winning scientist Ernest L. Rossi writes, 'Many of the so-called miracles of healing via spiritual practices and therapeutic hypnosis probably occur via ... gene expression in stem cells throughout the brain and body.'

Precisely how stem cells are involved in wound healing is not yet fully understood. They contain DNA, just as normal cells do. In terms of healing through visualization it is likely, as Rossi implies, that neuropeptides deliver messages to DNA in stem cells and produce proteins that tell the stem cells what cell type they should morph into.

• • •

The mind really does have an incredible ability to affect the body. In the next chapter we will learn of some of the new scientific evidence that visualization directly affects the area of the body that we are visualizing.

The Power of Visualization

Visualization is daydreaming with a purpose.
Bo Bennett

If you visualize a part of your body, that part feels it. Other parts don't. In a 1996 scientific paper published in the journal *Psychological Science*, scientists from the University of Connecticut reported that when volunteers who had experimental pain induced in them expected to have less pain in one finger, pain was indeed less in that finger but not in any other. The study involved 56 volunteers who had a placebo cream that they believed was an analgesic rubbed into their index finger on one hand but not into the index finger of the other. Pain was then induced in both fingers, but the volunteers only really felt it in the finger that didn't have the cream rubbed on it. Their pain was much less where they had the cream applied, even though it was a placebo.

Fabrizio Benedetti later reported the same type of effect. He induced burning pain in the hands and feet of 173 volunteers by injecting capsaicin (it's the chemical that makes chilli peppers burn). Prior to the injections, some of the volunteers had a placebo cream rubbed on a hand or foot, and again they believed that it was an anaesthetic. One group had the cream rubbed on their left hand and another group on their right hand and left foot. Two other groups didn't receive any cream so that they could serve as a control. The study, published in the *Journal of Neuroscience* in 1999, reported that there was much less pain in the areas where the placebo cream was applied. If it was rubbed on the left hand, for instance, then there was less pain there but the levels remained high in the other hand and in both feet. In the groups who didn't get any placebo cream, there was no reduction in pain. Pain relief only occurred where volunteers expected it to occur.

When we have a pain and receive a placebo but believe it to be a painkiller, our awareness of where the pain is located and our expectation that it will go away seem to cause pain to disappear exactly where our awareness is directed and nowhere else.

In his research, Benedetti showed that endogenous opiates (which we learned about in Chapter 2) were only released in the area of the brain that corresponded to the part of the body where there was an expectation of pain relief (where the volunteer's thoughts were focused). He wrote, '...endogenous opioids do not act throughout the nervous system but *only* on those neural circuits linking specific expectations to specific placebo responses' (my emphasis).

In other words, there is a release of chemicals in specific locations of the brain that brings about what we expect to occur. Our awareness seems to be the directing force, the force that instructs which chemicals should be released and where.

So, when a person expects to have pain relief in any area of their body, neural circuits in the brain are activated for that specific part and endogenous opiates are released there. The whole brain is not flooded with opiates, just the bits that control the areas that a person's awareness is focused upon.

The same type of thing would most likely occur if a person had two different conditions and was given a placebo for one of them, believing it to be a drug. In Chapter 2 we learned of the study where a person was given an inhaler that they believed contained allergens and pollen and went on to develop asthma symptoms as well as hay fever symptoms. Next they were given an inhaler and told that it only contained allergens. This time they only developed asthma symptoms. In the third experiment they were told that the inhaler contained allergens and pollen and, once again, developed asthma symptoms and hay fever symptoms. Their awareness of what was supposed to happen directed which chemicals were released and what, therefore, actually occurred. So, if a person who had asthma and hay fever was given a placebo for asthma but believed it to be a drug, their asthma symptoms would disappear but their hay fever symptoms would remain. Conversely, if they were told that the placebo was for hay fever, those symptoms would disappear and asthma symptoms would remain.

Just as in the pain experiments, our awareness of what is wrong with us and what is supposed to happen when we receive medicine seems to be the directing force that instructs the brain and body which chemicals should be released, which genes should be activated and deactivated, where chemicals should flow to and, ultimately, what should happen. Imagine if we believed that we just needed to wish a disease away! An interesting thought...!

THE BRAIN IS CONNECTED TO THE BODY

Every part of your body is *wired* to the brain. Nerves connect the brain to the skin, muscles, bones, tendons and internal organs. This is the reason why when someone touches a part of your body you can feel it and if an organ is damaged you can feel the pain. But as well as touch being registered in the brain, just thinking about a part of your body does the same thing. This is how we can increase the temperature of our hand if we imagine it hotter and also why some pain goes away if we are distracted.

Though this was once just the realm of the mystical and was dismissed by academics as the stuff of quacks and 'alternative types', a great deal of research has now focused upon this. Neuroscience studies have now conclusively shown that if we think about moving a part of the body, the area of the brain that governs that part is stimulated. Thinking about moving your hand, for instance, activates the 'hand map' in the brain.

Publishing in the *Journal of Neurophysiology* in 2003, scientists at the Karolinska Institute in Stockholm (where Nobel Prize winners in Physiology or Medicine give their Nobel Lectures), demonstrated that when we imagine moving our fingers, toes or tongue, for instance, the area of our brain that governs each part is activated.

It is most likely that the brain is activated in the area that governs any part of our body that we focus upon.

USING OUR MIND TO BUILD OUR MUSCLES

If you think about any part of your body over and over again it has an even more powerful effect. Just as we learned in the last chapter that repetition of a movement increased the size of a brain map or the thickness of an area of the brain, when we repeat the thought about a movement the same thing occurs.

In a 1994 Harvard Medical School study, volunteers repetitively played a five-fingered combination of notes on a piano. The combination was thumb, index finger, middle finger, ring finger, little finger, ring finger, middle finger, index finger, thumb. They did this for two hours a day for five consecutive days. Another group just imagined playing those notes for the same duration of time and they also imagined hearing the notes. At the end of the five days, the groups' brain maps were recorded. The finger maps for the volunteers who had played the notes had grown, as you would expect, but the maps for the volunteers who had imagined playing the notes had also grown – amazingly, to the same extent.

And it's not only the brain that is activated. Since nerves connect the brain to the muscles, muscles grow stronger if we imagine using them. A 2004 study by scientists at the Department of Biomedical Engineering at the Lerner Research Institute in Cleveland measured a substantial increase in strength through imagined exercise. Thirty volunteers were involved. Some did physical training of their little finger but some, instead, just imagined doing the training. In each training session, the volunteers did 15 contractions at a time, real or imaginary, followed by a 20-second rest period. Each session lasted 15 minutes and took place five days a week for 12 weeks. After the 12 weeks, the scientists tested the strength of each volunteer's little finger. As expected, the group who did the physical training got stronger; their muscle strength increased by 53%. But, incredibly, the group who did the mental training increased their strength by 35%, even though they hadn't actually 'lifted a finger'.

I know a young athlete, a sprinter named Thomas, who had to have an operation on his shoulder and was advised that he would have to be out of training for the whole season. Not wanting to lose strength in his muscles, he went to the gym in his mind, doing lifts as if he was really there. Not only did he recover from his injury much faster than expected, but he returned to training almost as fast and strong as he had been before his operation.

And his improvement was rapid. Within a short time he was picked to run for his country (Scotland) for the first time.

Recent research has even shown that if we imagine lifting heavy weights, the brain and muscles are stimulated more than if we imagine lifting lighter weights. In a 2007 report by scientists at the University of Lyon, 30 volunteers either lifted or imagined lifting dumbbells of different weights. Significantly, the scientists found that the activation of the muscles was appropriate for the type of weight that the volunteers imagined lifting. If they imagined lifting a heavy weight, for instance, their muscles were activated more than if they imagined lifting a light weight.

Athletes have understood for a long time that muscles are affected by visualization and therefore mentally seeing themselves achieving at the highest level frequently separates champions from athletes that history does not record. But now we know, scientifically, that the brain is stimulated by the visualization and it then stimulates the muscles. This is fact!

I was once a long jumper and was jokingly mocked for spending lots of time imagining jumping. But it worked, because after only two months of formal training I reached the Scottish Championship long-jump final in 1996, in a high-level competition that attracted UK Olympic hopefuls using it as an event to make the Olympic standard. Now we know just how beneficial visualization can be. I often wonder how much I would have achieved if I had kept training at that level, but I was actually more interested in coaching and thus I became a long-jump coach the following season.

If you imagine jumping far, or running fast, your muscles will be stimulated to develop so that you can do that. But if you set the bar higher, so to speak, and imagine yourself jumping a world-record distance or running a world-record time, and do this regularly, then your muscles will develop in that direction instead.

In July 2008 the BBC showed a one-hour documentary featuring Colin Jackson, the ex-world record holder for the 110 metres hurdles. Genetic analysis of Colin's blood performed at the University of Glasgow found that he had little genetic advantage, but analysis of his muscle fibres found that he had an exceptionally high level of 'super-fast twitch muscles'. On the basis of genetics alone, Colin would not have had such a level of these fibres. It is likely that his determination to be the best played a significant role in how his muscles developed.

If an athlete regularly imagines running a world-record time, imagining their movements at the required speed, then their muscles will be stimulated differently and grow differently than if they imagined running a time that might just get them selected to run in a championship. It's what we focus on that counts.

BRAIN–COMPUTER INTERFACES

One of the powerful applications to evolve from the research findings that imagining moving a hand activates the hand-movement part of the brain is in prosthetics. The research uses brain–computer interfaces (BCIs) that record the stimulation of neurons caused by imagined movements. It then converts the stimulation into a computer signal that instructs the limb to move.

In pioneering research published in *Nature* in 2006, a tetraplegic person with a tiny chip inserted into his brain was able to move a computer cursor on a computer screen and even open email with his mind. He also played a computer game, controlled a robotic arm and changed the channel and volume of a TV while he was having a conversation.

And in a research paper called 'Walking from thought', published in 2006 by scientists from Graz University of

Technology, paralysed people were reported to be able to walk down a virtual street in a virtual-reality simulator.

MIRROR NEURONS

Research has now shown that, incredibly, even just watching someone exercising affects our brain and muscles.

In 2001, scientists at the University of Parma in Italy, publishing in the *European Journal of Neuroscience*, scanned the brains of volunteers as they simply watched people move their hands, mouth or feet. Amazingly, the areas of their brains that controlled the hand, mouth and feet movements were activated as if they were the ones making the movements.

Taking it further, in a fascinating 2006 paper called 'Bend it like Beckham: embodying the motor skills of famous athletes', scientists at the Centre for Clinical and Cognitive Neuroscience at the University of Wales found that we don't even have to watch people moving. We only need to see a photo of someone known for a particular skill and our brains and muscles are stimulated. Looking at a photo of a famous footballer, for instance, activates parts of the brain that govern leg and foot muscles.

As unbelievable as it sounds, watching a great athlete performing makes you better at that event. Watching Tiger Woods play golf makes you a better golfer. Watching someone not as expert also improves your ability, but not as much. If you want to learn something, there's a lot to be said for hanging out with people who are masters at it. This is why 'modelling', in the NLP (neuro-linguistic programming) sense, works. In NLP, we are encouraged to study and learn from experts. Neuroscience research shows that our brain and body are then actually stimulated like an expert's.

And just as visualization of our muscles working improves our strength, so does watching muscles working. In a similar experiment to the one described earlier in this chapter, scientists conducted an experiment where volunteers watched other volunteers flexing their little fingers, instead of imagining flexing them. In the group who did the actual training, muscle strength of the little finger of their right hand (the one used) increased by 50%, but amazingly, in the group who merely watched the training, finger strength in their right hand increased by 32%.

An interesting by-product of the experiment is that little-finger strength of the left hands in both groups also increased. In the group who did the actual training, the strength of the little finger on their left hand increased by 33% and in the watching group it increased by 30%.

Actual physical training of the little finger, imagining training and watching training all activated neurons in the part of the brain that controlled the little-finger muscles. Extending this, if you had impaired movement in any part of your body, just watching fully able people move (without any envy or negative thoughts regarding your own condition) would improve your own movement.

Indeed, in a pioneering study into stroke rehabilitation published in the journal *NeuroImage*, scientists from the University Hospital Schleswig-Holstein in Germany studied eight stroke patients over a four-week period as they watched able people perform routine actions such as having a coffee or eating an apple. The patients also received normal rehabilitation during this period. At the end of the four weeks, the patients who had watched the actions had improved much more than patients who had not watched the actions and, incredibly, MRI brain scans showed that their damaged brain maps were actually regenerating.

The brain mirrors what we pay attention to. If someone is sad, for instance, and you are paying attention to them, your brain will mirror the sadness on their face. If you spend enough time with them, then there's a good chance that you will become sad too. Similarly, if you spend time with happy people, your brain mirrors their expressions and actions too and your mood is likely to improve.

The neurons in the brain that are stimulated by what we see are aptly called 'mirror neurons'. They help us to learn new things as we watch people doing them. For instance, in a 2004 study, scientists at the Department of Neuroscience at the University of Parma took brain scans of volunteers who had never played the guitar while they were watching someone playing one. The scans showed that their mirror neurons were activated as if they themselves were actually playing.

And recent studies have shown that such is the power of our awareness and our brain that just listening to sentences describing motion activates our brains as if we were doing the movements. Scientists from the Department of Neuroscience at the University of Parma showed that when volunteers listened to people talking about hand movements, the area of the brain that controlled their hand movements was activated. When listening to people talk about foot movements, the area of the brain corresponding to foot movements was similarly activated.

Interestingly, studies have shown that when we hear a person speaking, our tongue muscles are also activated, especially if the person is speaking clearly. So, if you had impaired movement and listened to someone describing perfect movements, your ability to move would increase and your brain map for the muscles required would expand. Similarly, in sports, if you, say, listened to an expert tennis player describe a great serve that they had performed, your ability to serve would improve.

I once did a demonstration of this type of effect with a roomful of workshop participants. I learned it from a great book called *Neurospeak* by Robert Masters. For about five minutes, I just talked about moving our right arms and rotating our right shoulders. When I finished speaking, I asked each person to stretch both arms and shoulders. To the surprise of the group, their right arms and right shoulders were considerably looser and more flexible than their left ones. Note to sports coaches: what you say really matters!

Extending this, if you were sick, just listening to people talk about perfect health would aid your journey to wellness, especially if they happened to mention how amazing the body was and how wonderful its regenerative capacity was. The last thing any of us need when we are sick is people around us constantly affirming how sick we are.

The brain is incredibly sensitive to what we are aware of. Think of a movement and the brain is stimulated as if you are performing it. See a movement take place, or even hear about it, and the same type of thing occurs. Even looking at a part of someone's body increases the sensitivity of that part of your own body. Indeed, studies at the University of Wales have shown that looking at someone's hand or neck increases the sensitivity of our own hand or neck.

This is why if we see someone hurt themselves we feel a twinge. If we see someone fall over on their ankle, we may feel a sudden twinge from our ankle right up our leg. This is also why we can come out in sympathy with a person who is in pain and get phantom pains and symptoms of illness when a loved one is suffering. Some men even experience contractions when their partners are in labour. The awareness of our loved one suffering puts our unconscious attention upon our own body part, and neurons in the brain are activated, bringing us some pain. But the fact that we can create pain and discomfort in our bodies like this shows that we can also rid ourselves of pain and discomfort. Any doctor will tell you that a great many illnesses have their roots in the mind. Therefore the mind should be able to cure them.

The brain doesn't seem to know the difference between real and imaginary, which is great if we want to visualize ourselves recovering from illness. To the brain, we really *are* recovering and it is likely that, just as in the placebo studies described at the beginning of this chapter, the right chemicals are released in the right places and the right genes are activated and deactivated so that we ultimately become what we are imagining.

GUIDED IMAGERY

In 2004, medics at Tai Po Hospital in Hong Kong used 'guided imagery' relaxation to treat patients with chronic obstructive pulmonary disease (COPD). Guided imagery relaxation is where a person listens to a recording of someone guiding them through a series of relaxing visual images. Twenty-six patients were involved in the study. Thirteen of them had six sessions of guided imagery while the other 13 just rested during these times. At the end of the study, there was an increase in oxygen saturation in the blood of the group who did guided imagery.

A 2006 study conducted at Purdue University School of Nursing in Indiana found that guided imagery benefited older women with osteoarthritis. Of the 28 women in the study, half used guided imagery for 12 weeks and half did not. At the end of the period, the women who used guided imagery had a significantly improved quality of life compared with those who hadn't used it.

A 2008 study at William Beaumont Hospital in Royal Oak, Michigan, used guided imagery in the treatment of interstitial cystitis. Fifteen women used guided imagery for 25 minutes twice a day for a total of eight weeks. The imagery focused on healing the bladder, relaxing the pelvic-floor muscles and quietening the nerves involved in the condition. Fifteen women in a control group rested during these times. The results showed that the women who used guided imagery had significantly reduced symptoms and pain compared with those who didn't.

And a 2008 study published in the *Journal for the Society of Integrative Oncology* found that guided imagery reduced the risk of reoccurrence of breast cancer. The study involved 34 women who participated in an eight-week imagery programme. It found that the women had reduced stress and improved quality of life and that cortisol rhythm, which is an indicator of the probability of the reoccurrence of cancer, was improved.

Guided imagery even affects wound healing. This was shown in a 2007 study at Southeastern Louisiana University School of Nursing involving 24 patients undergoing surgery to remove their gallbladders. Patients who used guided imagery not only experienced reduced levels of anxiety and stress hormones, but they also had much lower levels of surgical wound erythema. This is the redness around a wound that is usually associated with infection or inflammation. In effect, guided imagery speeds up the healing of our wounds.

Guided imagery has also been used in treating fibromyalgia pain. Publishing in the *Journal of Psychiatric Research* in 2002, scientists at the Norwegian University of Science and Technology compared 'pleasant imagery' (which used pleasant images to distract the patients from their pain) with 'attention imagery' (visualizing the 'active workings of the internal pain-control systems'). Fifty-five women were involved in the study and their level of pain was monitored every day for a period of four weeks. The pain level in the 'pleasant imagery' group was significantly reduced, while it wasn't in the 'attention imagery' group.

I too have made similar observations. Some people find that actively visualizing reducing their pain is difficult. Thinking like this can cause them stress and this only intensifies the pain.

The type of visualization used can be important. Some visualizations can be stressful, especially where pain is involved. If you ever find a visualization stressful, then stop! With pleasant imagery, stressful daily images are gradually replaced with pleasant ones, thus reducing stress and lessening pain.

Our ability to visualize also affects our success in healing ourselves. In a 2006 study published in *Alternative Therapies in Health and Medicine*, scientists from the Department of Health Promotion and Human Behaviour at Kyoto University measured levels of stress hormones (salivary cortisol) and mood in 148 people who received two guided imagery sessions.

First, the study found that salivary cortisol levels were much less after the first and second sessions. The scientists wrote that, 'Unpleasant information, a cause of mental stress, is replaced by a comfortable image, and this replacement affects a person's salivary cortisol level.'

Second, by measuring the vividness of each person's imagery, the study found that those who had the best ability to visualize had the biggest reduction in salivary cortisol levels.

Don't be concerned, however, if you are not a good visualizer. The part of your brain involved will expand with practice and your ability will improve. It's just like getting better at a sport. And even if at first your ability is low, you are still always having a positive effect. Thoughts and words stimulate the brain too.

MENTAL IMAGERY

Several recent studies have shown that stroke patients and people with spinal cord damage could regain some movement by imagining themselves moving. Similarly, people with Parkinson's disease could move more easily and more accurately.

In a 2007 study conducted by scientists at the Department of Physical Medicine and Rehabilitation at the University of Cincinnati College of Medicine, visualization (scientists call it 'mental imagery') was used in a six-week study to help stroke patients regain some movement. Thirty-two chronic stroke patients were involved, half of whom did visualization as well as physical therapy sessions. The other half only did the physical therapy sessions. At the end of the six weeks, the patients who visualized could move much better than the group who didn't. In standard tests, their 'arm impairment' was much reduced and 'arm function' was much better. When stroke patients imagine moving their arms, their brain is stimulated in the area that controls arm muscles. If it has been damaged by the stroke, then the brain maps begin to regenerate.

Most studies on the use of visualization for recovery from stroke have shown it to be most effective when it is used along with physical exercise. So visualization needn't be a substitute for medication or therapy but something that we do *as well*. No matter what drugs or therapy we take for an illness, we have to think something. Sometimes we think that the therapy will work and other times we think that it won't. Visualization *targets* our thinking in a positive, constructive way.

This ability of the brain to regenerate is important for any kind of injury that requires regeneration to bring back movement. In 2007, publishing in *Experimental Brain Research*, scientists taught visualization to patients who had suffered a spinal cord injury. Ten tetra/paraplegic patients were instructed to imagine moving their tongue and feet and gained a better ability to move their tongue and feet.

Research published in the journal *Neurorehabilitation and Neural Repair* in 2007 showed that visualization could help patients suffering from Parkinson's disease. Twenty-three patients were involved in the study; 11 were given one-hour physical therapy sessions twice a week for 12 weeks and the rest used visualization as well as having these sessions. At the end of the 12 weeks, tests revealed that the patients who used visualization were much more improved than the patients who didn't visualize.

Visualization has also been successfully used to help asthma sufferers breathe more easily. In an Alaskan study involving 70 asthma patients, patients either did visualization where they imagined reduced bronchospasm and inflammation (which was called 'biologically targeted imagery') or they received education in the management of asthma. After six weeks of two two-hour sessions a week, both visualization and education had substantially improved the symptoms of asthma, but the greater improvement was with the patients who had visualized.

Most interesting about this study is that, unlike the others, it did not involve focusing on movements, which most of the recent visualization research has focused upon. The peripheral nervous system describes the connection between the brain and the muscles in the body. When we focus on moving muscles, we activate the area of the brain that governs them. The asthma study was concerned with the link between the lungs – an internal organ – and the brain, which are connected by the autonomic nervous system (ANS), an unconscious process. Through the ANS, the brain is linked with the eyes, parotid gland, salivary glands, the lungs, heart, liver, spleen, stomach, pancreas, intestines, kidneys, bladder, skin and reproductive organs. We maintain these systems unconsciously. But as the contents of our conscious minds seep into our unconscious minds, our conscious thoughts gradually influence the ANS.

Together with placebo studies, the asthma study shows that it's not only focusing on muscle movements that activates the brain;

focusing on, or even just being aware of, any body part activates the brain too. All cells in the body are bathed by nerve fibres that connect them to the brain, so when we put our attention upon any part of our body – muscle, organ or cell – we stimulate the area of the brain that is linked with that part and, in so doing, we stimulate that part too. Therefore, through both the peripheral and autonomic nervous systems, the mind can have an effect upon every part of the body.

The peripheral and autonomic nervous systems are undoubtedly involved in some healing but it is likely that higher centres of the nervous system are also involved in some recoveries. These higher centres link our specific thoughts, intentions, mental images, hopes and wishes with individual processes in the body. Most placebo effects involve the autonomic nervous system, but I am convinced that many also involve these higher centres. Thus our beliefs (conscious and unconscious) can influence specific parts and systems of the body in specific ways. What we expect to happen can actually affect what does happen.

In placebo research, a person who heals while taking a placebo is not actively visualizing healing. But their attention, either conscious or unconscious, is directed to the parts of their body that are injured or in pain, whether these are muscles and linked to the brain via the peripheral nervous system, or internal organs, which are linked via the autonomic nervous system. When the person receives a placebo, thoughts of wellness, hope or relief replace thoughts of sickness. Different thoughts therefore mentally describe the illness and so the brain areas and body areas are probably stimulated differently from when the person thought they were sick.

THE POWER IS WITHIN US

So we know that attitude has a substantial effect upon health. A positive attitude can protect us from illness, especially heart disease, and it can help us to live longer. Placebo studies show that when we take a drug or a placebo, what we think really matters. Healing starts with us. The mind can make an inert medicine work or a good medicine seem inert.

We've also learned that our thoughts even change the structure of our brains and that they send chemicals from the brain throughout the body, where they interface with cells and even DNA.

We also now know that when we focus on a part of our body, the area of the brain that governs that part gets activated and the body part is activated too. And through this connection, when we visualize healing, then healing occurs.

Before we move on to instructions for the best way to visualize, the next chapter discusses stress and its role in disease. It is important with any illness to work on reducing stress in our lives because stress has a negative impact upon almost every condition.

To Stress or Not to Stress

**Do not dwell in the past, do not dream of the future,
concentrate the mind on the present moment.**
Buddha

I feel that it is very important to devote a whole chapter of this book to stress because it has such a negative impact upon the body.

Stress has been linked with a large number of conditions. For instance, long-term stress has been linked with anxiety and depression, sleeping problems, hypertension, heart disease, stroke, cancer, ulcers, colds and flu, rheumatoid arthritis, obesity and even the rate of ageing. It also depresses the immune system and therefore lowers our ability to fight infection. Indeed, that was the conclusion of a 2004 meta-analysis of 293 scientific studies examining the links between stress and the immune system. It conclusively showed that stress weakened the immune system. Therefore, if we can reduce stress in our lives, we can enjoy healthier lives. And studies have shown that if we reduce stress, we even recover faster from illness and disease.

A 2003 study conducted by scientists at the University of Auckland investigated how stress affected the rate of healing.

It involved 36 patients who had undergone an operation. The scientists took samples of wound fluid after the operation and found that the chemical composition of the fluid was different depending on whether the person was feeling calm or stressed before the operation. The fluid in the stressed patients had fewer substances necessary to heal the wound.

Stress even affects how well medicines work for us. Scientists at the UCLA AIDS Institute, publishing in *Proceedings of the National Academy of Sciences* in 2001, reported that stress not only enabled HIV to spread faster in infected persons but that it prevented antiretroviral drugs from doing their job properly.

The scientists measured the viral load and CD4 cell count of 13 HIV-positive men who had never previously taken combination antiretroviral drugs. They also measured their blood pressure, skin moisture and heart rates at rest. The patients were then given a powerful regime of antiretroviral drugs. Over the next 3 to 11 months, their viral load and CD4 cell count were measured and compared with measurements taken before they took the drugs. The results were dramatic. The higher the patient's stress level, the less they responded to the antiretroviral drugs. The average reduction in viral load was more than 40 times for men with low stress, but less than ten times for men with high stress. The drugs worked four times better for the patients who were calm than for those who were most stressed. The authors concluded: 'Our findings suggest that the nervous system has a direct effect on viral replication.'

In another paper, published in 2003 in *Biological Psychiatry*, the same scientists described the results of an 18-month study involving 54 HIV-positive men. They measured each person's 'stress personality', the way they reacted to stressful events, and found that 'shy people with high stress responses possess higher viral loads'.

Instead of lowering viral loads, which the drugs were supposed to do, this study showed that the virus replicated between 10 and 100 times faster in the shy people with high stress than it did in the other patients.

Faced with stressful situations, some people tell others how they feel, express their emotions and explain the challenges that they are facing. Doing this can really help them to deal with things because it means that they have someone to talk to and being honest with them acts as a release valve for their emotions. A problem shared is a problem halved, as they say. And earlier we learned that talking a problem through can affect the structure of the brain. But others suppress how they feel and don't tell anyone because they are afraid that people will think that they are not good enough or because they are afraid of people's reactions and think that they might judge them.

Much research has found a link between suppressed negative emotion and disease. In my first book, *It's the Thought that Counts*, I described several studies showing a link with cancer. One study found that tumours were thickest in people with a 'Non-verbal Type C' personality. This type of person was described as being 'co-operative, unassertive, and suppressing negative emotion', which is very similar to the HIV studies above, showing that shy people with high stress responses had higher viral loads. Shyness is often associated with suppressing negative emotion.

These research studies tell us that we need to share our problems with people. Storing up our worries and emotional pains inside does us no good. Eventually it can have destructive effects upon our health.

The growth of suppressed negative emotion is like a balloon inflating in the psyche. As the balloon gets bigger, so symptoms of disease express themselves in the body. We need to find a release valve where we regularly release a little of the air from our stress balloons.

LET IT OUT

Some studies have shown that simply writing down how you feel can release the air from the balloon. In the 1980s, University of Texas psychologist James Pennebaker had half of the students in one of his classes write for 15 minutes on four consecutive days about their deepest thoughts and feelings about traumatic experiences in their lives. The other half of the students was asked to simply write about everyday things. At the end of the year, the two groups were compared and it was found that the students who had written about their life experiences were the healthier of the two.

In a similar study, published in 1995 in the *Journal of Consulting and Clinical Psychology*, medical students either wrote for four days about traumatic experiences that they had had or wrote about everyday things. They received a vaccination for hepatitis B on the fifth day. When blood samples were taken after four and six months, the group who had written about their traumatic experiences had much higher antibody levels against hepatitis B than the group who just wrote about everyday things.

And a 2004 study reported in *Psychosomatic Medicine* showed that writing about emotional topics even improved the health of HIV patients. The study involved 37 patients, around half of whom wrote for 30 minutes per day for four consecutive days. Those who wrote about their emotional experiences had significantly lower viral loads and higher CD4 cell counts.

In a 2007 paper published in the journal *Brain, Behavior, and Immunity*, scientists from Ohio State University showed that emotional support sessions that were designed to reduce stress improved the health of cancer patients. The study involved 227 breast cancer patients; approximately half of them had the sessions. At the end of the one-year study, the women who went through the sessions were healthier than those who hadn't, according to tests on their heart, liver, kidneys, immune system and even emotional health.

Just as in the previous studies mentioned in this chapter, these four studies also show that talking about our worries and stresses improves our health. And when we do share how we feel with another person it also gives them the opportunity to help, which is a deep desire that we as a species crave – the need to be needed. So not only are we doing ourselves a favour by expressing how we feel, but we are doing others a favour too.

RELAX

As well as talking with people, a well-known antidote to stress is meditation. With regular practice, meditation can have a dramatic impact upon stress levels. Regular meditation calms the mind and makes it much easier to face life's challenges.

That was one of the first things that I noticed when I first learned meditation – the things that bothered me at the time and caused me stress no longer had the same impact. And since most meditation techniques focus upon breathing, then through meditation practice I was able to induce a state of relaxation in a challenging situation just by taking conscious breaths, which is breathing *on purpose*. So when I was challenged in a way that might have previously caused me stress, I would take a breath and pay it my full attention. Then I would take a few more. Doing this made me feel differently about the situation. I no longer reacted. Instead, I chose what I would say and do. I felt much more in control.

This was my personal experience, but it is an experience shared by many millions of people who meditate daily. If you want to meditate and don't know how, then I would suggest that you enrol in a good class, or read a book on it, or just sit for ten minutes and pay attention to your breathing. Listen to the sound of your breathing and the feeling as the breath goes through your nostrils. This is a very simple meditation technique but very effective.

Such is the recognized power of meditation that it is now frequently used in clinical practice to treat a variety of illnesses and diseases where stress is an aggravating factor. Many studies of meditation involve mindfulness-based stress reduction (MBSR), which is based upon the Buddhist technique of sitting quietly and being mindful of your breathing and any thoughts that arise. When thoughts arise, we just let them dissolve. MBSR also usually involves gentle yoga sessions.

A 2007 study looked at the effects of an MBSR programme on the health of early-stage breast and prostate cancer patients. It involved 49 patients with breast cancer and ten with prostate cancer. Scientists measured their mood, symptoms of stress, cortisol (stress hormone) levels, immune cell counts, blood pressure and heart rate before the study, after six months, and again after 12 months. They found a large improvement in stress symptoms, a reduction in blood pressure, decreased levels of cortisol, and an increase in immune cells counts.

A 2007 study conducted at the Department of Emergency Medicine at Thomas Jefferson University showed that MBSR could be used to control glucose levels in type II diabetes mellitus patients. After practising MBSR, patients had lower glycosylated haemoglobin (HbA1c) levels (0.48% lower on average) and also had lower blood pressure, less anxiety, depression and psychological distress than patients who didn't use it.

Meditation has even been evaluated on healthy people. A 2007 study published by scientists at Duke University Medical Center involved 200 healthy adults who learned a simple mantra-based meditation technique over four small one-hour group sessions and then practised it during the study for 15–20 minutes twice a day. The study showed that there were significant improvements in mood as well as reduced stress and anxiety. The scientists also found that more frequent practice produced better outcomes. More meditation was better than less, or none at all.

A powerful 2008 Harvard study has shown that meditation affects us at the genetic level and sheds some light on why it has such a profound impact on health. Twenty volunteers were trained in various relaxation response techniques for eight weeks (the relaxation response is the physiological response to techniques such as meditation, yoga, repetitive prayer, tai chi, qi gong, breathing exercises and guided imagery). Genetic analysis of the volunteers' blood found that 1561 genes were expressed differently (switched on or off) after the training: specifically, 874 genes were upregulated (dimmer switch turned up) and 687 were downregulated (dimmer switch turned down). This was after only eight weeks. Longer-term practitioners of the techniques were found to have 2209 genes differently affected.

Many of the genes affected were involved in the body's response to oxidative stress. This is stress that can result from mental and emotional pressures. It has a negative effect in many diseases. This therefore means that relaxation techniques can have a positive effect on many medical conditions.

It is also clear that meditation benefits us after only a little practice. The above studies show the health benefits even at the genetic level, but we notice almost immediate benefits to our state of mind. I was invited by the Brahma Kumaris World Spiritual University on a one-week-long meditation retreat in the mountains of Rajasthan in India in 2002. Days typically involved a 45-minute meditation at around 6 a.m., followed by a half-hour silent walk. After breakfast the delegates attended a few classes. Some free time in the afternoon was followed by another 45-minute meditation and yet another in the evening after dinner.

When I returned home I noticed that my mind had never been so still. I couldn't help noticing that there was an absence of thoughts buzzing around in my head. It was a strange sensation at the time, feeling just emptiness in my mind, although it was a good sensation. I felt great physically, mentally, emotionally and spiritually. I felt motivated to make some lifestyle changes that easily became permanent. And this highly peaceful mind stayed with me for about a month before I gradually drifted back into my daily thoughts, although I have never rescinded the lifestyle changes.

Stress can creep up on us. I've worked in a corporate environment where I 'had' to get certain things done. But did I really 'have' to? Would the world have ended if I hadn't? Sometimes we need to stop our busy-ness and ask ourselves what's more important, the job or our health. Is a job worth a life?

Sometimes it's only when we have a health scare caused by stress that we sit up and take notice and suddenly realize that it is our choice how we handle situations. Many people have re-evaluated their priorities in life after suffering a heart attack or stroke and have emerged with a completely different attitude: 'Nothing is more important than my health.'

Handling stress is something that can be learned. The skill lies in making a shift in what we think is important. And, as we've seen in this chapter, sharing our worries with people helps, and meditation helps. Having a positive attitude also helps.

We should also recognize that it is not so much the events of our lives that cause stress, but our attitudes about them. Recognizing that the stress comes from our own perception of a situation gives us the ability to control things. Because sometimes stuff happens. But how it affects us is up to us.

For just as we have the ability to heal ourselves, so we have the ability to see things differently in life, to shift our priorities.

In doing so, we reduce stress. And visualization always works best when we have less stress. That's when we can really begin to heal – provided we know how to visualize and how to apply it to specific conditions.

This is what the next chapter will show us.

How to Visualize

**Imagination is everything. It is the preview
of life's coming attractions.**
Albert Einstein

As we have learned so far, the mind constantly affects the body. Visualization is a potent way to influence this. With visualization, we add some direction and purpose.

This chapter contains some guidance for using visualization effectively so that you will be able to construct a visualization for any disease or condition. In Chapter 6 I described the results of some research that used visualization. Most research has so far been conducted for muscular movements (stroke, spinal cord injury, Parkinson's disease, prosthetics). These involve the peripheral nervous system. But many recoveries due to the placebo effect involve the autonomic and also higher centres of the nervous system, which suggests that placing our attention upon any part of the body stimulates that part in a specific way, related to what we expect or wish to happen, as well as the part of the brain that governs it.

The key to using visualization for healing is to imagine the healing process unfolding inside the body. Having your attention focused upon the diseased area activates that area and the part of the brain that governs it. I believe that, in line with what you imagine, brain maps change and chemicals are released in the brain and throughout the body, genes are switched on and off, and stem cells receive instructions on which type of cells to become.

And this is easy to do when you imagine yourself inside your body, as a tiny person – I call it a 'Mini-Me' (this term was coined by my friend June and some women who attended one of my workshops). As a Mini-Me (or a Mini-You), you play a role in the healing process. For instance, if you had a cut you could imagine yourself as a 'Mini-You' pulling the two sides of the cut together. You could use imaginary ropes or magic thread and pull the two sides of the cut together so perfectly that there is no trace remaining.

While you are doing this, cells around the cut would be getting stimulated and the brain area that governs that cut would also be stimulated. The more your attention was focused there, the more the brain map for that area would change; as we learned with the 'piano study' and other similar research, the brain doesn't seem to know the difference between what's real and what we are imagining. Neurotransmitters and neuropeptides would bathe this area of the brain and genes would be switched on and off in this area too. And neuropeptides would be released into the bloodstream.

Genes throughout the body and specifically at the site of the cut would also be switched on and off. In particular, growth hormone genes would be activated that would accelerate the healing process. Genes in stem cells would also be activated so that the stem cells would grow into new skin cells. Stress genes would also be turned down, assuming you feel no stress or tension when you visualize (I will suggest how to easily accomplish this later in the chapter).

On account of your visualization, healing would speed up. And because you imagined the wound closing so perfectly, this would also have an effect. It is likely that the wound would heal much more cleanly than if you weren't imagining this. It is most likely that when we fear that a wound will leave a scar, we influence the healing process to tilt it towards what we are imagining.

The exact movement of chemicals and genes that I have just described has not been thoroughly investigated in science yet, nor has it been hypothesized in a scientific paper (to the best of my knowledge). But I believe that it is just a matter of time. People have been achieving amazing results using visualization for centuries. It is only in the past ten years or so that science has been moving in the direction of exploring the power of the mind–body connection, but it's always existed. Science is now only just scratching the surface in its exploration of why some astounding miracles of healing take place.

In true science fashion, I may be wrong. But that doesn't matter so much. What is most important is that, somehow, healing is affected by our minds. Visualization is a way to use our minds in a highly positive way and to give us a sense of control in our lives. Too often, people feel powerless when they are diagnosed with an illness. Perhaps just the feeling of regaining some power and influence by using their minds in such a direct way is all that is needed. Perhaps, indeed, this is why the healings described in the stories later in this book were made possible.

Ultimately the how is not too important – which chemicals go where, which genes go on and off, etc. Having some knowledge of it helps us to build our faith, and that's mostly why I have described it. But, perhaps, just the feeling of hope that grows as we visualize on a daily basis moves mountains in the body, just as it plays a huge role in the placebo effect.

The point of much of this book is to give people who want to use their minds something to focus upon when they are diseased or sick. This chapter is about how best to visualize.

HEALING SCENES

I call the visualization of the type described above a 'healing scene'. It's just like a movie scene, but you are the main character in the scene (Mini-Me), participating in the healing process. This helps you to feel a sense of power over the disease or condition.

In the example described for healing a cut, you imagined yourself actively pulling the two sides of the cut together. For this, you had some anatomical knowledge of a cut – that it has two sides and that the two sides come together as it heals. For more serious conditions, having some basic information can help. Knowing that a tumour is a lump, for instance, gives you something to build a healing scene around. You could imagine it as an ice lump and just regularly picture it melting, just as a block of ice would melt. You could let this occur gradually in your mind, over several days or weeks, so that every time you visualize you see it getting smaller, or you could picture it dissolving to nothing every time you visualize. If you are taking medication or are receiving radiation treatment, then you could imagine the chemotherapy agents or radiation as little bullets of heat that dissolve the tumour.

The key is that your attention is focused upon the area and therefore that area and the brain area that governs it are activated. Chemical changes thus take place in the brain, throughout the body, and at the site on which your mind is focused.

Notice that the degree of anatomical knowledge required is minimal. If you have a high degree of anatomical knowledge, then you can use it. It is not ultimately better or worse to have more knowledge. My understanding at this point is that it seems to mostly depend upon what you believe (just like a placebo). If you know, through science, that a particular thing has to occur for healing, then you can imagine that if you like. It probably doesn't make any difference if you don't know. It's fitting, then, that everyone can use this method for healing, not just highly educated people.

For instance, imagining a tumour melting to nothing would probably have the same effect as imagining growth genes in the tumour switching off and immune cells recognizing the tumour cells and ingesting them. Construct your 'scene', then, with elements that fit your personal knowledge and understanding.

Sometimes, having some knowledge and not using it could have a negative effect. In and of itself it does not; but if you believe that you *should* be imagining something, but don't, then it is your own belief that affects the healing. It would be just like not taking all your placebos, as I described in Chapter 3.

I have noticed, in some cases, that just using symbolic images is enough. For instance, getting rid of the cold or flu faster than normal by imagining bubbles in a large cavern uses the bubbles as symbols of the illness. Each time Mini-Me bursts a bubble it symbolizes the illness weakening. Eventually you burst all the bubbles in the cavern and this symbolizes that the illness has gone.

Perhaps this type of visualization – a symbolic visualization – would work for anything. Imagining popping bubbles of cancer, while even mentally saying, 'Cancer cancel!' for extra power, may work miracles. Once again, perhaps the feeling of power over the cancer instead of feeling power*less* is the important thing. Or perhaps your unconscious mind, which has internal knowledge of the disease, activates the autonomic nervous system appropriately so that cancerous systems in the body are affected. Ultimately, the how isn't too important. The fact that it works is all that matters to people who are sick.

One of the things that we tend to do when we are sick is focus upon the disease, or how sick we are. By using visualization, we feel a sense of power or hope and engage ourselves in the mental act of doing something about it. One of the great things about using visualization is that for periods at a time the mind is focused on a positive outcome.

And while thoughts are engrossed in the scene, we are not giving any attention to suffering or to any thought that we won't get better. And, just for a while, we believe in what we are seeing. I mean, you *can* see the disease disappearing, can't you? Sometimes, just a few moments of faith a day, or replacing hopelessness with hope, is all you need.

Doesn't the Bible say that if you have faith as a mustard seed, you can move mountains?

HOW TO CONSTRUCT A SCENE

The most important thing is to decide what you want. This means that you can then decide how to get to this point from where you are now. For instance, deciding that having no cancer is what you want means that you can construct a scene for getting from cancer to no cancer.

This may seem like an obvious thing, but quite frequently we sell ourselves short. We just shoot for a little instead of going for what we really want. 'It would be kind of nice to be rid of this pain' is different from ridding yourself of the condition that's causing the pain. If you want to be rid of something, then let that be your goal.

In one of the examples above, we imagined a tumour being made of ice. Then we melted the ice so that the tumour was gone. If you had a lung or kidney infection, your goal would be to be rid of it. As a Mini-Me, you might imagine the infection like ground black pepper scattered over the organ. Then you could use an imaginary vacuum cleaner and suck it all up, seeing the lung or kidney cleaned and restored to normal.

As I've pointed out, having no anatomical knowledge doesn't matter. Having some can sometimes help, though, because it gives us a sense of knowing what we are doing, which adds to our feeling of power. It is not too difficult these days to find information. Public libraries contain books that have pictures of what body parts look like. You can get information on any disease or condition from the internet. And I'm sure your doctor would be happy to discuss your condition in detail with you, and might be quite interested to know that you are taking a positive mental approach to it. If you prefer, though, using a scene that symbolizes healing is great too. Later in the book, I shall describe Quantum Field Healing, which is a powerful symbolic visualization.

Once you've decided what images you want to use, go ahead and create a story that involves Mini-Me helping to get from illness to healed. If you had an arthritic joint, for instance, you might imagine two bones painfully rubbing together at first, without any fluid separating them. Your goal is to have a joint that is lubricated with fluid so that the bones don't rub together. For your scene, you could imagine Mini-Me walking up to the joint, and then squeezing lots of lubricating fluid into it. The joint is now perfectly lubricated. You might then imagine the now-lubricated joint moving freely and easily.

You could, of course, imagine the scene unfolding in a different way. At a workshop that I ran, my friend Kevin suggested imaginary diggers driving up to the joint. They had special cutting tools to cut away any excess bone that was rubbing together, to create a space. Then he imagined the diggers erecting girders to keep the space there so the bones couldn't rub together again. Then another digger drove up with a bucket full of lubricating fluid (maybe you could be driving it) and poured it into the gap. Then the girders were removed and the two bones sat comfortably upon the fluid.

There's no single 'correct' visualization. There's just what works for you. If you are imagining healing a part of the body by repairing damaged cells, you can imagine the cells in any way you want. Some people might imagine healthy cells as clear blobs, with little dots at the centre – like frogspawn. Others might see them as pink circular jelly balls. Others might imagine them as rubbery bricks on a wall or like uncooked eggs after they've been cracked in a pan. One person might see a damaged cell of an organ looking shrivelled-up and dark, like a raisin or prune. Then in their scene they might imagine cleaning it with a cloth or brush and watching it restored to its healthy shape, colour and texture. Then they move on to the next cell and do the same again until all of the damaged cells are restored to full health. Another person might imagine nursing the little prune back to full health. They might imagine taking care of it and giving it magic medicine and see it regain its strength and colour. At the unconscious level, giving cells magic medicine will probably symbolize them getting all the right nutrients that they need to return to health. This will most likely stimulate the correct brain areas in such a way that they will indeed receive nutrients.

To ensure that your scenes are free of stress and so that you have less fear of your condition, it is good to occasionally add some fun to your scene. For instance, in the first arthritis scene above, when you squeeze the lubricating oil out of the can, imagine the squeaking sound as it squirts out of the can. You can exaggerate the sound if you want. Or imagine all the individual atoms of oil as little balls with smiley faces. See them shout, 'Whahhheeeeeeyyyyyy!' as they slide out of the oilcan funnel as if they are having a great fun time on a slide. Adding bits of humour or light-heartedness to your scenes often brings a smile to your own face.

And because this is your imagination, you can imagine anything you want. You can use magic to transform one thing into another. What's to stop you using a magic wand? To your unconscious mind and your brain, all that has occurred is that you've gone from diseased to healed. How you get there in your scene is completely up to you. You can imagine that the lubricating fluid is everlasting so that it never wears out. Thus the joint could never become arthritic again. Maybe you can imagine it as 'gymnast joint' fluid or 'yoga master' fluid.

Another thing you can do to increase your sense of power is to make the scene feel more real. This can help if you feel that you are not good at visualizing. To do this, just engage more of your senses. Notice what your surroundings look like. Notice how the ground feels and how the things you hold in your hands feel. For instance, if you are cleaning cells, notice how the cloth and fluid feel on your hands. Notice how it feels to make the rubbing motions with your arms. If you are squirting lubricating fluid, notice how it feels to squeeze the can. Notice how it feels to vacuum up pepper (infection) from an organ. Feel the suction and hear the sound of the vacuum.

Once you are happy with your scene you can use it as often as you want. You can also evolve it in time, or change it altogether if you feel you can improve upon it. Each time you evolve it or change it, you make it better for you. Sometimes you may even feel that your condition has improved and naturally feel that you therefore need to adapt your scene.

HOW OFTEN SHOULD I VISUALIZE?

Visualize regularly. A tiny hammer can break a huge boulder if it makes regular taps upon it. Similarly, if you want to be an Olympic champion at a sport, going to the gym just once won't get you there. Going to the gym every day might. Remember the earlier report of improving finger strength through visualization? The same level of mental work as physical work was required.

If your doctor prescribes some medicine for you, the chances are the bottle or pack will tell you to take it three times a day. Use this prescription, then, for visualization. Take your mind medicine three times a day. Visualize in the morning, afternoon and at night. Or you can visualize more if you wish. I am convinced that repetitive visualization has the same effect as conditioning in the placebo effect, which I described in Chapter 2. But, unlike with conditioning, we can powerfully alter systems in the body on purpose. So listen to your own body tell you how often you need to visualize.

The length of each visualization session can vary too. Ten minutes for each session can be a good length of time to thoroughly work through your scene, and this equates to 30 minutes per day. Of course, you can go for longer if you wish. Sometimes, we can get totally absorbed in our visualizations. And you can do it for shorter periods too. If you do just a couple of minutes at a time, then you should do a couple of additional sessions. If you find it tiring work, on account of your condition, do not stress yourself. Start with just once a day for around a minute. Then build up to two sessions of one minute a day and gradually work it up from there to as much as you are able to do.

SOME EXTRA HINTS AND TIPS

Here are some hints and tips that you might also find useful. You don't need to use all of them. They are just guidelines and pointers – things that can help if you are having some difficulty.

Draw or Paint your Images

If you have difficulty with visualization, try to draw or paint your scene. While you draw or paint you will still activate the desired area of your body as well as the area of the brain that governs it, as if you were visualizing. If you are not so good at art, then trace some images from a medical book or from the Internet and make up your scene that way. Then look at your creation at least three times a day, while imagining or telling yourself that it is happening in your body.

If you have advanced computer skills and have the time, create an animated healing scene.

Patience

Don't get anxious if you are not healed in a day or two. Sometimes it can take days, weeks or months. Some illnesses take a year or more to heal, depending upon how much reconstruction is needed and upon whether you really believe that it is possible or not. Be patient with the process.

Don't lose heart and think it's not working just because you're not 100% healed within an hour of visualizing.

Improve your Lifestyle

Try to make some positive lifestyle changes that benefit your recovery. Examine your diet, habits and lifestyle. Do you eat a good nutritious diet? Be honest with yourself. Do you drink lots of alcohol, take drugs or smoke? What kind of attitude do you have? Are you able to take some exercise?

Ask your doctor about exercise and try to work in their recommendations. Sometimes a few changes in diet, attitude and lifestyle can have dramatic results on health.

Ask your Body What It Needs

Although some people may find this silly, you can ask your cells, organs or body what they need. Get into a relaxed state first. In a relaxed state you will be conversing with your unconscious mind, just as a hypnotherapist would, so you will be able to receive more information on the types of changes that you might be best to make in your life. It might feel like you are having an imaginary conversation but if you receive any wisdom that feels that it makes a lot of sense, then trust it.

A diseased organ might tell you, for instance, that it needs the nutrients from a particular food, or even that you should cut out a certain food because it contains substances that are harming your particular biology. You may even learn that you should give up smoking, drug taking or that you need to quit drinking alcohol.

You might even feel your cells telling you to ask your brain to send certain substances. So you go ahead and ask the brain to produce them and send them to where they need to go. Or you may get information on the type of visualization that you need to do. Perhaps there's a specific scene that you need to play.

Do a Victory Dance

This is something that I personally sometimes do in visualizations. It brings a sense of light-heartedness into what can sometimes be a stressful time. It's just a silly dance that celebrates the success that the scene is showing. I saw it being done in an episode of the US hospital sitcom *Scrubs*, as one of the lead characters celebrated a victory. It made me laugh.

Now, for instance, if I'm vacuuming up some bacteria and notice that I've cleaned up quite a lot, I'll see myself break out into a victory dance in the scene as a celebration of my success. Or sometimes I physically break into my victory dance, then go back into my scene where I left off (you might find it less embarrassing to do this if no one is around to see you) or I do my dance at the end.

You can do your dance in the shower, in the bathroom, in your bedroom, or wherever you wish. I often visualize when I'm out walking. I do much of my book writing in coffee shops in Windsor in the UK, where I live. The walk to the coffee shops takes me around 25 minutes. As well as visualizing healing, I also visualize things that I want to happen in my life. But whatever the nature of my visualization, I almost always do a victory dance at the end.

Of course, you might want to be a little discreet with your dance if you are walking along the side of a busy road. I do a little dance with my fingers at these times. However, around halfway into my journey I have to walk through an underpass that goes underneath the road. It's about 25 metres long, so I do my dance as I go through it. There's not usually anyone around at 6.50 a.m. when I arrive there, so I can really break out the moves. It always makes me smile.

One time I had broken into a few moves that I had seen in the film *Saturday Night Fever* and was totally absorbed in them when I got to the end of the underpass and looked up – to see a line of builders looking at me. It was close to Christmas and they must have been working all night to get a block of apartments finished. They had stopped eating breakfast and were staring at me.

This is where I made one of those regrettable split-second decisions. As my right hand was pointing in the air to my right, as in John Travolta's famous dance routine, I drew my hand to my ear and said, 'Hello!' as if I was on the phone. They must have thought I was insane. And then, as 'luck' would have it, my phone actually rang as I passed them. I just kept my head down and walked as fast as I could until they couldn't see me anymore. The experience did make me smile, though. Eventually.

Some of the real power of a victory dance lies in the fact that you can't experience anxiety, stress, worry or frustration at the same time as you experience humour. It's one or the other. The fun of your dance replaces the worry of a life situation. In time, whenever you think of the situation, instead of feeling worry you find yourself smiling because you have started to associate the condition with the dance – a great way to reduce stress!

OTHER WAYS THAT VISUALIZATION WORKS

Visualization works on more levels than just having direct biological effects. In addition to giving your body instructions for what you want it to do, the scenes drip into your unconscious mind.

When a thought drips into your unconscious mind, it influences how you behave. For instance, if the colour red were dripped into your unconscious mind without you noticing, if you were later shown some colours and asked to choose one, you would probably choose red and you wouldn't know why you chose it. Similarly, if you were to imagine the colour red several times a day, you would start to notice more red things than you normally would and you might also, seemingly accidentally and without even realizing what you were doing, walk a different path from normal, or drive a different route, that took you to a place where there was much more red.

So, when we visualize healing, we often change our behaviour without even realizing. We start to behave in a way that is more conducive to healing than how we normally behave. We sometimes find ourselves in the company of different people who end up sharing knowledge or information with us that's just what we needed to hear. We also sometimes develop a craving for a particular food, which probably contains some nutrients that we need for our healing. Sometimes we find ourselves changing the products that we use around the home. Perhaps one of them had an allergen that was having a negative effect upon us.

You might even find that life circumstances change without you having to do anything. It is not uncommon for people to be made redundant at just the right time. It might be upsetting at the time but turns out to be the exact tonic that they needed for their health.

I have noticed that when people recover from illnesses, they mostly put it down to a particular medicine or a change in their diet or other personal circumstances. And sceptics use this argument to say that visualization doesn't do anything. They point out that it was obviously the medicine, diet or the change in personal circumstances that led to less stress. And, of course, this *is* true. But what is usually missed is that it was the person's desire to get well again that *inspired* the necessary changes. It all starts with us.

Taking medicines, changing our diet and lifestyle, *and* our desire to recover work seamlessly together. It is rarely just one or the other, but a combination that produces the results. At the end of the day, you get well. Is it really that important how you get there?

That's why I never suggest that people give up their medicines. Take your medicines *and* visualize, and, at the same time, improve your diet, improve your attitude and adopt a healthier lifestyle.

The Power of Affirmations

One comes to believe whatever one repeats to oneself
sufficiently often, whether the statement be true or false.
Robert Collier

Affirmations can be used independently of visualization or along with it. An affirmation is a statement of fact, or what you intend to be fact, and you make it over and over again.

There are three things to remember about affirmations:

1. Repetition
2. Repetition
3. Repetition

When we say something over and over again, we create neural connections in our brain. The more we say it, the more connections we create and the stronger they become. As we learned earlier, we form the same connections when we are imagining something as when we are actually doing it. Evidence from mirror neuron research suggests that it's the same for speech. Talking about your hand, for instance, activates the hand area of the brain.

Therefore repeating a statement about something being true will create neural connections as though we were experiencing the thing as true and were merely making a statement of fact.

For instance, say you were holding a sandwich and were looking at it and feeling how it felt on your hands. Neurons would fire in your brain in the areas that processed the sensory data from your fingers as well as your thoughts and attitudes about the sandwich. If you didn't have a sandwich in your hands but just imagined what it looked like and how it felt on your skin, then the same neurons would fire in your brain with the same intensity as when you were actually holding it. And in both circumstances if you affirmed, 'I love sandwiches,' your brain would fire in the same areas, regardless of whether you were holding a sandwich or not.

Many people, if they have been sick for a long time, affirm their condition with statements like 'This is terrible', 'I'll never get better' and 'I feel tired.' While these statements are accurate reflections about how they feel, they also back up the condition on a biological level as neurons are stimulated in the appropriate areas of the brain, chemicals are released and genes are switched on and off. So the cells linked with the disease are encouraged to produce proteins and other substances that sustain the diseased state.

Of course it can be difficult to say, or even think, something different from how you feel, and when you are suffering the last thing you need is someone badgering you to be more positive. A friend of mine who was having some difficult challenges in her life once made me laugh when she said, 'If one more person tells me to think positive, I'm going to punch them.' But when you are ready – and you may not be in that space right now due to the overwhelming experience of an illness – then a change of attitude will help.

When a sick person changes their attitude and their language and affirms, over and over again on a regular basis, 'I am recovering' or 'I am getting better' or the well-known 'Every day in every way, I am getting better and better' or even, to begin with, 'I am determined to recover fully' then appropriate neural connections will form and neuropeptides will be released that interface with cells and DNA to bring about healing. The awareness of the illness and which systems of the body are affected ensures that the right neurons are activated to target the right systems of the body. The relief of 'knowing' that you are recovering will also ensure that stress hormones reduce in quantity, which will also speed up healing.

COMMENTATE

You can use affirmations in your healing visualizations. Sometimes it can be helpful to give a verbal commentary on what is happening. For instance, during a healing visualization, as you, say, sucked up bacteria using an imaginary vacuum cleaner, if you were to affirm that 'All of the harmful bacteria are disappearing from my body,' which is really pointing out what is happening, the appropriate neurons will fire in your brain as if the bacteria were indeed disappearing, which of course they are.

Affirmations also draw extra attention to what you are visualizing, helping you to focus upon that part of your body, thus helping to stimulate brain cells and instigate the healing process. They can be useful if your scene isn't very clear in your mind.

As another example, while firing a green laser to burn off cancer cells, you could be affirming that 'The cancer cells are burning off the bone and leaving it intact.'

And as another example, let's say that you were visualizing yourself pouring some magical lubricating fluid into an arthritic joint. As you pick up the container of fluid and the rubber tube that you are going to use to pour the fluid into the joint, you could acknowledge, 'This fluid is a magical, 100% efficient, everlasting lubricating fluid.' And as you pour the fluid into the joint, point out to yourself that 'The fluid is seeping into the joint. The joint is looking totally free now.' And as you imagine the joint moving, point out that 'The joint is moving freely and easily now.' So, basically, you commentate your way through bits of your healing scene. You can add as much or as little commentary as you wish, or none at all.

Commentating is useful if you really can't visualize clearly, as neurons in your brain will still be excited regardless of whether you see the picture or not. If you can't picture the inside of an artery, for instance, just the awareness of the words 'inside an artery' will excite neurons in the brain as if you were actually looking inside one.

HOW OFTEN SHOULD I DO AFFIRMATIONS?

Aside from commentary, different amounts of affirmation work for different people, but I have found that the more times I affirm something and the more gusto I say it with, the faster the changes. Repeating something ten times a day in the morning and ten times at night is a good place to start, or you could just do an affirmation whenever the thought arises in your mind. For instance, an affirmation of 'I am in recovery' might be something that you say whenever you feel like it, which might turn out to be 20 or 30 times a day.

You don't have to structure your times for affirmations, but it helps to do so. Ten times in the morning and ten at night would be structured. And you would do this for as long as you needed to until the thing you wanted to change had changed.

You can affirm more than this if you wish. You might be so determined that you saturate your mind with 50 or more affirmative statements a day.

In 1994 I went to see a doctor because I found a lump on one of my testicles. I was very afraid. He arranged for me to see a consultant in a few days' time, which made me even more afraid. I remember getting into my car and crying. Then I got angry that I had allowed some aspects of my life to be not what I wanted. I committed to make some serious changes after I got through this, which I became totally and absolutely determined about.

Over the next few days I affirmed with conviction, 'It's gone!' several hundred times. I also made a sweeping motion with my hand, as if I was cutting, which was symbolic of actually cutting the lump away. No matter what else I happened to be doing at the time, if a doubt that it had gone crept into my mind, I stopped and did my affirmation and hand movement several times until the doubt was gone.

I was in the second year of my PhD at the time and was on placement with the pharmaceutical company that was funding my studies. I recall that I ruined quite a few delicate experiments in those few days because a doubt always seemed to enter my mind just when I was at an important stage of an experiment and was using some rather expensive chemical ingredients. But, to me, my health took precedence over them. It was actually a powerful symbol of what was more important – my work or my health.

When the consultant examined me a few days later, the lump was indeed gone. It might have been a tumour. It might not have been. Personally, I didn't care. All I was concerned with was that it was gone.

Most of the times that I said my affirmation, I said it with conviction. I really meant it. When I was in a place where I couldn't say it out loud, I would say it out firmly and directly in my mind. If I was at home, I walked around my room saying it out loud with conviction.

HOW TO CREATE AN AFFIRMATION

So how do you work out what to say? Affirmations are statements of 'fact' – what you intend to be a fact – so write them as positive statements.

Here's a list of some positive statements about healing:

'I am in recovery.'
'I am getting better and better.'
'I am feeling better.'
'I am improving.'
'The cancer cells are burning off.'
'The tumour is dissolving/melting.'
'It's gone.'
'I can move freely and easily now.'
'My blood pressure is returning to normal.'
'My heart is getting healthier and healthier.'
'My breathing is getting easier.'

And make them really positive. For instance:

'I am recovering fast' is more positive than 'My cold is going away.'
'The tumour is dissolving' is more positive than 'My cancer is becoming less severe.'
'I am in recovery' is more positive than 'I'm not feeling as bad anymore.'

Remember, affirmations can be useful together with or independent of visualization. We can see these strategies at work in the next part of the book, which is a collection of true stories from people describing their healing journey and the role that their mind played in it.

PART II
TRUE STORIES

Introduction

The following section contains some true stories from people around the world who have used visualization as all or part of their journey to recovery from illness.

As you will see, many used visualization alongside other modes of treatment. They used it not so much *instead of* but *as well as* their medication or therapies.

In all of the stories that I've collected, one thing that I've noticed is the striking similarity between them. These are stories from people who have never met each other, yet each has used a similar strategy to heal themselves. Each person has created a 'healing scene', as I call it in Chapter 8, involving some form of imagined removal of the unhealthy cells or disease from the body.

There are not many books telling people how to do this type of thing. I've since come to believe that many people seem to intuitively know what to do, as I've found in my own personal life when I've had to create healing scenes for myself. We are not taught it, but we just seem to know what to do.

None of the stories has been medically verified. I have taken them in the spirit in which they were sent to me. People have been kind enough to send their stories in the hope that their experiences will inspire others to be able to heal themselves too and, most of all, to *believe* that they can.

There is a chance that some of the people featured in the stories would have got better anyway in the normal course of their illness. But to say that this is true for everyone would be to deny the powerful and usually underestimated human mind. As I've stated elsewhere in the book, there are many factors that influence healing. The mind is one of them and I hope that through reading this book, and indeed this section, we will begin to use our minds in a more positive way.

In the chapters that follow, I have grouped the stories together under the headings of each illness or medical condition: cancer, heart problems, pain, chronic fatigue and ME, viruses, allergies and autoimmune conditions; and have included accounts relating to weight loss and physical regeneration.

Cancer

IRIS'S STORY

I minute myself and sit on my shoulder. There is an imaginary helter-skelter there that can take me to any part of my body and I slide down this to reach the area I want. I decided in advance to make a comfortable place there to sit in, i.e. some grass/carpet and a soft chair, a place where the sun always shines and you feel calm and peaceful. [That grass/carpet and chair will always be there every time you do your visualization.]

I like to work with sound as well as seeing visuals, as it adds to the fun. As I work with crystals I always take my pendulum with me, as it acts as a magnet to the cancer cells and you can actually watch it drawing the cells from the area. It's great to watch it happening, as you can really achieve the feeling of knowing you have taken those rogue cells and dispersed them down the helter-skelter and out through the toes.

OK, here we go.

When I sit on my shoulder I talk to myself and say, 'OK, Iris, it's fun time. Let's go down and see what the rogue cells are up to.'

I slide down and use sound as I go down like you would as a child. I find my chair and sit and look at the cells and talk to them. 'You know how much I love you all and I love talking to you each day but you know you can't stay here and you'll have to leave.'

I visualize the cells talking back to me and saying, 'We love you too and we do understand.' They start to get excited and ask me, 'Did you bring your pendulum with you?'

'Yes, I did,' I say, and I take it out of my pocket and hold it up. It starts to spin and I can hear the laughter from the cells as they fly onto it like a magnet. I check the area in my body to see if it is clear but I can always find a couple of cells hiding. I call out, 'I can see you and you'll miss all the fun going down the helter-skelter if you don't hurry up,' and they rush out chuckling to join the other cells on the pendulum.

I keep spinning them around and they shout out, 'Have you opened the taps on your toes?'

I bend over and open the five taps and say, 'Are you all ready?' I take them to the top of my leg, blow them off the pendulum and I can hear them screaming with delight going down the helter-skelter in my leg and as they fly out of my toes into Mother Earth they shout, 'Love you, Iris,' and I call out, 'Ditto.'

This Worked Because...

Iris had an upbeat, positive attitude and there was a strong element of humour in her scene. This would have minimized any stress that she might have ordinarily felt relating to her condition. She also created a comfortable place in her scene where she would always feel peaceful.

In her scene, Iris saw the removal of cancer cells. Her scene played the story of 'cancer cells to no cancer cells'. Her awareness of where the cancer cells were located would have stimulated those areas as well as the part of the brain that governed them.

And the fact that her scene was so clear that she could 'really achieve the feeling' that the cancer cells were leaving would have amplified the power of the scene and the speed of the result.

Also, notice that Iris treated the cancer cells with love and saw them leave her body in a happy fashion. Some people prefer to do this type of thing rather than use force of any kind. Love is a powerful state and can have really powerful effects upon the course of disease. In the end, however, we will get the same result as long as the scene describes going from the presence of cancer cells to having no cancer cells.

PETULA'S STORY

I was diagnosed with inoperable breast cancer over ten years ago. I was only given a 15% chance of survival. The cancer had spread into my lymphatic system and into my neck. I had chemotherapy and radiotherapy to shrink the tumours and then if anything was left in my breast it was to be surgically removed.

While I was having my treatment I visualized a rabbit, whom I called 'Pure Health', jumping into my body and eating all the cancer cells. The cancer cells were food for the rabbit and he loved eating them. They didn't harm him because they were his food. He looked so healthy and had a really glossy coat. When he was full up he jumped out of my body and ran off into the woods where, at a certain spot, he excreted all his waste products. At that spot, in time, a beautiful tree grew. Everyone that saw the tree, or sat under it, felt great peace and well-being. It was called a healing tree.

I did this visualization at least two or three times a day and every time I had my treatment. At the end of my treatment the doctors were amazed at how well I had responded to it. The cancer had disappeared and I didn't need an operation.

Another visualization I did was to see the cancer cells as balloons and to see, two or three times a day, the balloons popping. The empty shells were then flushed through my body and came out as waste products and were sent into the earth to be changed to positive energy for the good of all.

The third visualization was for me to stand under a shower of pure, healing water. The water entered through the crown of my head and flowed down the inside of my body, flushing all the cancer cells out. The water came out of my feet as black, thick liquid at first. This gradually changed to a brown, thinner liquid and then to clear water when the cancer cells had been removed. This water went down the drain to the earth, again to be changed into a positive energy. Then I visualized a pure white healing light filling the spaces in my body where the cancer cells had been.

Also, every night I say to myself, before I go to sleep, 'I have a wonderful body that is glowing with perfect health,' and 'Every single living cell in my body is whole, normal and perfect.' I also visualize my body full of pink healing light, as this is the colour for love and harmony. Another thing I do is to chant 'Om' into my left breast and at a certain note I can feel the tissue vibrating. I am sure that all this has helped me, as I am still alive and well 11 years later. The doctors and nurses still marvel at the fact that I am so healthy.

This Worked Because...

Petula's scene described moving from having cancer to not having cancer. Notice the creative way that she did this with her first visualization. The use of the 'Pure Health' rabbit also established a light-hearted scene which would have reduced stress associated with the condition and it also made the scene more interesting, which makes it easier to stay focused. And the name 'Pure Health' was also symbolic of how she was imagining herself, as was the fact that the rabbit was so obviously healthy with its glossy coat.

I also like the bit about the cancer cells being recycled. This reflects an attitude of knowing that there's a positive side to everything and a desire for things to work out for the best all round. And we know that a positive attitude aids health.

Notice also that she visualized *and* she received chemotherapy. It doesn't need to be one or the other. And putting her attention on the cancerous location would have stimulated that location and the brain area that governed it, altering the brain map there and causing numerous chemical changes. Genes in the brain, throughout the body and at the cancer sites would also have been activated and the genes in the stem cells would have encouraged the growth of healthy new cells.

Repetition of her visualization played a key role too. She visualized at least two or three times a day.

The use of balloons was a good symbolic visualization and represented the bursting of the 'cancer bubble' in her body. To her unconscious mind, the cancer was being eliminated. This would have stimulated the correct brain and body areas so that it was, indeed, what eventually occurred.

The shower visualization was also a powerful symbolic visualization because, just like the other two, it described moving from having cancer to not having cancer. As she progressed with this visualization and the water became lighter until it was clear, this sent a powerful unconscious message to her brain that the cancer was gone. Higher levels of her nervous system would have been working, then, to make that a reality.

The use of three separate visualizations was a very good thing because sometimes we get bored with the same scene. This is where many people give up; they can't motivate themselves to visualize the same picture time and time again. But when we chop and change our scenes it keeps us fresh.

Last, her affirmation would have contributed greatly. It focused her attention upon what she wanted and, just as with the visualizations, would have stimulated her brain and body in the appropriate ways to bring about healing.

CATHIE'S STORY

Ten years ago I was diagnosed with non-Hodgkin's lymphoma. I had very large tumours in my abdomen and groin. I was scheduled for chemotherapy but was told to wait for five weeks to see how my disease was going to evolve. It was believed to be a slow-growing type but because the tumours were really large it was thought that the cancer might be about to mutate to a more aggressive form.

During my wait, I did a lot of reading and had reflexology three times a week. I had started to train as a reflexologist so I knew it could help. My reflexologist told me of the real dangers of chemo – something I had not been made aware of. To cut a long story short, I decided not to have any conventional treatment and relied on an organic diet and vegetable juicing, long walks in nature and lots of laughter with friends. I also gave up teaching.

But I did use visualization to focus my cells on getting rid of the cancer. First of all, I told myself that my body was not my enemy, but that some of its cells had lost their way somehow. I drew a picture representing my cancerous cells as grey blobs without much shape or substance. I then drew my T-cells as little piranha fish – they had very focused friendly eyes and very sharp teeth! None of the grey blobs stood a chance! I visualized them taking great big mouthfuls out of the cancerous cells, and vacuuming them up into their little stomachs … they obviously enjoyed their food … I even 'heard' them go, 'Miam, miam, miam!' as they ate (that's 'Yum, yum'… I am French).

At first I had to make a point of going through this visualization several times a day, but very soon it became part of my every waking moment. It was as though I had a little TV screen in the corner of my mind that was constantly showing the same cartoon. It made me smile a lot.

I also used affirmations, which varied. At the very beginning, when I still had a lot of anxiety about being diagnosed and dying, I made one up, a variation of 'Every day in every way I am getting better and better.' Mine was, 'My immune system is very strong and every day my cells are getting cleaner and healthier, my immune system is very strong.' Somehow the repetition seemed to be necessary in order to imprint on my brain.

It worked, because whenever I woke up during the night in the grip of panic, my affirmation would kick in and I would be able to go back to sleep after focusing on it for a while. Then the next night I would wake up again and, this time, virtually as soon as my eyes opened I would hear the words in my brain and go back to sleep immediately, reassured that, even in sleep, my body was still working for me. After a while, I would barely open one eye and hear my head filled with my affirmation: the tape was playing without my having to switch it on, so to speak! After I realized that, I never woke up during the night again.

I had also played with the affirmation during the day: I would take a mirror and pretend to be talking to somebody else and say, to the mirror, 'My immune system is very strong, you know!' and more often than not I would end up laughing at the thought of somebody walking in on me while I was having this demented conversation with my mirror.

I also used affirmations to tackle certain emotional issues that were at the root of my cancer. The very simple one suggested by Louise Hay, 'I love and approve of myself, all is well,' proved impossible at first. I could not look at myself and say, 'I love and approve of myself,' without either crying or laughing hysterically...

Still, using Louise Hay I looked at the affirmation to do with cancer as being a deep hurt, a longstanding resentment, etc. ... and it hit home. So I also did my best with 'I lovingly forgive and release all of the past.' I still use this one today and feel my heart open up as I say it.

I was diagnosed in April, for my 45th birthday, and by December my cancerous tumours had decreased by 70%. By the beginning of the next year they had all disappeared. You can check all these facts: my consultant at the Vale of Leven Hospital (in Scotland) is Dr Patricia Clarke.

Here's to a life of no limits!

This Worked Because...

Cathie created a scene that saw her T-cells swallow up the cancer cells, so it described moving from a state of having cancer to not having cancer. This would have stimulated the cancerous areas of the body as well as the areas of the brain that governed them, leading to beneficial chemical and genetic changes in the brain and at the sites of cancer.

And by affirming that her body was not the enemy, she was treating it with love. When we dwell on things having gone wrong and think that there is something wrong with us, we generate stress and it has a negative effect upon us. Instead, Cathie affirmed that some cells had just somehow lost their way. This also showed love and acceptance, which, I believe, would have made a positive difference.

The use of reflexology would have helped too. Although, like many alternative therapies, there isn't yet a great deal of positive evidence that supports it, I do believe that it is just a matter of time before better evidence becomes available. Her belief in it would also have contributed to its efficacy.

Introducing some exercise and switching to a healthy organic diet and vegetable juicing would also have been beneficial for her.

There is some evidence to indicate that increased consumption of fruit and vegetables and less meat in the diet can affect cancer.

Having lots of laughter would have reduced stress and also flooded the body with some happy chemicals, which most likely played some sort of positive healing role. The little introduction of 'Miam, miam, miam' would also have brought a smile to her face while visualizing.

Giving up teaching was also a good idea, as this would have eliminated a possible source of stress and allowed Cathie to focus more of her energy on healing. It is clear that she had a very positive attitude and was determined to rid herself of cancer.

Cathie's strong positive attitude also meant that she did lots of visualizations. Her scene became part of her every waking moment, which would have had substantial positive consequences.

Her use of affirmations would have contributed very positively to her healing by improving her immune system.

And by viewing her cancer as being a deep hurt and longstanding resentment, she was empowered to deal with those emotional issues. In my opinion, there is a link between suppressed negative emotions of this type and some forms of cancer. I mentioned some evidence for this in my book *It's the Thought that Counts*.

SARAH'S STORY

Following investigatory surgery for a lump in my groin in 2005, I was diagnosed with non-Hodgkin's lymphoma. Further investigations showed evidence of the disease on both sides of my body and also in my bone marrow. I understand that this categorizes the disease as stage IV (in medical speak).

It was explained to me that chemotherapy would be the treatment, with the possibility of a bone-marrow transplant in the future. It was also explained to me that, as the lymphoma was low grade, there would be no treatment immediately, only active surveillance until my symptoms changed. I was initially very confused about this course of action, as I had always understood that early intervention produced the best outcome in the treatment of cancer. But as I became more knowledgeable about the disease I felt more comfortable with the situation. I realized that there could be long periods where there was little or no change in the disease. This therefore gave me time to explore other avenues.

Back in the eighties I had bought Creative Visualization by Shakti Gawain, discovered meditation and lived my life through affirmation and visualization for a while. I had even participated in one of Shakti's workshops in London, but for many different reasons that part of my life had since ceased to exist.

The field of complementary medicine/therapy, however, still remained a source of interest to me, so I started to explore this in more detail in relation to my current situation. Brandon Bay's book The Journey (which describes Brandon's journey of healing cancer through the release of many years of emotional pain) had been sitting on my bookshelf at home for a year or so and I had not yet got around to reading it, so that is where I started.

I set off on my first 'journey' two weeks after diagnosis and found it to be a life-changing experience. I then discovered a holistic consultant who had developed a complementary approach to cancer treatment. It was there that I began to develop meditation and visualization techniques.

I had used homoeopathy in the past for minor ailments and had been very impressed with the outcome. Therefore I sought advice and guidance once again from a homoeopath. The one that I used was able to support all aspects of my current approach to well-being. She also introduced me to Reiki, which I found to be the most profound method of intervention. I found that it reinforced the meditation and visualization techniques that I was using.

Over a period of time the use of Reiki has intensified my visualization to the point where I only need to use initial intention to produce spontaneous visualization. It has become effortless. Vivid visualizations manifest almost as soon as I close my eyes.

I have had many different experiences of visualization through meditation, journey work, Reiki and just when I'm out walking the dog, and I believe that these have had a profound impact on my healing journey.

I feel passionately that if those diagnosed with cancer could only change their relationship with the disease, this would have a profound effect on the long-term prognosis. Too many people feel powerless when faced with a diagnosis of cancer and accept the medical prognosis without question. Sadly for many, this then becomes their reality. I, too, was in that place for a period of time.

In my situation, however, I did not have to rush into treatment and this gave me time to explore other options. Two years on, I'm convinced that health is a state of mind. All aspects of my life have improved and I'm in a much better place. I still see my consultant on a regular basis. However, the frequency of visits has reduced significantly as my symptoms remain stable.

I suppose the most measurable results of visualization have been the physical ones. Following a scan in 2005 I was told that enlarged nodes were evident in both groins. I actually did not have to be told this, as they were quite noticeable! They felt like a series of large peas in the groin area. When I first started visualization I would imagine the lumps as blocks of ice slowly melting until they disappeared. I repeated this visualization every night before I went to sleep. Within six months the lumps on the left side had reduced significantly and today they are hardly noticeable. The enlarged nodes on the right have also now reduced in size.

I practise visualization and Reiki every day. I also receive Reiki from a practitioner once a month for one hour. As I have now undertaken the initial training to become a Reiki practitioner (level 1), I'm able to channel the flow of Reiki energy for myself. As Reiki is a form of visualization, I have now developed my own technique where I use the two together. I believe that this intensifies the visualization. I start with an initial intention and, quite frequently, it is to have a perfectly healthy body. The visualization then quite often starts to manifests itself with little effort from me.

The most memorable visualization that manifested for me is one that I now repeat on a regular basis. This is where all the cancer cells in my body are waiting to get on a bus!!!!! I watch them get on to the bus one by one and as the bus pulls away all the little cancer cells are smiling and waving at me until they have disappeared out of sight.

Another noticeable physical result of visualization over a two-year period is the state of my general health and well-being. Before diagnosis I experienced frequent chest infections and was prescribed antibiotics on a regular basis. I also had a distinct lack of energy and I was always tired.

Now, however, I have not had a chest infection for over two years, I'm very rarely unwell and have an abundance of energy.

This Worked Because...

Sarah believed that health was a state of mind, so she focused on using her mind in a highly positive way. Her 'journey' would have played a key role in her healing because it would have facilitated emotional healing, which would have impacted the state of the disease. She also used Reiki and found that it intensified the visualizations that she was using. Undoubtedly her regular Reiki sessions helped to tilt the body towards healing. Recent scientific reports into 'hands-on' healing show that it alters the rate of cell growth in skin and bone cells.

Sarah's scenes featured the enlarged nodes as blocks of ice, which she saw melting, as well as the memorable one of watching the cancer cells leaving on a bus. Thus they described moving from having tumours to not having tumours. This would have affected her brain maps for the areas affected by the disease as well as the areas of the disease.

Ultimately, as I've said earlier, I don't believe that the brain registers the difference between real and imaginary. As Sarah imagined the tumours melting and the cancer cells leaving on a bus, it is likely that the brain released all the right chemicals and all the right genes were affected to bring about the real disappearance of cancer, because that is what she was imagining.

PAT'S STORY

Pat's story is related by her sister Carol.

My sister Pat woke up one morning and found she could not move. She was taken to Peterborough hospital, and from there to Addenbrookes Hospital in Cambridge, where a cancer was diagnosed that was wrapped around her spine between, I think, the third and fifth vertebrae. She was given radium treatment and after several weeks was able to walk with a frame, but the medical opinion was that she would only live six weeks. That was in 2002. My sister now visits me regularly, driving herself. The frame has long gone.

Pat, my daughter and I and several of our friends are all of spiritual bent. As soon as Pat was diagnosed we all started visualization.

I can only tell you what I did. I used to ground myself and then look into Pat's back like an X-ray. I would use a blue-white laser to burn away the cancer on some days, then on others it would be a special green acid that only burns away cancer cells, not bone. I did this every day for about a year. When I did see my sister I would always lay my hands on her and ask for God's special healing force to come through.

Whatever we did, it worked, because although the doctors told my sister they could not treat all the cancer with radium because of the position of it, in her last check-up no cancer was found. She has been told she is completely clear.

I do believe that the mind is a powerful tool but it needs exercise to make it strong. I also believe in God, angels and the power of prayer – a very strong toolkit to my mind.

This Worked Because...

Pat and her family and friends collectively visualized her healing. Carol's scene told the story of the cancer cells being eradicated. This would have stimulated the cancerous area and the part of the brain that governed it, leading to biochemical and genetic changes in the brain and at the site of the cancer.

Notice also that Carol wasn't even in the presence of her sister much of the time when she visualized. Healing can be sent to people. All we need to do is imagine the healing scene inside their body.

Carol also had a strong belief in the power of the mind, which would have helped. Coupled with her belief in God, angels and the power of prayer, it did indeed prove to be a powerful toolkit.

JEANNINE'S STORY

In July 2007, after a smear test, I was diagnosed with abnormal cells on the cervix. The degree was mild. I was asked to attend a colposcopy clinic on 11 October. You may be aware that this is quite common with women of my age (52) and it is treated quickly there and then. But I found this very alarming. So after the initial shock, which I expressed in a poem in my diary and by telling my closest friends, I set about doing something about it.

In September I wrote to Mr Jan de Vries (a world-renowned doctor based in Scotland), who prescribed me a herbal remedy (Indolplex with DIM – estrobalance). I took one tablet per day but realized just two weeks before I was due to go to the clinic that I should have been taking at least two a day.

I also believe in the power of the mind, relaxation, etc. For probably about two weeks before the appointment I set my mind to erasing the abnormal cells. I visualized the rows of cells (three or four rows) with the huge black spot (larger than it should be) and changed each one into a healthy looking cell, row after row, until I felt they were all looking healthy. I also took an imaginary rubber and erased each abnormal cell, replacing it with a normal looking cell, and visualized rows and rows of healthy cells. I did this every night.

I attended the Colposcopy Department on the due date and the consultant found that there was no evidence of abnormal cells. And the obstetrician even said that the vagina was looking younger than he expected for my age! I am not sure, mind you, what he was meaning by that!

I forgot to say that I also received two distant healings during that time, quite quickly after diagnosis. One healing was a bi-aura healing, the other one was a bi-aura friend sending the colour orange.

This Worked Because...

Jeannine's story describes going from abnormal cells to healthy cells. Her scene involved seeing rows of cells with a huge black spot and changing them into healthy cells. She also used an imaginary eraser to rub out abnormal cells. The brain doesn't know the difference between real and imaginary, so it is likely that the appropriate chemical and genetic changes took place to bring that about.

She also took a herbal remedy which probably had a positive effect, even though she didn't take it in the quantity that was prescribed.

Jeannine also wrote a poem and told her close friends of her initial shock. This may have facilitated the expression of stored-up negative emotion, which would have aided her healing process.

And, as I pointed out with Pat's story, we can send healing to other people. Jeannine received two healings in this way (distant healings), which were bi-aura healings. In one of them, her friend sent the colour orange. I am a fan of using colours in visualizations. For instance, as I pointed out in Chapter 3, blue is a calming colour. In one study, blue placebo sedatives were 66% effective compared with pink placebo sedatives, which were only 26% effective. Orange is often associated with joy, sunshine and enthusiasm. It is also sometimes associated with strength and courage. Both meanings are positive in the healing sense. Jeannine would either see herself as joyful and filled with enthusiasm to be healed, or she would feel strength.

LINDA'S STORY

Healing by visualization has been amazing for me. Five years ago I was diagnosed with diabetes and lived as a diabetic for two years. Three years ago I went to a doctor for asthma spray and was rushed straight off to hospital for blood transfusion. I had colon cancer. Tiredness was the only symptom, but thanks to an observant doctor who interpreted my white hands as a sign of little blood in my body, I am here today.

Whilst waiting for major surgery I began my visualization therapy. I had studied the mind for many years and was about to open my business Mpower Mindworks when I was hit with this news. The visualizations were great for dealing with the panic that hits one and took the trauma out of hospital treatments and long waits in hospital waiting rooms. I just escaped to a beautiful place and had no need for the valium, etc. that seemed to be dished out to other patients to avoid claustrophobia during scans, etc. During one 40-minute scan in a 'barrel', I mentally took myself on a bush walk, and when it was over and I had to stand up, my legs ached as if I had been on a long hike.

The surgeon said that most people needed to be off work for three months after the kind of surgery that I had. He said it only took seven days for the wound to heal, so the rest had to be in the mind. 'Great,' I thought. 'What a challenge!'

I was back at work full-time, using public transport, within three and a half weeks.

The cancer had spread to the lymph system and I was meant to have chemotherapy, but I believed that I had created this cancer by hanging on to heaps of negative thoughts of past events, so my mind must now heal the body. I did my visualizations three times a day and made sure I only ate food that I had prepared myself, so as not to put toxins into my body.

Here is the visualization that I use. It is adapted from the Silva Method (which is a powerful system of healing).

For greatest effect I either lie or sit in a quiet place, although this still works in busy places such as on a train. Then I count down slowly from 10 to 1 (feeling as if I am diving deeper into water). Moving my eyes from left to right I see the number 3 ... 3 ... 3. Then, moving my eyes back to the left, I repeat 2 ... 2 ... 2 and again 1 ... 1 ... 1. By now I am feeling very relaxed.

I tell myself that I am connected to higher powers (God, Buddha, etc.). I see myself reaching out grasping onto the hand of God. Then I feel the vibrations of the universe flowing through my body. I call on archangels and angels of the four corners to help protect me.

I tell myself to let go all negative past life experiences. I feel a light floating feeling as if I am free. I forgive all those people who have ever caused me pain and sadness. Initially, faces were very close to my face but over time these have floated off into the distance and it is hard to even remember who was there. They changed from angry faces racing towards me to just tiny dots now.

I then tell myself my mind and body are healthy and strong and working in perfect harmony: 'My mind is in perfect condition, working with all my bodily systems. My eyes see clearly, my ears hear perfectly.'

I imagine a vacuum cleaner sucking excess mucus from my nose and lungs, as I have suffered from asthma and sinus problems. Air flows freely into my lungs, where I celebrate the smell of the season changes.

I tell myself that my mouth is healthy and full of mucus to protect my teeth and allow me to speak words clearly. My mind and mouth are in perfect harmony, allowing me to speak my thoughts without causing offence.

I tell myself that my oesophagus and windpipe are perfectly healthy and that my stomach, colon and bowel are perfectly healthy and working well. I see, in my hand, a healthy liver, then my pancreas and blood working in harmony to give me perfect blood sugar levels.

I tell myself that my gallbladder, bladder and kidneys are healthy and working perfectly. Also that my heart is strong and healthy, with all veins and arteries open and clear, allowing blood to travel freely to all parts of my body.

Then I affirm that my immune system is strong, constantly fighting, repairing, restoring, healing and protecting my body.

Sometimes I see a little creature gobbling up any foreign germs in my body. These little creatures work throughout my body.

I affirm that my lymph system and all lymph nodes are very healthy (and I quickly scan my body). When I had cancer in the lymph, I visualized that my cells had the cell memory of 15 years before, when I felt I was strong, healthy and happy.

I affirm that my reproductive organs and tissues are healthy, my bones are healthy and strong from the inside out, and I go through my body as if inside my bones and travel from my tail bone up my spine, head, chest, arms, legs and toes.

Then I affirm that my skin is smooth, full of elasticity. Then I focus on my hand to rid myself of skin cancers that persist (they usually disappear after 48 hours).

I imagine a bright white light shining above my head. I draw it into my body via the top of my head. As it slowly passes through my body, cleansing and removing any negativity, illness and dead cells, I feel a warm glow.

I see a picture of my sick self and carefully erase the image as if using a rubber, starting at my feet. Then I see a beautiful white picture frame with myself in it. During the colon cancer I saw myself nailing up a barricade with the words 'NO cancer' across the entire image. This is no longer necessary.

In the picture frame I create a story doing all the things that I ever wanted to do – energy, friends, money, job, gardening, travel, dancing, etc. I live each thought out in detail to extend the relaxation.

Now I retrieve a real memory, something positive and happy. I relive the sounds, smells, feelings, changing the intensity to please me. I stay in this stage as long as I like.

To finish, I count one to five, wriggle my toes and tell myself that I am wide awake and feeling better than before.

I regularly have scans and each time the results are the same: no sign of cancer in my body. The doctors are impressed. I have never been so happy and healthy and full of energy in my life. I still spend 20 minutes every day doing visualizations and now teach teenagers at a high school the power of visualizations for anger management. The diabetes is all clear as well and I no longer use asthma sprays!

This Worked Because...

Linda's whole body-healing visualization would have stimulated all the parts of her body that she imagined as well as the brain areas that governed them. She would have given her body an all-over healing as her words and images described healthy scenes.

The visualization that she used was adapted from the Silva Method, which is a powerful system of using the mind and one in which I have faith and would personally recommend.

During her visualization, she not only imagined healing the cancer but also imagined that her pancreas was healthy and that her lungs and airways were clear of mucus. Ultimately, she cured herself of diabetes and asthma too.

She had a strong positive mental attitude and this would have helped her to remain determined to heal completely. The fact that she believed that the cancer was linked to holding on to heaps of negative thoughts of past events meant that she had a strong belief that she could heal herself using her mind. In the visualization she felt forgiveness and therefore released any built-up negative emotion. The repetition of her visualization played an important role too. She visualized three times per day.

She also ate food that she prepared herself so as to avoid any additives that often come in pre-packed foods, which could have had a negative effect upon her condition.

She also had a belief in a higher power and imagined the vibrations of the universe flowing through her. In this way she believed that some really strong healing power was flowing into her, which I believe it would have been.

Heart

KEVIN'S STORY

I'd finished working on my PC in my bedroom and had got the ironing board out. In those few seconds, my right thumb had become completely swollen and solid.

My immediate thought was that this could be a thrombosis and the last thing I wanted was for it to dislodge and end up in my brain or heart. I went straight to my local hospital's A&E department. By this time my thumb had started turning blue, which added to my fear.

I was referred to a local GP (I was told a referral from him back to the hospital would be quicker than waiting). He was very thorough and examined my fingers and eyes, told me I had a fever and said that he could hear a heart murmur. Putting all these together, he thought I could have a heart valve infection, which was potentially very serious and might involve me having to have valve replacement surgery. He explained that bacteria can form on the valve and that bits of it break off and can cause clots (which is what he thought was causing my blue thumb). He telephoned the hospital and told them he was referring me immediately. By this time, my thumb was completely blue and still swollen solid.

Walking back to the hospital, I thought how our lives can change in a matter of seconds. I became very aware of my mortality (not necessarily a bad thing but, wow, can it bring on lots of anxiety and raw fear!)

After further tests in A&E, the doctors also concluded that it could well be a heart valve infection. I was admitted to hospital very late that night with an echo-cardiogram and chest X-rays planned for the next day.

It was difficult to sleep and I lay there thinking of the things I still wanted to do in my life and how I didn't want to have major surgery with the possibility of dying. The more I thought along those lines, the more frightened I became. My fear fed on itself and grew until I suddenly shouted, 'Stop!' to myself in my mind. I reminded myself that there was an alternative way of responding to this situation. I made an agreement with myself that it was OK to acknowledge my fear rather than suppress it but it would do me more harm to let it develop into a downward spiral of negativity.

I decided I was not going to need heart valve surgery and that I could heal myself. I was not going to die and not going to allow my fear to have a negative impact on my situation.

I started to talk to my body, reminding it of how wonderful, powerful and strong it was and how it had amazing abilities to heal itself. I encouraged it to get into 'super-heal' mode!

I suddenly got a visualization in my mind that was so spontaneous and clear that it surprised me. I was inside my heart, looking at one of the valves. I saw the three parts of it that open and then close together to form a seal and I saw the bacteria on it.

I then saw that I had a pressure hose in my hand, the kind you use to clean paths, and I knew I was about to blast the bacteria off my heart valve. But I realized that if I did that, bits of bacteria would then be free in my circulatory system and could cause further clots. Suddenly I visualized big blobby immune system cells forming a protective line a little distance away. I knew they would envelop and absorb the bits of bacteria that would be blasted off and would prevent them doing further damage.

I started the pressure hose. Having used one before, I knew how it felt and the kick-back when the pressurized water hit something. I worked the blast of water over my heart valve and watched bits of bacteria flying off, to be swamped by my blobby cells.

I drifted off to sleep, but whenever I woke up (which was frequently!), I would replay the visualization, along with talking to my body in really positive and powerful ways. I would encourage it and tell it I had faith in the massive amounts of energy and healing abilities it had. I felt a determination to be totally healthy, vibrantly alive and remain so for many years to come.

The next morning I was examined by a consultant and team of doctors. Interestingly, I no longer had a fever and my thumb was less swollen and had started to soften. I then had my echo-cardiogram and chest X-rays, which both indicated I have a great heart! There was no sign of bacterial infection.

I cannot, in all honesty, say that I definitely had a heart valve infection before my visualization. However, no consultant or GP (at the time or in follow-up appointments) has been able to provide an alternative explanation for the symptoms I displayed.

At the very least, my visualization enabled me to get into a positive frame of mind and eliminate my fear. At best, who knows? It might just have saved my life.

This Worked Because...

First, I'd like to point out that Kevin displayed total determination. In my research in mind–body science over the past 13 years I have found that this state can sometimes accompany what we'd describe as miracles of healing.

Kevin began his determination with a simple word, 'Stop!' which he shouted in his mind. He decided that he would no longer pay attention to the fear that he was feeling but instead use his mind in a positive way. His determination made it clear that nothing was more important than his health, allowing his unconscious mind and nervous system to work more directly in healing him.

He did quite a bit of self-talk, reminding his body how wonderful, powerful and strong it was and that it had amazing abilities to heal itself. He even encouraged it to get into 'super-heal' mode. All of this talk would have activated parts of the brain that would, indeed, have encouraged the body to get into super-heal mode.

In the super-heal mode, images spontaneously arose in Kevin's mind. I have noticed that this sometimes occurs at times when we are asking the body or brain for direction. By encouraging his body into this mode, Kevin was open to any guidance that he might receive.

His resulting scene tells the story of a heart valve infection being eliminated. His focus on his heart valve would have activated the parts of the brain that governed it as well as the actual heart valve and interrelated parts. His scene was also played out in a light-hearted way – the image of the big blobby immune cells which would swallow up the bits of bacteria would have kept stress and fear to a minimum.

Kevin used a pressure hose in his scene. This was familiar to him because he had used one before. Therefore he could make his scene clearer by remembering how it felt when he switched one on. The clearer we can make our scene, the better.

HELEN'S STORY

Two weeks ago I was told that my baby had an irregular heartbeat of 167 bpm. After doing healing work every day (going into the cells of my baby's heart and putting in pink hearts with angel wings on them to represent love and the words 'normal, regular heartbeat'), I was told yesterday that the bpm had come down to 147 and that the beat was totally normal and regular.

Not sure whether it was all the love and healing that did it, but I'd like to think it was.

This Worked Because...

Helen's healing attention was on her baby's heart. I firmly believe that our intentions are picked up by the unconscious minds of those we direct our thoughts to. The Institute of HeartMath demonstrated a synchronization of heart coherence waves in two people separated by one kilometre when they consciously conjured up a feeling of appreciation (love). As adults, we sometimes get in the way of healing intentions, but babies don't. They haven't learned the rules that we have learned.

Helen's healing intentions would have stimulated her baby's brain and heart in a healing way. She put a tremendous amount of love into her visualization (pink hearts with angel wings on them), which she coupled with the intention of a normal, regular heartbeat. Love is good for the heart.

FLORA'S STORY

About nine years ago I was quite unwell and thought I had bowel cancer. All the tests were negative. But before the test results were known, a blood test showed that I had a dangerously high cholesterol level and a blockage in the left carotid artery.

The trouble with the bowels had been because of the amount of cholesterol in my system!

One of the doctors had been sounding my heart and around the neck area, which I thought was rather weird at the time. He later told me that when he decided to practise in Scotland he would always check for heart/stroke potentials. It was thanks to him that the blockage in my carotid artery was found. This was why I was having dizzy spells.

At that time I knew nothing of cholesterol problems but, as is my wont, I read everything I could. My cholesterol reading was 11 and I was put on statins. I had a vegetarian diet but was very fond of cheese and butter and cream, so they were all cut out and I lost a stone in weight.

After about nine months, during which time I was telling the doctor about the muscle pains and tiredness, etc., to no avail, I was taken to hospital with a suspected stroke. I had woken up with no movement in the left side of my body. Thank God I had not had a stroke, but my muscles had been paralysed by the statins.

The doctors wanted to change the drug type, but I refused any more. I was a great follower of Louise L. Hay and positive thinking, so I set to with my visualization exercises.

I pictured my carotid artery with the blockage. I thought it was probably not a good idea to blast it, as I did not want bits floating along the arteries. Many years ago, the very first computer game my daughter had was 'Parkie', where you were the 'parkie' chasing round the flowerbeds to catch these 'things' before they gobbled the flowers. (They were like a yellow ball that opened like a mouth and ate the flowers.) So I pictured the blockage dissolving slowly and good cells, just like the 'gobblers', coming along and sucking up the dissolved cholesterol and taking it out of my system and disposing of it safely.

It worked. I no longer have a blockage. I now control my cholesterol by positive thinking and diet and exercise.

This Worked Because...

Flora understood the power of positive thinking and made a determined decision to use her mind in a positive way.

In her scene she used images that she was familiar with, which always helps to make a scene clearer. By seeing the blockage slowly dissolving and gobblers sucking up the dissolved cholesterol, she stimulated her brain and body in such a way that this is what occurred. Chemicals would have been released and genes would have been expressed in the brain and in appropriate areas of the body.

Regeneration

TOM'S STORY

In October 1996 I had a serious car accident. A double-decker bus ran full-force into the driver's side of my car. The result was that I broke my collarbone, my ribs, my pelvis, my hip and my back, fractured my skull and twisted my kneecap round the back of my leg. I remained in hospital for three months and was told that I would probably regain 75% of my agility but only over a long period of time. I told the doctor there and then that I would be fit enough to run a full 26-mile marathon the next year in Glasgow and have 100% agility back.

The doctor stated that he would give £1000 to any charity I wanted if I succeeded, and he laughed.

Day by day I focused my thoughts on healing. In my mind I created a little healing system whereby I visualized a tiny version of myself going inside my body to the affected areas and also a team of tiny workmen all doing their different jobs, sanding down all my affected bones and knitting together all my injuries with their special tools. For example, the welder welded the seam on my pelvis, the joiner sanded the rugged edges of my bones and the French polisher polished them.

Day by day I got stronger. When I received a scan on my hip, the doctor looked at me, surprised, and said that it actually looked as though the bones had been sanded down!

I ran the marathon the next year in four hours and eight minutes and received £1000 from the doctor, which I donated to charity. The doctor was absolutely amazed at the results.

I still heal myself in this way when there is anything wrong with me.

This Worked Because...

Tom's scene would have activated each part of his body that he imagined healing, as well as the brain areas that governed them. This would have led to genetic changes in the brain, at the sites of injury and also in stem cells, instructing them to evolve into whichever cell type was necessary.

Tom also showed total determination to fully recover, which resulted in dedicated visualization, and this would have played a major role in his recovery.

ED'S STORY

Several years ago I tore a calf muscle while training for a ten-kilometre race. I saw a sports therapist who did some very good work but told me that the muscle would never be the same again. It was a very Western-medicine approach based on the fact that there was scar tissue.

Naturally I didn't really like this diagnosis! However, I did accept it. And despite resting/stretching, etc., every time I got to a certain speed and intensity of training I broke down again.

Some time later I read and very much enjoyed It's the Thought that Counts. *I also heard you talk, David, at a 'Firewalk' about the athlete whose shoulder healed much more quickly than predicted with visualization.* [I mentioned this in Chapter 6.] *So I decided that my calf would heal itself completely.*

I kept telling myself that my body knew how to grow healthy tissue. I've never consciously broken down what I did, but I guess I actually saw and felt my body repairing the muscle – almost like tiny, tiny workmen! I definitely sent attention to my calf and clearly felt that the unhealthy tissue was being broken down and replaced with healthy tissue.

I haven't had the calf re-examined to see if there is any scar tissue, but can say that it has healed 100% in terms of the way it feels – and it's been that way for a year and a half. During that time I have run 30–35 miles a week training for other ten-kilometre runs and achieved my goal/speed time with no pain or discomfort in my calf at all.

I know lots of runners and sportspeople will be told that their injuries won't heal completely. I believe that they can!

This Worked Because...

Ed began with the belief that it was possible for his calf to heal itself completely, despite what his sports therapist had told him and despite the pain that he had experienced ever since the injury. From this state of positive belief, his healing became possible.

He regularly affirmed that his body knew how to heal itself. Undoubtedly, this would have caused his unconscious mind to direct the right centres of his nervous systems towards a full recovery.

Hs scene helped this by telling the story of his muscle being repaired. He conjured up tiny workmen, which symbolized that work was really being done.

MARY'S STORY

About ten years ago (I am now 70), I had a very painful swollen knee joint following a fall when walking in mountains in Wales with my husband. The GP's diagnosis was a cartilage problem and I was told I would need an operation to snip a portion of the cartilage out. I was put on the list to see the consultant.

I was determined to get this better using alternative holistic therapies. I had spiritual healing and shiatsu and took various health supplements, among other things.

I do an hour's Buddhist meditation every morning before breakfast. Sometimes I get into a very peaceful state where all thoughts subside and I am fully aware. When I was in those states I did my visualization.

I visualized an enhanced blood supply flowing into my knee joint, where phagocytes (immune cells that ingest and destroy foreign invaders) engulfed the damaged cell tissue and carried it away. I then visualized an enriched blood supply carrying the necessary nutrients for repair flowing into the joint, enabling the growth of new cells. Then I saw my knee joint completely whole and healed and, finally, myself hiking again.

I kept the appointment with the consultant, who sent me for X-rays. Although they don't show cartilage, he wanted to see if the ends of my bones were healthy considering my age. Result – all perfect. After manipulating my leg he found no evidence of the cartilage problem.

I told him of all I had done. His reply: 'Oh, I don't know about all that.'

I do get twinges when walking down steep paths, but I now use walking poles to help myself.

This Worked Because...

Mary saw her knee joint completely whole and healed and also saw herself hiking again. She also saw blood, nutrients and immune cells flowing into the joint, giving it all that it required for healing. These regular visualizations would have seeped into her unconscious mind and stimulated the correct areas of her brain and the area of injury so that her scene became reality.

LUCCA'S STORY

A few years ago I ate something that had dried herbs in it and a small piece of herb lodged between my teeth. When I flossed that night I probably managed to push the herb under the gumline. By the next morning I had a full-blown gum abscess. I thought it would go away, but it got worse. Soon I was running a low-grade fever and couldn't chew without a lot of pain.

I saw my dentist, who relieved the pressure and drained the abscess before she sent me home to rinse with salt water. She suggested antibiotics, but I'm not keen on using them unless it's absolutely necessary. I went back a few days later so that she could check it out and found that it was getting worse again. The dentist suggested that I see a periodontist, who then said that I had an infection that extended down the root of the tooth to the jaw.

The periodontist cleaned the abscess out by cutting the gum open, scraping the tooth and packing it with a disinfectant before closing it up again, and the infection cleared up within about four days. The only drug I had was a non-blood-thinning painkiller that was a little stronger than I would normally take for headache.

While I was in the chair, the periodontist tested the tooth for reaction to cold, in order to find out whether the root was damaged. She also tested one tooth to the left and one to the right of the tooth she had worked on. Her opinion was that I would need a root canal in all three teeth and that it was possible that I would lose the middle tooth altogether. The gum had receded during the surgery and she predicted that it would recede further and therefore wouldn't be able to hold the tooth.

I didn't like this prognosis. I didn't want root canals, or to lose one or more teeth. I had managed to heal third-degree burns with my mind 20 years earlier, so I decided that I could heal my tooth and gum as well. I set about using the same technique I had used then.

Just before I went to sleep each night I pictured a healthy root going into each of the three teeth (in the form of emerald-green light) and I pictured healthy pink gums holding them in place. If I recall correctly, I did this for about a month. My gum healed well and I haven't had any further problems. I told the dentist I wouldn't need the root canal after all.

I was back in the dentist's office for a routine scaling about three months later and she had another look at my tooth and gums to see how they were doing. She asked her assistant to check the chart again to make sure she had the right tooth, because she couldn't find any evidence of the abscess. Not only had the gum healed, but it had regenerated as well. Everyone in the office had to have a look at the 'incredible regenerating gum'! The dentist said she had never seen anything like it, but that 'seeing was believing'.

This Worked Because...

Lucca had faith that she could heal herself. She had healed third-degree burns many years earlier, so she had a memory of what was possible.

Her scene described healthy roots going into her teeth and she used green light in this part of her scene. The colour green symbolizes regeneration and healing in some cultures, so undoubtedly this would also have assisted the healing. She also pictured her gums being healthy.

Through her scene she would have stimulated her brain and her gums and nerves. Genes would have been activated in the brain and in the gums as well as in stem cells so that her gum was able to fully regenerate according to how she had imagined.

Pain, Chronic Fatigue and ME

LISA'S STORY

If I have a headache or other pain, I focus my attention on my heart. I feel, see or sense it beating. Then I imagine a small bright light pulsing in the middle of it. I hold this for a few minutes. Then I move the pulsing light into the part of my body where I feel pain or discomfort.

I hold this intention and watch the light as it sends waves of healing energy throughout the area (this can be increased until the light and waves are pulsing throughout the whole body, muscles, circulatory system, etc.) for as long as I wish.

It doesn't always totally take the pain away, but it reduces it.

This Works Because...

Through concentrating upon her heart, Lisa is distracted from her pain. But in addition, her scene of the pulsing light symbolizes loving, healing intention, which she then moves to the part of the body that feels pain.

This will stimulate those parts of the body and also the part of the brain that governs them, as well as the neural pathways that are responsible for the pain. Most likely, endorphins are released in the area of the brain that governs the painful part, therefore neutralizing the pain.

Lisa's expectation that pain relief will accompany her visualization will also encourage this endorphin release, and that expectation will build with every success.

SASHA'S STORY

A couple of years ago I became severely ill with chronic fatigue syndrome (CFS). Previously I had been a very active individual with a successful career lecturing in the performing arts and I had several qualifications in holistic therapies.

The descent into CFS was rapid, leaving me completely disabled – I was unable to put on my own socks and had to be lifted out of the bath. But my story does not really start there. It starts at the turning point when I realized the power of my mind to help me heal.

It is important to understand at this stage that I am not saying that CFS is in the mind – it is a physiological condition affecting the neurological and immune system. What I am saying is that I discovered the extraordinary power of visualization and intention to aid my recovery.

My turning point was one particular day when I was lying in bed feeling especially miserable. It was what was then an average day – I was spending 20 hours plus per day in bed, rising only to wash, eat and use the bathroom. And on this average day I was doing what I always did, although I was not aware of it consciously. My subconscious pattern was to play a series of messages to myself over and over again. They consisted of things like 'This is dreadful,' 'I'll never recover,' and 'My life will never be the same.' But in the midst of all this I heard another voice from inside my head, and the voice asked me who *was making it dreadful.*

Everything stopped, there was silence and the small voice inside my head answered, 'Me!' In a sudden flash of understanding I realized that although the pain that I was experiencing was inevitable, given my physiological state, the suffering was a choice. I lay in peace and silence for the rest of the day. There was a huge sense of relief. I was no longer a victim of CFS and I realized the power I held to aid my own recovery.

What followed was a journey to health and self-realization that was so profound that I am actually grateful to CFS for the lessons that it taught me and the way it changed the course of my life. I stopped labelling myself as someone who had CFS, and started to refer to myself as being 'in recovery'. I realized the power of my intention and focused clearly on my goal of health. I also began to visualize myself in great health. I visualized my nervous system healing and all my cells and organs healing. Each day I lay in meditation, gently commanding various body parts to heal and sending them positive energy.

I saturated myself with information that supported my new belief system. And as I began to do so, all the tools that I needed to heal seemed to fall into my path. Books by Bruce Lipton, Candace Pert, David Hamilton and Donna Eden helped me to understand that the mind and body are one. Inspiring material such as The Secret, Way of the Peaceful Warrior and What the Bleep Do We Know!? helped me to focus and visualize on my healing. I also stumbled across Emotional Freedom Technique (EFT) and found it helped to alleviate my symptoms and to clear my past, and PSYCH-K, which helped to reprogramme my subconscious mind.

I am now 100% healed and I reached this point in remarkable time for someone who has CFS. I have had a career change and am running my own business, working with others who have

CFS and helping them to overcome their self-limiting beliefs to intend, visualize and create health. I have also written a book called Joyful Recovery from CFS/ME.

It was the EFT and the PSYCH-K that did it in the end. I got over the majority of the condition using EFT, but there was still a bit hanging on. And then I did a 45-minute PSYCH-K session known as the 'Core Belief Balance'. At the start of the session I still had ME, and at the end I didn't! I felt the overactive HPA axis [the HPA, or hypothalamic-pituitary-adrenal, axis is a system connecting the brain and body that controls stress and thus affects many of the body's systems] *switch off when I rebalanced the belief that the world is a dangerous place! And interestingly, my resting heart rate, which I had monitored on biofeedback software for some time, went from its usual 106 bpm to 72 bpm after the session and has stayed there ever since.*

I feel that overcoming illness has helped me to find my path in life, and at the heart of this path was the intention to heal and the belief that it was possible.

This Worked Because...

Sasha recognized that she was running a daily subconscious pattern that was keeping her sick. Her turning point was recognizing this and realizing that suffering was a choice. Two people can have an identical illness but one may suffer much more than another. The difference is in each person's attitude.

Sasha developed a powerfully positive attitude, which she directed towards healing herself. As she visualized her various body systems and parts healing, she would have stimulated these systems and the parts of her brain that governed them, tilting her body towards healing. Undoubtedly, new subconscious patterns would have started running, such as, 'I am getting better' and 'I can do this', which would have hugely aided her recovery.

She also saturated herself with information that supported her belief that she could heal herself. Sometimes, when we are in recovery, our belief that we can get better wavers. But when we feed ourselves positive information that supports our beliefs, then those beliefs become strengthened and our healing speeds up.

Sasha also used energy healing techniques like EFT and PSYCH-K. I have personally witnessed some quite dramatic and rapid recoveries in people who were treated with these healing modalities. I am absolutely certain that they played a large role in her recovery.

JULIETTE'S STORY

I have been recovering from a number of illnesses for some time now (ME/fibromyalgia and a nervous breakdown) and although still yet to be fully well, I am a lot better than I was. Some of this may be due to the visualization that I have done on and off.

In the earlier stages of my illness, I would often lie down and imagine water pouring through my body, clearing out all the debris and illness. Also, sometimes images of a beautiful rose would help. I would imagine it in my body – usually my heart centre – and this would help on the emotional side, healing hurt. I would also hold in my head images of myself functioning healthily and well, often walking in mountains, as I used to enjoy this before I got sick. Sometimes this last visualization is a little vague – I find it hard to see it clearly at times, as I have been through so many changes. I guess I was never very regular with these images, though.

Also, for the last six months I have been working with a therapy called GIM (guided imagery and music) and this has been very powerful. Images arise naturally in response to the stimulus of the music and I have found the experiencing and

159

sensing of these images extremely powerful in both my physical body and my emotional body. As these images arise during the session, I find it is easier to maintain them with an awareness throughout the rest of the time, and I use them in times when I need to feel strong.

One of the prominent images for me is having white angel wings and my body being a light luminescence. I have found this extremely spiritually strengthening, and remembering that I am a spiritual being on this Earth and have dignity, value and inner composure has helped me to feel stronger, daily. Images of myself amongst mountains, on beaches and with a healthy vibrant supple body are often present. Often I am being very free in myself – flying, etc.

I am currently doing this work so am in the middle of seeing how I progress but I am definitely moving forward in my life with it. This year I have visited places that I have been unable to go for 12 years (beaches, mountains!) and have started to swim a lot more as well as become more assertive with others. I feel that it is giving me the spiritual and emotional strength to deal with making the changes that I have been trying to make for a long time too.

The therapist is also encouraging me to draw the images, which reinforces them and gives me something tangible to look at.

I have this treatment once a month and then regularly visualize/ sense the images during the weeks in between.

There is one more image that has been coming up a lot in the GIM therapy that I also use a lot and I forgot to mention. It is a unicorn. In the therapy I am often riding it on a long beach and it is very strengthening. In between sessions I often visualize a unicorn near me, too, and again I find this brings me a source of support in a spiritual way, I guess.

This Works Because...

Juliette is using some powerful symbols in her scenes. Imagining water pouring through her body and clearing out the debris and illness will filter into her unconscious mind and stimulate the brain and relevant areas of the body so that the illness will indeed be flushed out of her body.

The image of the rose at her heart, which symbolizes love, will undoubtedly help heal past hurts, which frequently contribute to (and in many cases cause) our current illnesses.

The use of GIM has been powerful for her. Music often helps people to get clearer images. One of the powerful symbols that GIM has given rise to is Juliette seeing herself as a light luminescence. It is helping to spiritually strengthen her and establish the belief that she has value and is worthy of health and fulfilment. A lack of self-worth can be an underlying cause of some illnesses. Drawing or painting her images will also help to further establish their power.

The symbol of the unicorn is also highly spiritually strengthening. When we feel spiritually strengthened we feel powerful, worthy and that we can achieve anything that we put our minds to, including healing ourselves. We also feel emotionally more complete. These states of mind will be stimulating Juliette's brain and body in such a way that healing is inevitable.

Viruses, Allergies and Autoimmune Conditions

BARBARA'S STORY

I am fairly new to the conscious level of realizing that we have the power of our subconscious mind available to us. On a number of occasions (now more so than ever) I have realized that the important question to ask is not 'How is life treating you?' but 'How are you treating life?'

I am generally a healthy person and have just realized that it is the power of my subconscious that is keeping me healthy – my thought processes on health have always contained positive wording. I do not allow myself to be ill.

Being an 'away from' person, I don't like pain and suffering, and being ill is not an option. Being self-employed is also a good enough motivation for not becoming ill.

I am in an industry where I see people at close quarters and touch their hands on a regular basis. Because of this, people used to phone me when they were ill to say that they wanted to cancel their appointment because they had fallen ill with some virus.

I knew that if I cancelled the appointments I wouldn't get paid, so my reaction to them was always, 'Don't worry, I don't do viruses. As long as you are up to it, I will be there.' They were usually amazed by my reaction, but ever since I have been doing this, I have never fallen prey to bugs going around. I just do not do 'flus and colds, and that is the way it is.

I am sure this is all to do with what I tell my subconscious.

This Works Because...

Barbara has a positive attitude. Her comment that it is far more important to ask how you are treating life than how it is treating you is very empowering. Having such an attitude gives us the power and this is far better than seeing life as something that we have no control over.

This attitude has helped Barbara to strengthen the belief that she doesn't 'do' viruses. This is a very powerful affirmation and will be contributing to the strengthening of her immune system, which is keeping viruses at bay.

SUSAN'S STORY

I woke up feeling pretty lousy with what I immediately labelled as the start of a bug or the 'flu, but I decided I didn't want it and pictured my immune system kicking into gear – I saw all my fantastic white blood cells multiplying like crazy and devouring all the ugly dark unwanted germs with speed and ease. I also imagined my immune system like tiny soldiers (I pictured something like the toy soldier from The Nutcracker!*) and they kicked into action and destroyed and eliminated all the rubbish.*

Then there were tiny wee sweeping brushes and pans to clean up any remaining mess, so there was no debris to reignite any infection, and I imagined every cell working perfectly, just as it was designed to, and I sent love and gratitude to every tiny cell and molecule.

I also believe in something bigger, so I pulled down pure divine healing energy from the heavens through my crown and throughout my entire body, balancing this off by sending down roots from the soles of my feet right into the healing earth.

The outcome of all this? Well, I've been feeling surprisingly OK today – not 100% perfect (yet!), but I've had a really productive day at work and now at home it's time for some tlc: a nice dinner, a hot bath and an early night!

This Worked Because...

Susan's scene described her immune system eating up any unwanted germs. This would have stimulated her unconscious mind and autonomic nervous system so that her immune system would be strong enough to tackle any unwanted germs.

The use of 'tiny wee sweeping brushes' also brought a slightly light-hearted feel to her scene. And her focus on the complete removal of any debris in this way would have ensured that there were no unwanted germs left over.

She also generated a state of love and gratitude, which is a powerful healing state, and sent this into her cells, symbolically – and therefore actually – strengthening them.

Her belief in something bigger would also have contributed to her healing. She symbolized this belief by imagining divine energy from the heavens flowing through her body, connecting her to the divine source.

KEVIN'S STORY

Somehow I developed a verruca on the inside of my right big toe, towards the top. It showed all the typical signs – a raised area of skin with a black centre where the virus that caused it had taken hold.

I was tempted to use one of the freeze kits you can now buy at chemists. However, the location of the verruca, on a sensitive part of my toe, made me squirm. So I decided I'd try a visualization.

I sat down and closed my eyes and relaxed. I created an intention of a visualization that would be appropriate in this case.

Almost immediately I had a clear picture in my mind of being underneath the verruca. I could see the black centre of it above me. Suddenly the lower area resembled a building site! A criss-cross mesh of protective skin formed between the verruca and the skin below. The mesh looked like the metal framework around which concrete is poured to strengthen it. There was a clear inner intention that the virus would never be able to penetrate this protective mesh of skin. In fact, this layer was slowly moving up, to push the verruca off my toe.

Although I had this visualization only once, it was very clear and powerful with a feeling of intention behind it.

About a week later, after my shower, I wondered if anything had happened. To my disappointment, the black centre of the verruca was still on my toe. However, to my delight, when, out of curiosity, I put my fingernails either side of it, off it came! The skin is now almost healed.

This Worked Because...

Kevin used a scene that described a mesh of skin growing underneath the verruca and therefore the virus that caused the verruca wasn't able to penetrate it. This would have given instructions to his nervous system for this to occur.

I also like his use of having an intention to have a visualization that would be appropriate. This would have caused his unconscious mind, which had a detailed knowledge of the verruca, what caused it and how to get rid of it, to show him what he needed to imagine. His visualization would therefore have stimulated the brain and his toe in just the right way so that the verruca could just be lifted off. This is also probably why his visualization was so clear – he was seeing exactly what he needed to see and nothing else.

Interestingly, Kevin only visualized once. Sometimes that is all that is necessary. It is likely that this was helped by his intention to have the appropriate visualization.

TOMEK'S STORY

I had two giant verrucas on my feet. The one on the left foot was taking almost the whole surface of my big toe. You told me that I could heal them with visualization. I did so and they disappeared! Wow! Hehehe. I had them for five or six years and I tried everything (burned them, took drugs, herbs) and now they are gone. Now I will go and have a foot massage. Hehehehe.

This is how I visualized. First I imagined that I was burning them with acid. Sometimes I was just brushing them with an acid brush and sometimes I had a gun that fired acid and I fired it on my verrucas. After one week the results were impressive. After that I tried also to visualize my feet and toes without any verrucas, just nice skin, and sometimes I imagined that I was burning them.

Ah, yes, the best part – I had on a regular basis (couple of times a day) a victory dance in the toilets at work or at home or in the car. Good fun.

I also noticed that I was always negative about the verrucas in the past. Every time my girlfriend told me try to do something with them, I would say, 'No, it won't work.' So thank you very much – 100 million times.

This Worked Because...

Tomek created a scene that told the story of the disappearance of his verrucas. This would have stimulated his brain, the areas where the verrucas were situated and also his immune system, so that the verrucas, despite their large size, quickly disappeared.

You can also see from his description that he has a good sense of humour. I met him after a talk that I gave in 2008 and this was definitely true then. This would have minimized stress.

He also did a regular victory dance, which would also have reduced stress and helped his brain to develop the neural patterns of belief that the verrucas were indeed shrinking, stimulating it to release all the right chemicals to ensure that this was indeed what occurred.

LYNN'S STORY

In December 1978 I had the 'flu. I didn't like having it because it rendered me useless, aching and feeling thoroughly miserable. I made a vow that I would never have it again! And I never have!

I have managed this with the use of visualization and affirmations; each year, I state that I have no use for being laid up with influenza and that I am healthy. Each year since 1978, upon feeling what might be the beginning of a simple cold or 'flu, I have visualized my immune system as my own personal army.

In the beginning 'Lynn's Army' was equipped with bows and arrows, but over the years they have evolved into an army of light fighters using beams of red light to annihilate the attacking enemy, followed by blue light for healing and green light for regeneration. I visualize myself inside a bubble that alternates between blue and green and all the shades between.

This Works Because...
Lynn's story describes her army defeating the enemy of cold and 'flu. This ensures that her immune system is strong and is, indeed, attacking any enemies.

However, Lynn's story continues below. As you will see, her opinion is that viewing her immune system as an army that attacks an enemy has had some negative effects. Compare this with how some of the previous visualizers showed love towards diseased cells.

LYNN'S STORY, CONTINUED

However, this did not prepare me for another illness, diagnosed on Christmas Eve 2002. I was admitted to hospital suffering from kidney failure and a biopsy revealed systemic lupus erythematosis. This is an autoimmune disease that is caused by the body's immune system turning against itself. My troops had turned mutinous!

During my four-month stay in hospital I was too ill to do anything other than sleep. I was being treated with a toxic cocktail of nuclear drugs, including chemotherapy, and having to spend four hours, three times per week, on dialysis.

I am a very spiritual person and during this time I felt as though I was surrounded and protected by angels; I guess this was how my subconscious interpreted the feeling of trust I learned to have in those who were in charge of my care and well-being. During my waking hours, I was convinced there was an aura of rainbow colours around me, healing me and protecting me, and I never doubted that I would recover from my ordeal.

When I was eventually discharged from hospital, I couldn't walk due to muscular apathy. I hated being confined to a wheelchair and this resulted in a recurring dream in which I was enjoying the freedom of being able to run with the wind in my hair. Considering that all my hair had fallen out due to the effects of chemotherapy, this was a rather positive dream!

This dream started the deliberate visualization of seeing myself walking, followed by actually carrying out the task and walking further each week until I was finally able to get rid of the wheelchair. I am still a long way off being able to manage the walk of eight miles per day I enjoyed before I became ill and I am still registered disabled. But with the use of visualization, I remain hopeful that my ability will improve.

Coping with the lupus forced me to review my use of visualization. Mutiny is the result of disharmony amongst the troops. I began to see my illness in a different light; lupus is the Latin word meaning 'wolf' and I guess my interest in mythology played a big part in learning to deal with my affliction. The following is taken from an article I wrote for Lupus UK's official magazine, News & Views, *which I entitled 'The Beautiful Beast Within':*

For many years, since childhood, I have been fascinated with mythology, particularly the legends of shape shifters, humans who can take on the shapes of animals, birds or fish. I have spent most of my adult life in some form of spiritual training, which has included walking the shamanic path and learning about power animals.

I met my power animal many years ago. She appeared to me in the form of a beautiful wolf with silvery-grey fur. We have travelled together and she has taught me many things. In the Native American Indian tradition, Wolf is teacher and Rudyard Kipling used this description in his Jungle Book stories. Arkela is the alpha male wolf, who finds the orphaned Mowgli and rears him as his own. This is why the Scout movement adopted the name for their pack leaders.

In Celtic mythology, Wolf is the mentor. Wolf is seen as the companion of the God of Nature, Cernunnos, and also the Goddess of Childbirth, Bridget; both are thought to take on the shape of the wolf and walk between the worlds. For the wolf, communication and community are of the utmost importance. The alpha male and female are chosen for their abilities to teach and lead the others, so co-operation is of vital importance amongst the members of a pack. These qualities are things that most people regard as vital in a society that wishes to live harmoniously.

For me, lupus is much more than a disease. She is the beautiful beast that resides within me. Just like any wild animal, I have to be careful how I approach her; she needs special care and consideration, but is happy enough to accept the offering of steak every so often! If I have overworked her, she howls and makes me suffer for my inconsideration and I know to step back and leave her in peace to rest for a day or so.

Sometimes, I step back and take a good long look at her; she is wild and ferocious, yet she is beautiful and wise and I know she has something of the greatest importance to teach me and those working in the field of learning about lupus. Despite the scars I carry, accredited by my own carelessness in dealing with her, I love her. She is a part of me and I have learned that we can only walk side by side if I learn to consider her needs as well as my own.

Visualizing my illness as an alter ego has helped me to cope with having lupus. Six months after I came out of hospital my consultant remarked on how well I was, considering that I had been so devastatingly ill. Now, four years on, I am off all lupus-related drugs and enjoying remission.

This Worked Because...

Lynn showed trust and care and had no doubt that she would recover. This strong positive belief characterizes some recoveries that we put down to the miraculous and also underlies some recoveries of people who take placebos for illnesses.

Lynn visualized herself walking, followed by actually walking, which would have stimulated her muscles and the brain areas that controlled them so that she was indeed able to walk, just as the stroke patients, spinal cord injury patients and Parkinson's patients described in Chapter 6 recovered movement through mental imagery.

She viewed lupus as disharmony in 'Lynn's Army' – that they had turned on her – and this realization has dramatically helped her healing. Lupus is an autoimmune condition where the body's immune system attacks the body. Other autoimmune conditions include diabetes mellitus (type 1), multiple sclerosis, myasthenia gravis and rheumatoid arthritis.

The symbolism that Lynn used to make peace with her condition – learning to love the beautiful beast within – ultimately facilitated her recovery. This would have stimulated her nervous system in the appropriate way so that all the relevant parts of her body were able to heal and the immune system ceased its attack upon her.

I asked Lynn if she felt that her use of 'Lynn's Army' was aggressive and maybe had a link with lupus. This was her reply:

That is exactly what I was getting at, that perhaps my tactics were aggressive. Something I never mentioned before was that after I learned I had lupus, I started visualizing 'it' as Jabba the Hutt from Star Wars, and zapping it. But my guides told me that this was wrong because it was hate/aggression/ negative, etc., and that the way to overcome the illness was to send it love. Then the whole 'wolf' thing came to me and

*because I love wolves, it was much easier to learn to love my
illness.*

*I think that maybe instead of fighting illness, we need
to embrace it and learn what it is trying to teach us about
ourselves. In my case, I've meditated on it and done some
past-life regression with my partner Matt's help. Louise Hay
says that lupus is about 'giving up; anger and punishment'
and this goes along with what I've been learning about
myself. I'm working on trying to love my body instead of
resenting it. So I guess what I'm saying is that we cannot fight
fire with fire, but that by 'starving' the flames, i.e., taking
away whatever feeds them, the fire will go out, the illness will
subside. We can only do that by surrounding ourselves with
Unconditional Love, and visualization can help.*

When we visualize, we don't need to use fear, hate or violence in
the sense that we see something suffer. It is OK to see the removal
of an illness, but we don't need to use violence to do it. So firing
lasers or bullets is OK when it's not done in an aggressive,
enemy-hunting way. For instance, Carol mentally used a blue-
white laser beam or green acid to dissolve cancer cells, but she
was not viewing them as an enemy or imagining them suffering.
It was, in a way, just like imagining scraping wallpaper.

But when we personalize a disease or diseased cells and see
them as an enemy that needs to be vanquished through violence,
then, although we may defeat the illness, the internal use of
aggression could open us to further attack. This is not always
the case and it really depends upon your own personal beliefs
and the strength of your own will, but there are real benefits in
making the scene more light-hearted, while still working with
removal, cleaning, or imagining the healing symbolically.

DREW'S STORY

In October 2004 I contracted myasthenia gravis, which is considered incurable. It is a breakdown of the immune system. It was controlled by medication. Then in October 2005 I went on a two-day educational vibrational medicine workshop in the north of Scotland, in Nairn.

At the end of the second day my condition was extremely acute. My eyelids dropped, I was seeing double and I couldn't move my jaw, so couldn't speak or eat or swallow, and then the myasthenia started to close down my lungs. A doctor came up to me and said, 'Drew, I'm afraid you are too ill to travel. You will have to come home with me and stay with my family and I will treat you.'

At this stage of the condition the only orthodox treatment available to me to counteract the symptoms was steroids or blood transfusion. However, I received three or four vibrational medicine treatments per week from Dr Petrow with no medication. The treatment was holistic. I came home to Fife in February 2006, a full three months later! (How many doctors do you know who would take a patient home with them for three months?)

On Christmas Eve 2005, after I had had 50 days of incapacity and lost 60 pounds in weight, I attended a service at Pluscarden Abbey near Forres. The monks there were conducting a service in Gregorian chant. And as I sat in a pew I listened to the singing and my eyelids suddenly lifted. I could see and also move my jaw freely and, hey, I could speak! All my symptoms just fell away! They returned shortly afterwards but at that point I knew that I would be healed.

During my recovery period of November 2005 to February 2006 I regularly used visualization. Myasthenia is triggered by antibodies in the bloodstream which lead to the breakdown of the immune system. David, you may recollect that I asked you how to visualize eliminating antibodies and your recommendation was to imagine being at an airgun stall at a fairground and shooting ducks (antibodies) off a moving conveyor belt. It is difficult to assess the precise contribution of visualization to my recovery and my own view is that it supported the intensive vibrational medicine treatments that I was receiving three or four times a week.

I had total faith in my doctor, the treatment, the visualization and that one day I could and would be well. Where this absolute faith came from I do not know, but I have no doubts about the power of the mind being a major contributory factor in the healing of the body.

Between that February 2006 and the following January I had 11 months of blood, muscle and eye tests.

On being fully discharged, the Head of Neurology said to me, 'Mr Pryde, you are the only person that I have heard of who has fully recovered from myasthenia gravis.'

Now I rejoice in my good health and live a full and happy life. Though sometimes I wonder, 'Why me? And what now?'

This Worked Because...

There are a number of factors that most likely contributed to Drew's complete recovery. One was his absolute faith that he would recover. Considering that myasthenia gravis is considered incurable, this demonstrates the power of faith to profoundly affect the body. Faith such as this is a state often associated with miracles of healing.

The love and care of Dr Petrow also played a huge role, as did the obviously powerful vibrational medicine treatments that she administered. Although there is little scientific evidence of the effectiveness of vibrational medicine at present, it is my opinion that it is a very powerful system of healing that works at a deep level in the body. Many breakthroughs in science take years to be fully embraced by the scientific community. In medicine, doctors who pioneer the new techniques are often called 'mavericks' or even 'quacks', until evidence eventually silences the critics.

Vibrational medicine is based on the fact that all matter vibrates at a certain frequency. It is not too hard to grasp this if you consider that all atoms, by their very nature, are pure vibrations of energy.

In mainstream science, one of the key vibrational frequencies of water (around 3300–3500cm^{-1}) is used in laboratory analysis in the technique known as infrared spectrophotometry, which is used routinely in university, pharmaceutical and medical research laboratories all over the world. Vibrational medicine administers vibrational frequencies that aim to neutralize diseases in the body.

Sound is a form of vibrational healing because sound is a vibration. Hence Drew experienced a dramatic improvement while listening to the Gregorian chants.

Drew's scene also played a part in his recovery. In myasthenia gravis, antibodies block the acetylcholine receptors in a key movement-control part of the brain. Drew imagined these antibodies being neutralized by a popgun on a fairground conveyor belt. This was a powerful symbolic visualization. The meaning would have seeped into his unconscious mind, resulting in activation of his nervous system in such a way that the presence of antibodies actually did diminish.

Note also that, even though you could consider the use of a gun as violence, Drew's scene did not use violence or excessive force. The location of the children's fairground set a light-hearted scene, as did the child's game of 'shooting the ducks'. The visualization was largely symbolic and what it symbolized was not only the removal of the antibodies from the specific area of the brain but also the removal of myasthenia gravis.

ELIZABETH'S STORY

I had terrible hay fever for years and had to take antihistamines daily. I decided to try visualization and after doing it once or twice I have only had to take an antihistamine two or three times in the last eight months. I have had no hay fever symptoms for the rest of the summer.

I saw a little 'Me' going towards my immune system, which I imagined was made up of hundreds of little people. As I was going towards them, I couldn't see them properly and vice versa, they couldn't see me too well, as there was quite a bit of fog. Because of this, my immune system was attacking me, fearing that I was an enemy. However, as the fog cleared, my immune system and I saw each other and I said, 'Hey, it's me, there's no need to fight. Just chill out and do only what you have to to keep me healthy. Take the rest of the day off.'

I then saw the head guy shout to all his troops, 'Hey, it's just Elizabeth – we don't need to fight.' His troops let out a cheer and started to play tennis and lie down on beds to sunbathe. I hugged the head guy and then walked off.

This Worked Because...

Elizabeth communicated with her immune system and asked it to relax and chill out. Allergies arise out of an overactive response of the immune system towards allergens (substances that cause an allergic reaction). Elizabeth asked her immune system to just do enough to keep her healthy. She then imagined her immune characters relaxing and enjoying a game of tennis. This communication would have seeped into her unconscious mind, stimulating the immune system to, indeed, calm down its sensitivity.

The presence of fog in her scene symbolized that things were not clear with the immune system, and that's why it was overactive.

Once she mentally cleared the fog, communication could take place and the immune system could function normally again.

There is a biochemical similarity between some allergies and autoimmune conditions, so this visualization could be adapted and applied to autoimmune conditions. I have done so and listed it in the Visualizations section in Appendix II towards the back of the book.

15

Weight Loss

TAMARA'S STORY

*I have struggled with being overweight all my life. It is my –
sorry – it was my safety net, the barrier to keep the hurt away
and finally I made the solemn decision that I didn't need the extra
weight anymore, so I started, a few months ago, to visualize a
Pac-man type of being eating away at my fat cells. I've lost about
a stone since January (three months ago).*

*It is a long process and, aside from the unconscious changes in
my eating habits that I sometimes notice, nothing in my lifestyle
has changed – it's still as hectic as before.*

I asked Tamara for a few more details on her visualization.
This was her response:

*I manage on average five times on a good week, mostly every
night before going to sleep. I have breaks in between where
I don't do any meditation. The visualization consists of some
Pac-man beings eating the fat in particular points of my body
and then just exploding and disappearing into thin air.*

Some others then actually transport the fat from the thighs and waist to my breasts (as you probably know, the first part of the female body to go down during weight loss is the breasts, but I gained half a cup instead by doing it this way; it's just marvellous!) and then I try to visualize my skin tightening up. I finish with a whole body scan/healing to raise the metabolism and check for parts that may not be in tune with the rest.

The results so far are:

Weight loss: 9.5 kg (1 stone and 7 pounds) in around four and a half months.

I have gone from a tight size 22 to a comfortable 20.

I have gained half a cup on my bra size.

I have gone from needing at least eight hours sleep to being comfortable with only six and not being tired.

No new stretch marks at all!

I eat what I want when I want when I'm hungry, takeaways included (very busy life), but it seems that I have lost interest in things like chocolate and sweets in general, and I feel fuller sooner when I eat.

The brain and the mind are two amazing tools!

This Works Because...

Tamara's scene tells the story of fat being eaten up, resulting in a slimmer and healthier body.

As I pointed out in Chapter 8, 'How to Visualize', visualization often results in us being unconsciously inspired to make some lifestyle changes. In Tamara's case, she has lost interest in eating chocolate and sweets. However, this isn't the only reason that she is losing weight. Her scene will have seeped into her unconscious mind, resulting in her nervous system creating the loss in weight, and her metabolism will probably have been stimulated in just the right way.

YOU CAN DO IT

These stories show that the mind has a really powerful ability to heal the body. I am aware that some people might require medical records to believe that these healings actually occurred, but I would like to suggest that these types of healing take place every day, all over the world. Overly relying on having the medical evidence in front of us reduces our ability to open our minds and believe that such amazing healings are possible. Our own belief or lack of belief can enhance or block healing. Therefore I would encourage you to open your mind and accept the possibility that the mind really did play a significant role in these healings.

I believe that the mind plays a major role in many of the recoveries that people experience using drugs. When we take a drug, we feel hope. Hope alters our biology, so part of the effect of a drug is the placebo effect.

Our visualizations change the microscopic structure of the brain, expanding and contracting brain maps. They stimulate cells in the area that we are visualizing and they produce neuropeptides in the brain that are released into the body. This causes chemical changes in many organs as well as in the target area that we are visualizing. Genes are switched on and off all throughout the body as well as at the target area, tipping the genetic balance of the body towards healing. And, as I've mentioned, it is highly likely that genes in stem cells produce proteins that cause the stem cells to morph into the exact type of cells that are required to replace damaged ones. The science of this has not been fully investigated yet, but I am fully convinced that this occurs. Eventually the body is healed in accordance with the images, real or symbolic, that we have held in our minds.

Many of the miracles of healing, including spontaneous remissions, that have been documented throughout history probably involve this process. The miracle really begins in the mind, which then brings about the necessary biological changes that produce the healing.

Indeed, when He healed the blind, Christ said, 'According to your faith it will be done to you' (Matthew 9:29).

PART III

IN CLOSING

The Power of Love

Where there is great love, there are always miracles.
Willa Cather

There is one other thing that I want to mention in regard to healing and I think it deserves a chapter of its own, such is its power to heal body and mind. It is love. Love nurtures the soul.

Aaron was so terribly stressed. He was struggling financially. He wasn't getting on so well with his boss at work. The recent pay rise he expected hadn't come through. Every day was like a nightmare for him. He just couldn't shake the constant feeling of anxiety, fear and dread. Then, completely unexpectedly, the woman he'd secretly been in love with declared her love for him. In an instant, all of Aaron's problems disappeared.

Of course, the situations still existed. But Aaron's experience of them drastically changed. The anxiety, fear and dread dissolved overnight.

Love shifts our perception of things. That's where the miracle occurs – inside us. Love reaches inside us and stirs our soul. Its light then shines upon our life. And life appears different.

My research into the mind–body connection has convinced me that emotional pain is at the root of many illnesses. But it can be healed with love. And so love has the power to heal our physical conditions.

The most obvious place to experience love is in relationships – romantic, familial or friendly. We need relationships. They are the foundation for our experience of life. Without them, life would have less meaning.

In *Aikido and the Harmony of Nature*, Mitsugi Saotome, founder of the Aikido Schools of Ueshiba, writes,

> *If you were alone in the Universe with no one to talk to, no one with whom to share the beauty of the stars, to laugh with, to touch, what would be your purpose in life? It is other life, it is love, which gives your life meaning...We must discover the joy of each other, the joy of challenge, the joy of growth.*

I believe that our main purpose in life is to deepen our experience of love. Many people, in their final days, reflect on what was most important in their lives. Most say that it was the quality of their relationships – the time they spent with their loved ones. Everything else was just detail.

And as we experience love, we also experience healing of mind, emotions and body. I am not suggesting that all we need is relationships to cure ourselves of serious illnesses. But love – real love – will change our experience of them. And then many of the things that mattered before won't seem to matter as much. We will discover for ourselves what is really important. Stress, which accelerates disease of mind and body, will fade away and be replaced with gratitude and a deep reverence for all forms of life. And from that space, if there's anything practical that we need to do to facilitate any physical healing, we are perfectly placed to do it. We have more energy, vibrancy and motivation at our fingertips than ever before.

Love enhances us. It makes us so much more. We stretch out further. We become so much more. We become the person we've always wanted to become. Our loved one sees in us so much more than we see when we look in the mirror. And from that space, we expand into ourselves.

In his poem 'Love', Roy Croft writes,

> *I love you*
> *Not only for what you are*
> *But for what I am*
> *When I am with you.*

Of course relationships, like all things, need continual attention. They need work. How would growth occur if we were not occasionally challenged to work at things? In the popular advice column 'Sweet Reason', Molleen Matsumura wrote,

> *Love is like a campfire: it may be sparked quickly, and at first the kindling throws out a lot of heat, but it burns out quickly. For long-lasting, steady warmth (with delightful bursts of intense heat from time to time), you must carefully tend the fire.*

Ursula LeGuin puts it another way:

> *Love doesn't sit there like a stone. It has to be made like bread; remade all the time.*

And there is a skill to remaking it, which we learn through experience. We learn that we have to occasionally put our own needs aside for the needs of another. All parents know this.

The welfare of the children must always come first. In romantic relationships, as our love deepens, we put our own needs aside so that we may contribute to the fulfilment of our loved one's needs. The desire to listen replaces the need to be right. And we discover great joy and experience deep healing in this.

I have learned that love is both the most complex thing imaginable and also the simplest: learning what we should and shouldn't do, what is best and how to deal with the emotions of our loved one. These things can be tricky. But when we do make the choice that love, if it were intelligent, would make, it is, and always was, so simple. We may have wanted to get our point across because we perceived it to be vitally important. It could help our loved one so much, we think. But in the period of time when we stay silent and give our loved one our full and undivided attention, when we really listen without our minds calculating what we'll say next, we discover great happiness. What we thought was so important often turns out not to be. In the moments that follow this choice, love shines from our soul and illuminates the face of our loved one, our own heart and our lives.

It was that simple all along. Only we made it complex.

● ● ●

We don't need to wait to be in a romantic relationship to experience love. It is all around us. In fact, it is inside us. It is how we choose to experience the moments of life, whichever form they come in, that allows us to experience love.

You can experience love in many ways. You can show kindness to a stranger. You can smile at someone in the street. You can allow someone to pull out ahead of you on the road while you drive your car. Notice how you feel when you do these things. The more you do them, the more they affect you. It becomes easier for your soul to illuminate your path.

You can also show compassion. You can show gratitude.

THE POWER OF GRATITUDE

Happiness cannot be traveled to, owned, earned, worn or consumed. Happiness is the spiritual experience of living every minute with love, grace and gratitude.
Denis Waitley

A friend once told me that gratitude changed his life in 30 days. He was depressed at the time and had been for a while. One day he decided to try a simple exercise. Every day he would write down 50 things that he was grateful for. He would try to go the full month doing this – 30 days.

It was hard at first, but he always managed to find 50 things. Sometimes it took him all day. He'd do a bit in the morning and add to it throughout the day, and he'd always have his list completed by the time he went to bed. As the days passed, it got easier. After two weeks, he was feeling so much better that he was writing 75 things a day in his gratitude list. By the end of the month he was a different person.

And funnily enough, as is often the case when we change from the inside out, our deepest hopes and dreams move towards us. He met the woman of his dreams and got the job he'd always hoped for.

Why not try this exercise for 30 days and see just how much of an impact it has on your life? It might be difficult at first, if you are struggling with your life, but it will get easier. As the power of gratitude causes a crack to appear in the veil of difficulties in your life, the light of your soul shines through. The first thing you feel is a tickle around your heart. Not a physical tickle, an emotional one. You just feel better. But then more cracks appear and your light gets stronger until soon, as if by magic, your *experience* of your life changes. And then your life changes.

GO THE EXTRA MILE

Elizabeth and I were recently driving to Scotland from our home in Windsor to visit our families. We stopped at one of the motorway service restaurants to have breakfast. We were both a little tired because we had left really early in the morning and, due to being very busy in the few days leading up to our trip, we had not had very much sleep.

But the tiredness left us when we encountered the woman who served us our breakfast. She was working behind a long counter and served us our order before we moved further along the counter to pay. She greeted us with a warm smile and some friendly comments. Her genuinely kind and positive attitude was like a refreshing shower. I think she could tell that we were feeling tired because she gave us an extra large portion of breakfast to accompany the big portion of joy, which was just what we needed. Within a few seconds, Elizabeth and I were feeling refreshed, and we hadn't even eaten yet.

While we were eating, I noticed a feedback form on the table. Highlighted was a new initiative being run by the restaurant. It was called 'Go that Extra Mile'. The form gave the opportunity for customers to comment if a staff member had gone that extra mile in providing good service. We had just experienced great service, so we filled out the form.

We had to include the staff member's name and the time and date, but we hadn't noticed the woman's name, so on our way out we went back to the counter and tried to read her name from her badge. The problem was that the restaurant was filling up and she was quite busy. She frequently had her back to us so we couldn't catch her name.

Now I have to admit we thought of just leaving because it felt a little out of our comfort zones to be standing alongside a queue of hungry people. We were aware that some customers thought we were trying to jump the queue. But, in life, love often stretches us and presents us with opportunities to burst out of our comfort zones. We either act on these opportunities and grow a bit more, or we walk away and wait for another opportunity.

So I shouted across to the woman and asked her name. I told her that I was filling out the feedback form and that we were really grateful for the way she had helped us feel when we had arrived earlier. Right then, her face just glowed. Her smile almost stretched the full width of her face. I suddenly felt inspired to point out the form to some of the customers in the queue too. I said, 'Doesn't she have a lovely smile? What a great way to be served ...with a smile!' They were now all smiling.

Then, as fortune would have it, the woman's manager appeared. I was on a roll now and had no intentions of stopping. I related what I'd written on the form to the manager, right in front of the woman and the customers. The manager's smile suddenly broke through too. And none of the customers seemed to care that I was holding up the queue. This was a little moment of magic and everyone was participating in it. I don't think anyone wanted to interrupt it.

The manager said it was a great pleasure to receive some positive feedback. Apparently we had been the first (I don't know when the initiative had started). She said that all they had ever received was complaints. It was really special to receive positive feedback, she said, and especially in such a personal way.

I'm sure that many customers had been pleased with their service in the past, but had not commented. Isn't it funny how most people reserve their feedback until they have something negative to say? How many people do you know who send a card to a restaurant when they've had a nice meal, just to say thanks? But how many people complain when a meal didn't meet their expectations?

In the absence of some form of positive feedback, people don't realize what a great job they are doing or what a gift their job is to others. We deprive them of knowing this. I think it's up to us to tell them.

I have said on so many occasions that the ones who complain have the loudest voices. Too often, things are changed to suit the minority because those who complain make a big fuss. I think it's about time we started to show more gratitude in the world. Let's make a fuss about the good things. Let gratitude have the loudest voice so that things change for the better. I feel that we could make a huge difference to others' lives, and our own, by going that extra mile to say or do something really nice for others. Don't wait until something bothers you before you offer feedback.

And have you ever noticed how good it makes you feel when you do something nice for another person? After the exchange in the restaurant, I felt on top of the world. Amazing isn't it? I was able to radically change my mood, Elizabeth's mood and our experience of the world, and inspire good feelings in a staff member, her manager and a whole queue of people, just through a simple act of kindness.

PINGING KINDNESS

Love cures people – both the ones who give it and the ones who receive it.

Karl Menninger

I love to 'ping' kindness. I might be walking down a busy street and when I see someone who looks sad I imagine pinging a little ball of kindness towards them. I visualize it flying through the air and landing on them. For effect, I usually flick my finger as if I am flicking the ball of kindness towards them.

I get quite creative at times. Usually I give the ball of kindness a colour – whichever colour I am inspired by at the time. I also ping whatever quality that I feel the person needs. So sometimes, instead of kindness, I might ping happiness and at other times I might ping fulfilment, or love, or joy, or forgiveness. I look at the person and just ping the first quality that pops into my mind.

Sometimes I ping more than a little ball. Sometimes I stretch it out and have it reach several people at once. Sometimes I break a large ball into little fragments and shower people with them. Other times, I send a ball rolling down the street and watch it blow through a whole line of people.

And a funny thing sometimes happens. When I ping something, people sometimes look towards me and smile. There have been several occasions when people who were looking sad or emotional just suddenly appeared different. I like to think that there was an exchange between us at those times and that the person did actually receive something that was helpful to them.

But it is always helpful to me too. You get back what you give out, as they say. To ping kindness puts you in a state of consciousness of having kindness to ping.

In *Romeo and Juliet*, Shakespeare wrote,

> *My bounty is as boundless as the sea,*
> *My love as deep; the more I give to thee,*
> *The more I have, for both are infinite.*

Love is infinite. When you give it out, in any form whatsoever, you receive some in return. From the consciousness of kindness, compassion, joy, or whatever quality you 'ping', your soul shines out of you, passing through your heart first. That's why it makes you feel good. And when you feel good, healing begins.

Kindness, of course, is also practical. Demonstrating kindness for others helps them, but it also helps us. Joining a charity makes a real difference in the lives of those who receive help. But there is something immensely healing in the act of giving of yourself in charitable work. It feels healing. It often takes away our own pain. Our inner dialogue of suffering gradually changes from 'How can I receive?' to 'How can I give?'

Many people have recovered from depression through launching themselves into charitable work. A number of years ago Patch Adams, the doctor featured in the movie of the same name that starred Robin Williams as Patch, advised my dear friend Margaret McCathie to 'Go out and serve and see your depression lift.' She did and it did!

I really believe that spiritual and emotional healing occurs like this. The more love we can consciously spread in the world, the more we heal ourselves. The word 'heal' comes from the Old English word *haelen*, which means 'to make whole'. When we give love, we make ourselves whole.

CHANGE YOURSELF AND YOU CHANGE THE WORLD

I have often spoken about the similarity between people and tuning forks. When we strike a tuning fork, other things begin to vibrate. When we are in a bad mood, just like a tuning fork, we inspire a gloomy mood around us. People start to act as we are acting. The same, of course, happens when we feel happy. Then we inspire happiness around us.

I think we send out mental and emotional vibrations everywhere we go. Neuroscience is beginning to shed light upon this phenomenon. We unconsciously perceive people's mood and our mirror neurons reproduce it in ourselves.

Imagine if these vibrations were colours. Some days we would send out red and other days we would send out gold. I think that each person has a colour that represents their average state, the person they tend to be most of the time. And the more we give love, the more our colour is love-coloured.

I have written in other books that science is painting a picture of an interconnected world – a world where you and I are connected on a deep level. Carl Jung described a collective field of consciousness that connected everyone, calling it the 'collective unconscious'. Each of us has an unconscious mind and they overlap. The edges between yours and mine are blurred. Thus, at some level, we share a connection, just as the internet forms a connection between all of our computers.

I have also used the analogy of a spider's web to describe this connection, but it is a web of intelligence. And the interesting thing about this is that to change the colour of the web, all we need to do is change ourselves and our vibrations will ripple along the strands of the web. So, if we want to see more love in the world, we start by becoming more loving ourselves. If we want to see more peace in the world, we start by becoming more peaceful inside ourselves.

His Holiness the Dalai Lama said,

Responsibility does not only lie with the leaders of our countries or with those who have been appointed or elected to do a particular job. It lies with each of us individually. Peace, for example, starts within each one of us. When we have inner peace, we can be at peace with those around us.

IT'S OK TO SUFFER

I have noticed that one thing that distances people from happiness is the word 'should'. We think that we should do this or that, or that we should have done something different. Or, more painfully, that we should be something different. But I think that we start to feel happiness and peace and experience healing when we love ourselves – when we say, 'It's OK to be me!'

If you are suffering right now, that's OK. Don't torture yourself by thinking you shouldn't be. If you are not happy right now, don't beat yourself up by convincing yourself that you should be happy. People who read self-help material often think that they are not enlightened enough, loving enough, forgiving enough or peaceful enough. Then they criticize every negative thing they do and, even worse, they beat themselves up for every negative thought. I know this to be true, because I still do it sometimes. But it's OK. It's all part of growing up. We'll all get there in the end. In the meantime, lighten up, for your own sake.

My dear friend Stephen Mulhearn, a shamanic teacher who runs a retreat centre called Lendrick Lodge in Brig o' Turk in Scotland, has a great sense of humour. He often makes light of the way we beat ourselves up. He had me in stitches of laughter once when he talked of a friend who was working hard on a new nutritious diet. Stephen told me that his friend had shaken his head and said, in a deadly serious and grave voice, as if confessing to a murder, 'My only vice is milk.'

The way Stephen described all this to me was just so funny. He has that talent. But it got me thinking about how we are our own worst critics. In fact, other people don't need to criticize us. We do a good enough job of it ourselves.

But it is when we accept that 'It's OK to be me; I don't need to be perfect, or healed, or enlightened right now; I just need to be me today,' we move towards wholeness. This is love for ourselves. This is the space that inner peace grows from.

Hermann Hesse, winner of the 1946 Nobel Prize for Literature, wrote,

> You know quite well, deep within you, that there is only a single magic, a single power, a single salvation ... and that is called loving. Well, then, love your suffering. Do not resist it, do not flee from it. It is your aversion that hurts, nothing else.

When we make peace with who we are, we begin to love ourselves. And from this space of not running away from ourselves, healing can be profound.

At the end of the day love in any form, for ourselves and for others, is powerful medicine. Therefore I would like to end the book with an inspiring little exchange. I couldn't find the source of it, but I am grateful to the author:

> A wise physician said to me, 'I have been practising medicine for 30 years and I have prescribed many things. But in the long run I have learned that for most of what ails the human creature, the best medicine is love.'
> 'What if it doesn't work?' I asked.
> 'Double the dose,' he replied.

I think that about says it all!

Appendix I

Quantum Field Healing (QFH)

An ocean traveler has even more vividly the impression that the ocean is made of waves than that it is made of water.
Arthur S. Eddington

I was once a scientist with one of the world's largest pharmaceutical companies. I resigned in 1999. I was fascinated with how healing could be achieved by using the mind. I had played around with visualization for years, researched mind over matter in my spare time and read many spiritual writings. Coming from a scientific background, with an understanding of the placebo effect, I knew that the mind powerfully affected biology. But I was curious to know at what level thought could affect biology. Was a thought a force that originated in the gap between the branches of neurons? Did it shift molecules around?

I had achieved very high marks in a few classes in the quantum sciences at university and had read up a lot more since then on my own. I did not believe that thoughts arose out of interactions between chemicals in the brain. I still don't. Of course, chemical changes do alter how we think and feel, but the actual thoughts are ours. And I believe that they originate independently of chemicals.

Science says that thoughts are products of chemicals because chemical changes can alter the mind. But now we know that thoughts cause chemical changes too. So which comes first – the thoughts or the chemicals? Each affects the other, but one has to come first. I am sure that thoughts ultimately come first and affect the very core of reality, at the level where the tiniest particles are created.

If you look inside your body you see cells. If you look inside them you find molecules, of which DNA is one. Looking at what DNA is made of, you learn that it is atoms. But if you look inside an atom, it's mostly empty space. Most people have heard of protons, neutrons and electrons, the subatomic particles that compose atoms (there are actually many, many more particles) but we don't realize what they appear like and how far apart they are. If a proton were the size of a grape, then an electron would be smaller than the thickness of a hair and would be around two miles away from the proton. That's how much space is between them inside an atom. And atoms are what your body is made of. At this 'quantum' level, reality is mostly empty space. We are mostly empty space.

And it gets even weirder, because the subatomic particles (protons, neutrons, electrons, etc.) are not particles at all, in the sense that they are not solid balls. They are vibrations of energy. The latest research in quantum physics tells us that they are actually tiny vibrating strings. As a string vibrates at a certain speed, our instruments detect the vibrations as a certain particle (a proton, for instance); but if it vibrates at a different speed, or if two vibrations interact with each other, then we detect a different particle (e.g. an electron). Think of it as one vibration creating a red particle and another, at a different speed, creating a blue one.

The bottom line is that reality is not solid, but constructed from vibrations of energy. And scientists believe that these vibrations originate in a larger field of energy, sometimes called the 'quantum field'. Therefore subatomic particles, which make up atoms, which make up molecules, which make up cells, which make up humans (and our diseases), are all born in the quantum field.

As far as I was concerned, this was where thoughts interfaced with matter, at the level where matter was created, because ultimately the mind was the instrument that created our picture of reality. The mind caused us to see matter where really only vibrations of energy existed. If we could align our minds with that level, I reasoned, then our thoughts could be much more powerful. We could consciously shape our reality and thus eliminate disease. I believed that our subconscious thoughts always interacted at this level but our many beliefs and assumptions about reality distorted the quality of our conscious thinking. That's why, in terms of healing results, we tended to get only what we were prepared to get – when we had faith or believed that something was possible or would happen (such as in the placebo effect), we bypassed some of our previous beliefs and assumptions and aligned ourselves more fully with our unconscious and the deeper level of reality.

I believed that faith was extremely powerful and that this could explain some miracles that mystics and great spiritual masters had performed. At their level of knowledge and understanding – their level of consciousness – their thoughts, uncluttered with conventional beliefs and assumptions, influenced matter much more powerfully than most people's.

A few years after I left the pharmaceutical industry, I wanted a powerful visualization that anyone could use, that could be done quickly and that would symbolically align the mind with the core level of reality, thus bypassing our limiting beliefs and assumptions. I actually awoke one night in 2001 with a series of images running through my mind. I wrote them down and this became what I called Quantum Field Healing (QFH).

Quantum Field Healing works symbolically at the source level of an illness or disease. The main principle in QFH is to look at a disease or illness not as a physical thing but as the energy waves (or vibrations) that it originates from in the quantum field. So you don't see a disease as a physical thing, but as patterns of energy vibrations that can be changed, just as you could change a wave on a pond by dropping a stone in it. The stone, in QFH, is a thought.

THE QUANTUM FIELD HEALING VISUALIZATION

Let's say that you have a specific disease (or illness, condition, pain, etc.). Visualize the body part or organ and then imagine going inside it, as if you were taking a camera inside so you could see the bones, muscle, flesh, tendons and joints. Now go inside the part until you see the cells that it's made of. Now go inside a cell and see the proteins, enzymes and DNA inside. Go inside the DNA and see the atoms that it is made of. Pick an atom and go inside it. See the subatomic particles – protons, neutrons, electrons and others. Imagine them as stars in the night sky.

The quantum field is a field of energy from which particles condense, analogous to the way in which raindrops condense from clouds. The particles begin their life in the quantum field. So, rather than imagining you are going inside the particles, go to their source – the quantum field itself.

Imagine the quantum field as a place in deep space of total stillness. Imagine this in any way that you want. It can be helpful to imagine it as a totally still lake of energy, like a still pond or lake early in the morning.

Now imagine the waves (vibrations) of disease and then mentally remove them, symbolically removing the disease.

Mentally say, 'Show me the waves (or vibrations) of _____.' State the name of the disease if you know it, or just call it 'the disease'. You are asking your unconscious mind to symbolically show you the waves. See the vibrations in any way that comes to mind. I usually see them as stormy seas.

Mentally affirm, 'Cancel!' and watch the waves collapse and disappear. You are now back to your place of total stillness and have just cancelled the disease.

Next, put new vibrations in its place. Imagine dropping a pebble into the still lake, only it is a pebble of light, which represents your intention. It may either be white or any colour that comes to mind. In the state of higher awareness that QFH brings you may see colours or even symbols. I have seen a face once or twice. You can imagine pebbles of anything you want and be as general or specific as you wish. For my intent I sometimes use 'perfect health' or 'healing' and I usually add one or two extra qualities as well. For instance, I often add pebbles of peace, love, compassion, kindness or forgiveness, or any other emotional or behavioural quality that I would like to see, think would help, or sense is related to the disease.

Imagine dropping the first pebble into the energy lake. Be aware if you hear any sounds, even just the sound of the splash. A 'peace' pebble, I find, often makes a 'ping' or 'Om' sound in my mind.

Watch the pebble make a small splash and then see light (of your colour) fanning outwards in the energy lake. These are waves of 'perfect health' or 'peace' or whatever your intention.

Now drop in the next pebble and observe the same process. You can add as many or as few pebbles as you wish and spend as much or as little time as you wish, adding several pebbles with the same intention. I have found that adding two or three pebbles just once is often enough. But how often you do it is up to you.

So you have now removed the waves of illness and replaced them with waves of health. The healing is technically done, but I like to further cement it, so to speak. Now we gradually return to where we started, noticing along the way that things are different because there are different waves at source. This reinforces your belief that the healing is done.

Imagine coming back out from the quantum field to see the subatomic particles. Mentally say, 'Show me that it is done.' This is giving you confirmation that the healing is complete. Imagine something slightly different from before – for example, instead of the particles being white like stars in the night sky, see them take the colour of the pebbles of light that you added. Thus they are particles that make up the now healed body. You may even wish to watch them shimmer or imagine a fine blanket of light ripple across the sky, a bit like the northern lights (aurora borealis).

Now come back out to the atoms. Mentally say, 'Show me that it is done.' See the atoms take the colours of the pebbles of light you added. If you wish, you could also see them shimmer or move around.

Come back out to the DNA and say, 'Show me that it is done.' Once again, see the DNA shimmer in the colours of the pebbles of light you added. You might even see some healing genes light up with great brightness.

Come back out to the cells and say, 'Show me that it is done.' Watch the cells shimmer with the colours of your pebbles of light.

Now come back out to the actual body part and say, 'Show me that it is done.' Again, watch it shimmer in your chosen colours. And you don't need to just see the shimmering colours at every stage. You can imagine a change in any way, maybe as your atoms or the DNA flexing like you flex a muscle. Maybe your cells will do the same, as they breathe with new life.

If you wish, at this stage you can visualize the disease being eradicated – a tumour dissolving, a virus leaving your body, or an organ or tissue regenerating. You can add an appropriate visualization from Appendix II, Visualizations, or create your own scene. It is not really necessary to add a visualization at this stage, but some people like to do so as if they are visibly watching confirmation that the healing is complete.

Finally, see your whole body and say, 'Show me that it is done,' and see it enveloped with the colours that you chose. You might even see yourself flexing your body in perfect health.

To close, mentally say, 'Thank you. It is done. It is done. It is done.'

Take a few deep breaths and open your eyes. It is done!

One of the unique advantages of QFH is that it expands your consciousness. At the moment where you go inside an atom and see the night sky, with subatomic particles shimmering like stars, it feels mind-expanding. It symbolizes bypassing the limitations of the body and the limitations of your beliefs and attitudes. This lifts you to a higher state of awareness or consciousness, thus aligning your thoughts much more with the foundation of reality.

You can also apply QFH to changing deep attitudes and beliefs or to removing old patterns of emotions that you no longer wish to experience. You would mentally ask to see the waves (or vibrations) of the attitude, belief or emotion and cancel it in the same way. Then add the new attitude, belief or emotion that you wish to have.

To summarize the technique:

1. Visualize the diseased body area.
2. Go inside and see the cells.
3. Go inside and see the DNA.
4. Go inside and see the atoms.
5. Go inside and see the subatomic particles.

6. Go to source and imagine yourself at the quantum field – a place of total stillness.

7. Say, 'Show me the waves/vibrations of _____ [the disease, illness, condition, pain, etc.],' and imagine these represented by stormy seas.

8. Affirm, 'Cancel!' and watch the waves collapse and disappear.

9. Say, 'Show me the waves of _____ [e.g. perfect health, healing, forgiveness, peace],' and imagine pebbles of brilliant light (any colour that comes to mind) dropping into the stillness and the ripples fanning outwards, as when pebbles are dropped into still water. Add one or more pebbles.

10. Come back out to the subatomic particles and say, 'Show me that it is done.' See them take the colours that you chose or change in some other way (e.g. a shimmering sky like the northern lights).

11. Come back out to the atoms and say, 'Show me that it is done.' Again, see a change in colour or some shimmering or movement.

12. Come back out to the DNA and say, 'Show me that it is done.' See a change.

13. Come back out to the cells and say, 'Show me that it is done.' See a change.

14. Watch a healing scene if you wish.

15. Come back out to the body area and say, 'Show me that it is done.' See a change.

16. Come back out to the whole body and say, 'Show me that it is done.' See the body enveloped by your chosen colours and flexing in perfect health.

17. Say, 'Thank you. It is done. It is done. It is done!'

The whole process should only take about five minutes, or you can stay longer at any part if you feel it is important. For instance, with every out-breath, you could imagine a pebble of peace.

For some healings, you might feel it necessary to add several pebbles of healing or perfect health or forgiveness over the course of several minutes, so that the majority of healing time is spent at that stage, heavily imprinting the quality of healing into the quantum field.

In time, when you become really expert at the visualization and have strong faith in the power of your mind, you will be able to go straight to the quantum field in a split-second and cancel the diseased state.

TRUE STORIES

The following section contains some true stories of people who have successfully used QFH.

Hayley's Story

When I got home, I was telling my partner and my visiting in-laws about the workshop and I came to the part about the illness visualization. I have an overactive thyroid and, as a result, a small goitre. It's not that noticeable, but to me it has been a very strong visual reminder of the condition. As I was telling my family of the visualization, unconsciously I put my hand up and touched the goitre, something I know I tend to do when talking or thinking about it.

It wasn't there!

I suddenly became aware of my hand gesture, because the unconscious touch didn't give me the expected result. I just couldn't feel the goitre. It had shrunk. I had to move my neck a long way back to even feel the smallest amount.

In my visualization I had seen it shrinking back from being a cloying pink fleshy mass, wrapped around my windpipe, to a grey shrivelled dried-up nothing. By the time I got home it had happened.

I managed to totally freak out my partner, my in-laws and myself in one go. They also could see it had changed, and my in-laws are generally quite sceptical people.

It was very odd, but in the last minute of the visualization at Regent's College (the workshop venue in London), I felt an incredible urge to cough. It was nothing major, just a slight throat-clearing, but there was a really heavy tickle in my throat below my thyroid. I really tried to hold on to it as I didn't want to disturb anyone else or break my concentration, but in the end I had to cough as I felt I was losing my focus. As I coughed, the weirdest thought came through my mind: that I was coughing out the thyroid (symbolically) – I know now that I did.

I have also realized that I need to slightly modify my visualization, as I do need to keep a well-functioning thyroid, so I now see it as a beautiful healthy gently glowing very soft green.

Pauline's Story

I was at one of your workshops, David, and we did Quantum Field Healing and the DNA visualization. I sent the healing (distant healing) to my daughter, Chloë, who was then four years old and had been diagnosed with asthma days before. She had been put on antibiotics, steroids and an inhaler.

When I was doing the healing I actually felt it being sent to Chloë and became excited. It was really clear. I could see and feel her DNA change colour and shape, becoming yellow and light green.

I was woken as usual the following morning by Chloë's kiss, and she told me, almost immediately, that her cough and breathing were better and she no longer needed the inhaler. She didn't know that I had been sending healing to her and, since that day (three years ago, at time of writing), she has never used steroids or an inhaler and doesn't need them.

This was amazing and I've used the method with other people since then. I haven't felt the healing being sent as strongly as when I sent it to Chloë, but I know that in some way the person receiving it will be changing for their highest good.

Ruth's Story

My friend Ruth came along to your workshop and she was so impressed with the Quantum Field Healing that she began doing it to get rid of a mole/skin tag that she had under her eye. She'd already had one removed by surgery and didn't want surgery again, so she focused on Quantum Field Healing instead. In addition, she visualized new skin growing from underneath and pushing the mole away and it falling off.

A couple of months later she was in the shower and it actually happened the way she had pictured it: the mole just fell off. And she had been told that that shouldn't happen. In fact, it doesn't ever happen!

Liz's Story

The day after I went to the DNA and QFH workshop, I was running an event when a candle exploded in the middle of the floor and I burned myself. I decided to use what you had just taught us and instantly the pain was gone.

The next morning there was no trace of the burn.

These are just a few of the many examples of healing that Quantum Field Healing has produced. Try it for yourself and see what results you get. Its power lies in the fact that our thoughts are aligning with the level of reality that all matter arises from. The limits of our ability lie only in what we believe is possible. What do *you* believe is possible?

Appendix II

Visualizations

I am enough of an artist to draw freely upon my imagination.
Imagination is more important than knowledge.
Knowledge is limited. Imagination encircles the world.
Albert Einstein

This section contains a list of common ailments and diseases and visualizations that can be used for them. For some conditions there is only one visualization, but for others there are two or more. This is to cater for some of the different ways in which we like to imagine things. A visual image that might feel good for one person might not feel so good for another.

Many of the visualizations are interchangeable or can be adapted for other conditions, so if you suffer from something that is not on the list, scan through and see if there's another visualization that you can use, or any elements that you can use, or even make up one of your own. In fact, the visualizations listed in this appendix may best be used as guidelines. I would suggest that you try to create your own – something that has greater meaning for you and how you perceive an illness or disease – or adapt these so that diseases and cells and other parts of the body are represented the way you see them.

You'll notice that some diseases and conditions are described symbolically, such as bacteria or viruses as black dots or inflammations as inflated balloons. It doesn't matter whether you know what something looks like anatomically, so symbolic images can make it easier to create a scene.

You'll also notice that some visualizations are very similar and repetitive, and many are variations upon a theme. However, the appendix is presented as an A–Z list so that you can dip into any condition and pick up a visualization without having to cross-refer too much to other pages.

You can even use the visualization to enhance any other treatment that you are receiving. For instance, if you are receiving radiotherapy for cancer you could imagine the radiation as laser beams burning cancer cells off and leaving healthy cells intact. Or you could picture chemotherapy drugs as little balls of light that dissolve tumours.

You can also do these visualizations for other people, either by just concentrating upon them or while placing your hands upon them. I personally believe in the power of prayer, therefore visualization for another person – with their permission, of course – is like an active prayer.

Remember that although this is a book about visualization, I am not suggesting that you give up your medicines or other treatments. In fact, I am suggesting that visualization is something that can be done *as well as* receiving treatment. When you take a medicine or receive a treatment you'll think something – either that it'll work or that it won't. Your mind is always present. So you may as well think something positive. Visualization is a way to target your thinking in a positive way. Just make sure that you don't get stressed while visualizing. If you do, then stop. Maybe there's a different scene you could use, or perhaps relaxation or meditation would be better for you.

For all we can say, visualizing healing of an illness or disease might prove to be one of the most powerful medical interventions we've ever known. In my opinion, new research is pointing in that direction. By visualizing, we may be activating pathways to health in our body that have never been considered. The mind may be the main factor with some people who live a normal healthy life even when they have been diagnosed with a serious disease.

Here is the list:

Acne

Acne is caused by a blockage to the oil-secreting glands in the skin, which is usually caused by too much oil (sebum) being secreted. This leads to pus being trapped inside or blackheads forming.

1. Imagine a pipe or hose that the oil is coming out of. See the oil flowing at whatever rate feels appropriate, based upon how your skin feels to you. If you feel that your skin is too oily, then you might see the oil flowing fast into the glands.

   Imagine that there is a valve on the pipe or hose. Now turn the valve down and watch the flow of oil reduce. Reduce it as much as you wish, to whatever level you feel is appropriate for your skin.

   Then imagine being underneath the pus or blackhead so that you are looking up at it. Take an imaginary suction hose and suck the pus or black stuff out. Feel the power of the suction and listen to the slurping sound. Clear the pore completely until it looks totally clean.

2. Imagine using a coloured acid or dissolving gel (any colour you want) and rub or spray it into a spot. It's a magical acid that only dissolves spots and leaves perfectly healthy skin underneath.

Watch the spot dissolve. See it shrink. Hear it fizzle as it does so, as if it were melting. Then move on to the next spot.

If there's any residue left when a spot is dissolved, use an imaginary vacuum cleaner and just suck it up. Take some pride in your cleaning so that there's absolutely no trace of the spot left, only beautiful healthy skin.

3. Just as models in magazines are airbrushed on computer screens to remove blemishes, imagine that you are airbrushing your skin. Imagine zooming in to each area and use a mental 'eraser' tool (like a photo-editing computer software eraser tool) to erase spots and scars.

Imagine the sensation of rubbing or gently erasing the spot or scar, restoring your skin to just the way you want it to be – blemish-free.

As a variation of this, scan a photo of your face into your computer (if you have one) and actually use editing software to airbrush your skin. But as you do, affirm that there is a link between what you are doing and neurons in your brain.

For acne scars:

Imagine the scar tissue as being made of bricks or other material. Now remove the bricks one by one and replace each one with a healthy skin cell. Notice how the scar is converted into perfectly healthy skin.

Ageing
To slow down the ageing process:

1. Imagine stretching out and flattening wrinkles. Take an imaginary iron and iron the wrinkles flat. Use an imaginary steam iron

with steam pouring out. If you wish, go right inside, to the cells, and watch old, wrinkled cells stretch and flatten out as you iron them.

Now take an imaginary oiling can and imagine oiling all of your joints. Go through all of them, one at a time, keeping them well oiled and supple. Imagine a light flowing into the top of your head and flooding your entire body with lightness, so that you have lightness in your touch and as you move.

2. Imagine going into your brain and seeing a dial that has 'ageing speed' written on it. Note the level that the dial is set to.

Now turn it backwards to slow down the ageing speed to whatever level you wish. As you do this, affirm that your body and mind are becoming fitter and healthier.

AIDS
See HIV.

Allergies
Allergies occur where the immune system is overly sensitive (hypersensitive) to certain substances. For instance, a hypersensitivity to pollen is hay fever.

Imagine that your immune system is made up of hundreds of little cells. You might even imagine them as little people. See them on edge, overly sensitive to the slightest movement. When you walk over to them, see them jump.

Go over to them and say, 'Hey, it's me, there's no need to be so edgy. Just chill out and do only what you have to to keep me healthy. Take the rest of the day off.'

Then see the chief shout to all his troops, 'Hey, it's just [your name] – we don't need to be so agitated.'

His troops let out a cheer and start to play tennis (or any game you enjoy) and lie down on beds to sunbathe.

Hug the chief and then walk off.

Anger

1. Imagine anger as a large ball of fizzling light inside your head or any part of your body where you feel the anger is situated (people sometimes feel anger focused in different parts of their bodies). Picture it like a sparkler or other firework and let it be any colour that you feel is appropriate.

Imagine a dial that represents the anger level and notice the level it's set to. Now turn it down to the level you want (zero, presumably?) Watch the light shrink smaller and smaller and smaller until it completely disappears with a tiny 'pop'.

A powerful version of this is to imagine some of the things that anger you and then do the visualization. Place the fizzling light inside the scene that you are imagining. This way you symbolically reduce the anger you feel about each thing, so that if the situation arises again in the future you won't feel angry. You may need to do this several times (ten to 20) in a row to neutralize your feelings about some situations, but it will be worth it.

If a person is your focus of anger, once you've 'popped' your anger, imagine saying something to them that reflects your new state – perhaps 'I forgive you.'

2. Imagine all the anger in you as being contained inside a pressure cooker. See it swirling around in you.

Now open a valve and let the pressure out. Hear it hissing and feel the pressure inside you dropping until the hissing has stopped and the anger has disappeared.

3. Use the victory dance. Imagine the thing that angers you. Get the thought really clear in your head. Once you can feel anger or irritation, break into your victory dance.

Now think of the thing that angers you again and, once again, break into your dance.

I would recommend that you do this about ten to 20 times in a row.

You can also apply this to things that you feel emotional pain about or even to emotional trauma. As Nobel Laureate Eric Kandel has pointed out, psychotherapy causes measurable changes in the brain. Doing a victory dance will also achieve this, because it will divert blood supply away from areas of the brain that process anger, thus helping to build neural connections in areas that process humour (and dancing).

Anxiety

Imagine an anxiety dial inside your brain. At one end it says 'Calm' and at the other it says 'Anxious'. Note what it is currently set at.

If you are feeling a little anxious, then imagine slowly turning the dial towards calm. As you do so, take deep steady breaths.

Arrhythmia (Palpitations)

An arrhythmia is an irregularity in the normal beating of the heart. There are different types, but the most common is palpitations, which this section refers to. They are usually harmless.

1. Imagine your heart and imagine little pink hearts with angel wings on them (to represent love), with the words 'Normal regular heartbeat' written on them. Watch the little pink hearts float gently down onto your heart. Imagine the rhythm of your heart return to normal.

2. Imagine that the timing system of the heart is faulty. So imagine going in and repairing it. See it like a clock mechanism or a metronome. Conjure up some magical tools and repair it. Take great care and attention as you fix the timing mechanism and even give all the bits and pieces a real good clean and polish, restoring the entire workings of your heart to perfection. Hear the 'tick-tock' of the clock in a beautiful sounding perfect rhythm.

Arthritis (Rheumatoid or Osteo-)

Arthritis is characterized by damage to the joint cartilage and to lack of fluid between the joints. Pain and inflammation arise as bone rubs against bone.

1. Imagine holding a big syringe or oilcan full of the magical frictionless everlasting oily fluid. Imagine it either clear or coloured (it's up to you – whatever feels best).

   Now imagine injecting it into the joint. Watch the viscous fluid go into the joint and see the two pieces of cartilage move apart.

   Now, while looking at the fluid-filled joint, see it move freely and effortlessly. If the joint is, say, your knee, then imagine effortlessly, painlessly walking or running. See into your joint as you imagine this and see the two pieces of cartilage comfortably kept apart by the fluid.

   Celebrate your success with a little victory dance (real or imaginary).

2. A slight variation of this would be to imagine going inside the actual fluid and seeing the atoms that it's made of. See them as little bubbles with smiley faces on them, and as they flow out of the syringe or oilcan, imagine them crying, 'Whaheeeeyyyyyy!' as if they were on a water slide. See the huge smiles on their faces. They are obviously having lots of fun as they slide out of the syringe or can and into the joint.

See the little atoms flood into the joint and flow right up the sides of a cavern that represents the gap between the two bones (if you are seeing the actual atoms, which are microscopic, then the gap between the bones will be as big as a cavern). See more and more atoms enter the cavern until it is comfortably full. They are soft squishy atoms, so they form a spongy fluid.

Now imagine moving back out of the joint so that you no longer see the atoms but a frictionless fluid holding the bones apart.

3. Imagine mechanical diggers driving up to the joint. They have special cutting tools to cut away any excess bone that was rubbing together, to create a space.

Now imagine the diggers erecting girders to keep the space there so that the bones can't rub together again.

Now another digger drives up with its bucket full of magical everlasting lubricating fluid. Watch it pour the fluid into the joint and see it fill the gap.

Asthma

Asthma is characterized by occasional constriction of the airways, which restricts breathing.

Imagine being inside one of your airways, like being inside a small tunnel. Now imagine teams of little workers pushing the inside of the tubes out and making them wider. Then see them adding magical strengthening rings to help support the new expanded size and keep the tubes from constricting again.

Atherosclerosis

Atherosclerosis is often called 'hardening of the arteries'. The walls of the arteries become thickened with scar tissue and cholesterol, and calcium deposits eventually build up. This can restrict blood flow through the arteries.

1. Imagine the inside of one of your arteries. If you have been diagnosed with atherosclerosis, then you might imagine lumps of white globular cholesterol lying around, like big chunks of lard. Or you might also see large build-ups of rocky calcium, like white jagged rocks littering all around the top, sides and bottom of the walls. Or use any other image that represents atherosclerosis for you.

    Imagine yourself holding a laser. It has a label on it that says 'Bad cholesterol and calcium deposit dissolver'. Switch on the laser and fire away. Melt the cholesterol or rocky calcium. See them dissolve in much the same way as warm water from a tap will dissolve an ice cube. Clean out all the bad cholesterol and calcium deposits from your arteries.

    Take an imaginary suction hose or vacuum cleaner and suck up all the melted residue.

Arteries are supposed to be flexible, like a flexible piece of rubber. With atherosclerosis, the 'tubing' becomes hard and inflexible.

2. Imagine the cells that form the walls of your arteries as rows of soft rubber bricks, but some are much harder, discoloured, misshapen and cracked.

    Remove the hard and damaged bricks from the wall one at a time and replace them with soft rubbery bricks. With each section you refit, imagine that the artery is really flexible. See it effortlessly bend and flex.

Athlete's Foot

Athlete's foot is characterized by dry, itchy skin on the feet and toes.

Imagine the skin cells like flaky, hardened cells that are cracked and separated from each other – like photos you may have seen of the bed of a river or sea that has dried up.

First, go into the cracks and vacuum up little particles of fungus (athlete's foot is caused by infection with the tinea species of fungus). Picture them in any way that you wish, for instance like little balls of moss.

Then start to moisturize the cells, one by one, using a magical moisturizer that also dissolves any stray bits of fungus. As it soaks in, watch each cell change shape, bending and stretching out and being restored to a normal healthy cell. See the cracks disappear as the cells join up with each other.

Autoimmune Conditions

Autoimmune conditions – e.g. type 1 diabetes, lupus, rheumatoid arthritis and multiple sclerosis – occur as the body's immune system attacks parts of the body. For example, in diabetes, the immune system attacks beta cells of the pancreas.

The following visualizations are intended to reduce the sensitivity of the immune system to the body. The first visualization is similar to the allergies visualization because there are biological similarities between some autoimmune conditions and how the immune system reacts to an allergen in someone who is allergic to it.

1. Imagine that your immune system is made up of hundreds of little people. You are walking towards them, but as you do so, you can't see them properly and they can't see you too well as there is quite a bit of fog. Since it can't see clearly, your immune system is attacking your body, fearing that you are an enemy.

   Now imagine the fog clearing so that you and your immune cells can see each other perfectly. Go over to the chief and say, 'Hey, it's me, there's no need to fight. Just chill out and do only what you have to to keep me healthy. Take the rest of the day off.'

   Then see the chief shout to all his troops, 'Hey, it's just [your name] – we don't need to fight.'

His troops let out a cheer and start to play tennis (or any game you enjoy) and lie down on beds to sunbathe.

Hug the chief and then walk off.

2. Imagine the cells of the immune system that are attacking the healthy cells as wild dogs.

Now walk among the dogs. They do not harm you. Command them to sit down. Mentally command, with absolute conviction: 'Down, boy.'

Watch each dog stop its attack and sit. Then see it totally change in personality and become a playful house-pet type of dog – totally obedient and loving. Stroke it and give it a hug.

Do this for each 'dog'.

Blood Pressure
High Blood Pressure – Hypertension

Imagine an inflated balloon representing your blood pressure. Notice how inflated it is. Now untie it and watch the air flow out. Listen to the whooshing and rasping sound as the air rushes out of the balloon. See it get smaller and smaller. And as it gets smaller (and filled with much less pressure), affirm that your blood pressure is reducing.

As well as visualization, try breathing. A great way to reduce blood pressure is meditation, where you just sit quietly and breathe. You can even do this as you walk, or just for a couple of minutes as you sit at your desk. Just take deep and even breaths.

Low Blood Pressure

Imagine a deflated balloon representing your blood pressure. Notice how deflated it is. Now use a pump or a dial and add air to the balloon. As the air enters the balloon, watch it get bigger and bigger and affirm that your blood pressure is increasing. Increase the pressure in the balloon until it's at the level that you feel is normal and healthy.

Bronchitis

With bronchitis, the bronchi (tubes in the lungs that air passes through) are inflamed and produce mucus.

Imagine inside the bronchial tubes. Imagine them red and inflamed, containing deposits of mucus. Now use a suction hose or vacuum cleaner and suck the mucus out. If the bronchitis is a result of smoking, then also suck out any little flecks of black residue that are peppered throughout the walls, which symbolize residue from smoking.

After you have sucked up the mucus and cleaned the walls, imagine spraying them with a green magical healing liquid. As it is absorbed into the walls, see the inflammation reduce to nothing and the walls return to a healthy pink colour.

Imagine a soothing air that you breathe in that calms the bronchi.

Broken Bones

These two visualizations can be used once the bone has been set by a doctor. Even though it has been set, there will still be a microscopic gap between the two ends, where new bone material will grow.

1. Picture the two ends of the fracture and imagine teams of construction workers repairing it. See them build scaffolding and construct hundreds of fibres of new bone that connect the two ends, forming a 3-D net of bone material between the two ends. As more and more fibres are added, gradually see the net

become denser and denser with new fibres until the workers have completely healed the fracture.

Affirm that the bone is as strong as or stronger than it was before the break.

This version is a bit more fun and might be preferred by children:

2. Imagine the two ends of the fracture. Now imagine yourself with powers like Spider-man, where you can shoot a web. Stand at one side of the fracture and fire a web strand to the other side. Once it sticks, connect the bit on your spidey wrist to the end you're standing on, so that the two ends are joined by your web. But this is no ordinary web. After a little while it hardens and turns to bone.

Fire hundreds of strands of web between the two ends of the fracture until they are completely fused together. You can have some fun doing this. See yourself swing from one side to the other so that you can fire some web from both ends.

Burns

Imagine using a soft brush and a bucket of magical, ultra-cool and soothing 'skin paint'. It has hints of blue and green light in it. Imagine gently brushing the burn with this magical soothing skin paint. As it soaks in, new skin cells set up camp underneath the burn. As you continue painting, more and more skin cells grow until the burn has completely disappeared and has been replaced with healthy skin.

Cancer

I've included more visualizations for cancer than for most other conditions because it is such a widespread disease and manifests itself in different ways in the body.

In addition to the following visualizations, you can read people's stories in Chapter 10.

If you are undergoing chemotherapy or radiotherapy, imagine the drugs or particles of radiation as balls of light that land on the tumour and melt it. Imagine globular immune cells with smiley faces lapping up the residue.

1. Imagine the tumour getting smaller and smaller and smaller. See it shrink until it disappears with a tiny 'pop'. For extra smiles, while it's dissolving you could yell, 'I'm melting! Melting!' You might even wave your arms and shiver your body as you act out the melting process (if no one is around to see you having this fun). It's a bit like a victory dance.

2. Imagine cells in a cancerous part of your body. Notice that some of them are perfect pink healthy cells but some are discoloured and covered in slime or some other substance. These represent the cancer cells.

   Now take an imaginary brush and some special cleaning fluid and start cleaning these cells, one at a time, until each one is gleaming and restored to a normal healthy colour.

3. Imagine the cancerous part(s) of your body and see the cancer as a black slimy deposit. Now take an imaginary coloured laser beam (any colour you feel) and burn off the cancer, leaving the healthy cells around it intact. It is a special laser, so it only burns cancer cells. Now take an imaginary brush and pan and sweep up any residue, or suck it up with a suction hose.

4. Imagine taking a magic wand and firing a spell towards cancer cells. You can even make up a magic word, or use one of Harry Potter's. See each cancer cell flex and change colour and transform into a healthy pink cell. Do this for every cancer cell.

5. Imagine a beautiful green flawless crystal and imagine placing it beside the cancer. See it give off a green light and watch this light dissolve the cancer cells. Place your attention upon the crystal several times a day, and watch the light dissolve the cancer. Plus, each time you imagine the crystal you energize it and make it stronger.

6. Some people prefer to see the cancer as part of them and thus they treat it with love and affection instead of attacking it. So, imagine sitting down with the cancer cells, hugging them and telling them that you love them (if cancer were conscious, it wouldn't know it was hurting you. It would think it was helping.) Imagine the cells saying that they love you too. Then tell them that you have to let them go now. Now imagine them leaving your body with big smiles on their faces.

DNA Strategy

The following two visualizations involve visualizing DNA.

Around 50% of tumours have been found to contain a mutation in a gene called the TP53 gene (although this doesn't automatically mean that having such a mutation means a person will get cancer, only that if their lifestyle is cancer-promoting then they stand a bigger chance of getting cancer than someone with a healthy TP53 gene. In other words, attitude, environment, eating habits and lifestyle play a significant role.)

The TP53 gene is known as a 'tumour suppressor' gene in that it helps to stop the growth of tumours. It has often affectionately been called 'the guardian angel gene'.

1. You could imagine the TP53 angel lying on the ground as though it's been hurt. See it like a little hurt organism. Now nurse it back to life again, giving it some medicine and nutrients. See it growing stronger, giving off a glow of light. See it gain its full angelic strength.

Then imagine it diving into the DNA. See a ripple of the angel's colour of light go through the length of DNA. Then imagine the tumour(s) simply deflating or dissolving and vanishing with a 'pop'.

2. If you are technically minded, see yourself writing a computer software program, only the program is to be translated into a genetic program to instruct your DNA to find a way to restore perfect health. The human body has the ability to use many different pathways to health. If one gene is defective, then, in many cases, the body often has an ability to use a different genetic program that will maintain health.

Go inside the body, to the site(s) of the cancer, and type a genetic program made up of simple written commands on an imaginary computer. For instance, you could type:

'Restore TP53 gene to normal function.'
'Create alternative genetic program to restore perfect health.'
'Switch off cancer-promoting genes.'
'Switch on tumour-suppressor genes.'
'Restore body to perfect health.'

You could even type, 'My body is in perfect health,' or write words of your own choice that represent what you want.

Imagine typing the individual letters. See these words appear on the screen as you type.

Once you've written your program of commands, press 'Enter' on the keyboard and see the words float off and merge with your DNA, one command at a time. Notice the colours of your commands. Are they coloured?

As they float off, imagine some genes lighting up and some turning off, indicating what genes are about to be affected. Imagine the DNA inside the tumour and see it radiate a coloured light (according to your commands) through the tumour. Then imagine the tumour shrinking to nothing and vanishing with a 'pop', as if it had a valve and all the air had just been suddenly let out of it.

Candida

Candida is infection with the candida species of yeast fungus and often manifests as candidiasis (thrush) or in the vagina. It is often noticed in immunocompromised people.

Imagine walking around the fungal area with a suction hose or a vacuum cleaner and sucking up all of the fungus. Try to feel the force of the suction and imagine its sound.

Alternatively, you could use the infections visualization. If you want to boost your immune system too, then you could also use the immune booster visualization.

Cellulite

1. Imagine the cells in the fatty cellulite areas. Imagine that they are like rows of fatty, lardy, jelly bricks.

   Use an imaginary suction hose or vacuum cleaner to suck up the cellulite cells. Feel each cellulite cell resisting as you suck, but gradually they are sucked up into the vacuum. Feel the force of suction vibrate the hose and hear the slurping sound as the fat is sucked up into the bag. Make sure you show great care and patience, since this is a beauty thing you are working on.

   And when the cells are sucked up or dissolved, see that there's only perfect healthy-looking skin left. See it tighten and resume your version of perfect and beautiful.

2. Imagine loads of little fat-eating cells like little Pac-men, piranha fish or cellulite-loving rabbits eating up the cellulite and leaving the skin looking beautiful and healthy.

Chickenpox

Chickenpox is a skin infection caused by the varicella-zoster virus.

1. Imagine taking a magical dissolving fluid (any colour you feel inspired by) and squirt it into a spot. Watch it soak right into the spot.

   As you stand beside the spot, see it dissolve right before your eyes, as if the fluid were an acid, and disappear with a 'pop'.

   If there's any residue left at the end, use an imaginary vacuum cleaner to suck it up. Take pride in your cleaning so that there's absolutely no trace of the spot left, only perfectly healthy skin.

2. Take an imaginary eraser and imagine erasing the spot cells one by one, until they completely disappear.

   If the thought of this is uncomfortable, then imagine using Photoshop (or other photo-editing software) on a computer. Imagine your face, or any other part of your body, on the screen, select the eraser tool and effortlessly rub the spots away. You could even do this for real on Photoshop if you feel up to it. Take a photo of yourself and then edit it. As you do, affirm that there is a symbolic link between what you're doing and the neurons in your brain and thus the cells in your body.

3. You could simply imagine talking to your spots and asking them to leave. Imagine the cells detaching themselves from your body, one by one, and flying away.

Alternatively, or in addition, use the viruses visualization.

For Scars
Scars are fibres of tissue.

Imagine cutting the fibres one at a time. As each cut is made, hear the fibre twang.

Once the fibres have gone, imagine using a magical skin paint to paint on layers of new healthy skin. As each layer of paint is applied, notice that it is a layer of perfectly formed, healthy skin cells.

Gradually add more and more layers of healthy skin cells until you see perfectly healthy skin.

Or, as in the second chickenpox visualization above, you could imagine your face on Photoshop and create perfect-looking skin.

Chlamydia

Chlamydia is a sexually transmitted disease that is caused by infection of the urethra (men) or cervix (women) with the chlamydia trachomatus bacteria.

The infections visualization is a good one to use here. You could also do the following, either at the end of the infections visualization or as a stand-alone visualization:

Imagine walking through the area that's infected and applying a magical blue healing gel to it. Rub the soothing gel in and try to imagine the cooling sensation. As you rub in the gel, imagine the swelling reducing and the redness returning to a healthy pink colour.

Chronic Fatigue Syndrome
See ME.

Colds (and 'Flu)

The common cold is mostly due to infection by the rhinovirus (as opposed to the 'flu, which is infection by the influenza virus). It usually causes a sore throat and mild fever.

Imagine the cold or 'flu as hundreds of bubbles floating in a room or cave that symbolically represents your body. See them pouring out of some large pipes (a small number of these – maybe two to five).

Go to the first pipe and imagine that it has a valve on it, like a wheel – like the ones used to seal the doors on submarines. Now turn the valve and stop the flow of bubbles. As you do so, gradually see the flow of bubbles become slower and slower. When the flow has completely stopped, put a lock on the valve so that it can't open again. Repeat this for the other pipes.

Now burst the bubbles. You can do this with any instrument you wish or you can do it mentally. See each bubble go 'pop' as you burst it. Burst every last bubble until the cold or 'flu has completely gone from your body.

Alternatively, use the infections or viruses visualization. Even though the common cold is a viral infection, the bacterial infections visualization is often more appropriate because people don't generally think of the common cold as a virus. And, ultimately, it is what you think that counts. If you wish, you could also use the sore throat visualization (see Throat).

Cuts

1. Imagine yourself inside the cut and see the two sides standing apart, like the walls of a canyon.

    Imagine using magical threads to stitch them together, from the bottom of the canyon to the top.

    With each stitch, pull the two ends of the cut together and see them fit seamlessly together. Imagine them coming together so seamlessly that they create a perfect join so that you cannot even see where the cut had been.

    Stand back and admire your great work. You may even see loads of skin cells applauding you on the great job you've done.

Give yourself a pat on the back (this will generate happy chemicals that will speed up healing).

2. Imagine a team of construction workers repairing the cut. See them build new skin. Imagine immune cells mopping up any bacteria in the area. Then see the two ends of the skin being pulled seamlessly together.

3. You could also imagine talking to the cut in a kindly manner. Imagine lovingly stroking its insides (touch generates growth hormones, which are required for regeneration). Imagine that the two sides of the cut love each other and no longer wish to be separated (maybe they – or you – have had an argument and that's why they are apart). See them reach out and lovingly embrace each other. You could even do this while listening to some romantic or inspirational music.

Cystic Fibrosis

Cystic fibrosis is a genetic disease that affects the mucus glands of the lungs, liver, pancreas and intestines, and causes thick mucus to be produced. This leads the airways to become clogged and the build-up can cause severe bronchitis and pneumonia.

In addition to the following, you can do the bronchitis visualization (minus the reference to flecks of smoking residue) or the pneumonia visualization.

1. Cystic fibrosis arises out of a mutation in the CFTR gene. Therefore you could visualize CFTR as a little character lying on the ground as though it's been hurt. You might even see 'CFTR' written on its T-shirt or cloak.

Now nurse it back to life again, showing great care, compassion and attention. Give it some medicine and nutrients. See it growing stronger, giving off a glow of light.

Once it's healthy, imagine it diving into DNA. See the DNA flex with great power and a pulse of light travel its length. Now imagine the mucus evaporating from your lungs and other areas where it is causing infection.

You could imagine writing a new genetic program to compensate for the genetic defect, instructing your DNA to find another way of restoring you to health. I believe that the human body is capable of many more miracles of healing than we have ever given it credit for. Just as in an aeroplane if one engine is faulty the others can compensate and bring the plane home safely, so if one gene is defective, then the body often has an ability to use a different genetic program that will provide health by another route.

2. Imagine writing a computer program, only the program is to be translated into a genetic program to instruct your DNA to find a way to restore perfect health.

As you write your program on an imaginary computer, affirm that your DNA/body can use different pathways to health.

Type a genetic program made up of simple written commands on an imaginary computer. For instance, you could type:

'Create alternative genetic program to restore perfect health.'
'Switch on healing genes.'
'Restore body to perfect health.'
'My body is in perfect health.'
'The symptoms of cystic fibrosis are disappearing.'

Alternatively, you could write words of your own choice.

Imagine typing the individual letters. See these words appear on the screen as you type.

Once you've written your program of commands, press 'Enter' on the keyboard and see the words float off and merge with your DNA, one command at a time. As they do, imagine some genes lighting up and some turning off, indicating what genes are about to be affected. Imagine the DNA radiating a coloured light throughout the infected area. Then imagine the infections reducing to nothing and the mucus dissolving.

Cystitis

Cystitis is a bacterial infection of the bladder and urethra. Use the infections visualization. Also, to help tackle the burning sensation:

Imagine inside the bladder. See the cells as red and swollen.

Now imagine you have buckets of magical blue cooling fluid. It's thick and gloopy and feels really cold to the touch.

Now rub the fluid onto the cells one at a time and watch them cool and the redness return to a healthy pink colour.

Depression

1. Imagine a ball of soft green, pink or white light in the centre of your brain or heart, or see it like a little candle flame. This represents your happiness. Note its size.

   Now imagine a dial and turn it up. As you do this, see the light get bigger and bigger and brighter. Mentally affirm that it is a symbol of your inner strength and happiness.

   Continue to turn the dial and watch the light get bigger and brighter. See it expand right out of your head or heart and throughout your entire body. See the light flow through your arteries and veins, through your heart and your internal organs. Imagine it tickling cells and organs and see them smile. See it flow over your skin and imagine your skin cells smiling.

See yourself surrounded by this powerful light and mentally affirm that your power and happiness are great.

2. If you are able to, think of a time in your life when you were really happy – really, *really* happy! Now capture that moment in a little transparent ball of light and move it into your heart or brain. See it multiply hundreds or thousands of times and watch the balls float all around your body so that your body becomes saturated with them. I would also recommend that you then burst into a victory dance to celebrate. If you can put on some happy upbeat dance music too then that would be great.

3. See the depressed you. Now walk up to yourself and give yourself a hug. Place your hands upon your depressed self's head and imagine healing light flooding into the head and circulating around the body. As you do so, feel the compassion and love of giving. This makes it a high-energy (high-vibration) light, so it helps to raise the energy of your depressed self.

Diabetes

Diabetes comes in two main types: type 1 and type 2. Type 1 diabetes is an autoimmune condition where the immune system destroys insulin-producing beta cells in the pancreas, resulting in high levels of blood sugar. Type 2 diabetes is a result of insulin resistance or reduced insulin sensitivity, which also results in high blood sugar. Type 2 is more common in overweight adults.

For Type 1
Use the autoimmune visualization.

1. In addition, imagine flooding your pancreas with a green healing light (green symbolizes regeneration). Imagine some of the

damaged beta cells as half-eaten, and as you flood them with regenerative green light, see them grow back to full strength.

2. Alternatively, imagine a team of construction workers wearing green and rebuilding the cells. See them work to perfectly regenerate the cells, one by one, so that the pancreas is as good as new again.

For Type 2

Some studies have suggested that the reduced insulin sensitivity in type 2 diabetes is due to the insulin receptor on cell surfaces. So for this visualization, imagine that the receptor is asleep and you are waking it up.

Picture a cell as a balloon with loads of little pieces of dough on the surface, of all different colours, shapes and sizes. These represent receptors on the surface of the cell. As we learned earlier, receptors are docking ports for molecules to transmit their information into the cell. Notice the insulin receptor. What does it look like? What colour is it?

See insulin molecules approach the insulin receptor, in any way you wish. But the receptor is asleep. You may even see or hear it snore.

Imagine giving it a little shake and asking it to wake up. Tell it that there are loads of insulin around that need to get into the cell.

See the receptor get up and give itself a shake. Listen to it if it says anything.

Then watch the insulin and the receptor embrace each other before the insulin disappears through the hole. Then watch a line of insulin molecules do the same, each embracing the receptor before disappearing down the hole.

Diarrhoea

Diarrhoea often results from some kind of infection; therefore use the infections visualization.

Emphysema

Emphysema is characterized by a destruction of the walls of the alveoli in the lungs, which limits breathing.

1. Imagine that you have a bag of new alveoli cells and start filling up the holes in the walls using these cells. Use a magical fluid to coat the edges of the new cells and fit them perfectly into the holes. As you fill in each hole, notice that the cells around the new ones join seamlessly with them.

2. Think of a time in your life when you could breathe effortlessly. It's even better if you can think of a happy time. Remember the feeling of being able to breathe in and out really easily. Imagine that moment and turn it into a ball of coloured light.

    Now bring the light into your lungs and see it multiplying and filling all the holes in the alveoli. As the light merges with the walls see it turn into new, healthy alveoli cells.

Endometriosis

Endometriosis is growth of endometrium (the tissue that lines the uterus) outside or beyond the uterus.

The deposits undergo periodic bleeding in synch with normal menstruation, which can lead to inflammation. In ovarian endometriosis, cysts can also develop. They are known as 'chocolate cysts' because of their dark brown colour.

1. If you have been clinically diagnosed with ovarian endometriosis, imagine your ovaries with dark brown deposits on them. You can imagine the deposits in any way you like – whichever images you

237

feel represent them. Maybe you see them as rocky or maybe you see them as sludgy.

Now use an imaginary suction hose or vacuum cleaner and go around your ovaries, sucking up every last piece, leaving your ovaries looking healthy and happy. Get them totally clean. Maybe even see them with little faces and see them smile now that they are so clean and healthy.

You could, instead, use a power hose or jet wash and blast them clean. Then clear up the residue with suction or using a dustpan and brush.

2. Imagine that there's a chocolate cyst-loving animal that just loves eating chocolate cysts. See it eat away at the chocolate coating, totally clearing every last bit until the ovaries are polished clean.

Enteritis (Gastroenteritis)

Enteritis is often called gastroenteritis, although the stomach isn't really involved. The same visualization can be used for both, however. Enteritis is inflammation of the small intestine that is usually caused by infection with a virus or bacteria.

Imagine the inflamed cells like inflated balloons and then let air out of them one by one, as if you were letting air out of a balloon. Listen to the whooshing (or rasping) sound as the air rushes out and the inflamed cells return to normal size. Now rub on a magical blue cooling fluid. It's thick and gloopy and feels really cold to the touch.

Rub the fluid onto the cells, one at a time. Watch them cool and see any redness return to a healthy pink colour.

And, being magical, the fluid has special properties. It acts like an immune paint that neutralizes any infection in the area, as well as preventing reinfection.

To help with this, try to conjure up the memory of a cooling gel. If you have some Deep Freeze-type stuff for cooling muscles after sprains, rub a little on your hand and feel the freeze. Or rub a little alcohol onto the back of your hand and feel the coolness as it evaporates. Or put some ice or cold water on the back of your hand and use that memory instead.

Alternatively, use the infections visualization.

Epilepsy

Epilepsy is the name given to any of a number of recurring brain seizures.

Imagine being inside the brain. Imagine little agitated characters looking on, alert, jumpy and a little afraid. These are epilepsy characters. Notice what they are doing.

Now walk over to the leader. Hold their hand and tell them that there's no need to be afraid. Everything is OK. They can relax. They can leave now.

See the leader give you a big smile and stop shaking. Then you hug. See them go over and spread the good news to the rest of the characters. Then watch them all leave your body in any way you wish.

'Flu (and Colds)

The 'flu is caused by an infection with the influenza virus (as opposed to the common cold, which is infection with rhinovirus). It usually results in fever, sore throat, cough and aches and pains over the body.

Use the colds visualization, the infections visualization, the viruses visualization or the sore throat visualization.

Gastroenteritis
See Enteritis.

Glands (Swollen Glands)

1. Picture the swollen glands like inflated balloons. Notice how inflated they are.

Now untie the balloons and watch the air rush out. Hear the whooshing or rasping sound as the air rushes out (it's fun to listen to it like this and it will make you smile) and the balloons deflate, one at a time. See each balloon get smaller and smaller until it is completely deflated.

For extra smiles, imagine each balloon shouting, 'I'm melting! Melting!' just like the Wicked Witch of the East from *The Wizard of Oz* when Dorothy accidentally throws water on her. If no one is around to see you (or if they are and you just don't care), wave your hands in the air and make melting actions. It's a little like a victory dance.

2. Imagine a bustling nightclub called Glands that's full to the brim with people. It's at bursting point. Now see the bouncers start to clear people out. As they do so, notice that there is much more space to breathe and move around. Glands is no longer full to the brim and your glands are no longer swollen.

You could also (or instead) use the infections visualization.

Gonorrhoea
Gonorrhoea is one of the most common sexually transmitted diseases. It is usually characterized by a burning sensation while urinating and sometimes a discharge.

Use the infections visualization or the following:

Imagine the site of pain or infection and rub a magical blue soothing gel onto each of the cells there, one at a time. See them at first as red and inflamed, but once you rub on the gel, see (or hear) them breathe a sigh of relief, then see their swelling reduce and them return to normal.

Alternatively:

Imagine the red and inflamed cells as inflated balloons. Imagine letting the air out of the balloons and hear the whooshing or rasping sound as the cells return to normal size and colour.

Haemorrhoids

Haemorrhoids are swollen veins in the anus or rectum.

Picture the haemorrhoids like balloons with air in them. Now untie the balloons and watch the air rush out. Hear the whooshing or rasping sound as the air pours out (it's fun to listen to it like this, and it will make you smile, especially as this is a sound quite familiar to that area!) and the balloons deflate, one at a time. See each balloon get smaller and smaller until it is completely deflated.

Hay Fever

Use the allergies visualization and, if you wish, in addition:

Imagine yourself walking through a field of freshly cut grass where there is loads of pollen. But you feel great and have absolutely no symptoms of hay fever. Laugh as you revel in the fact that you are no longer affected by pollen. Do a victory dance.

Heart Disease

Heart disease is a collective term for a number of different cardiovascular diseases.

1. Imagine the heart and imagine some of the damaged cells like shrivelled-up prunes or any other way that you imagine damaged cells to look. Now take an imaginary cloth and some magical pink or green cleaning fluid (pink symbolizes love, green symbolizes regeneration) and gently clean the cells one by one, restoring them to perfect health.

2. The heart symbolizes love, so imagine putting more love into it. Imagine speaking to your heart and tell it that you love it deeply and unconditionally. Give it a hug.

   Now imagine its beat. Maybe you can actually feel or hear it. Now imagine a soft pink or green light at the centre of your heart and watch it expand with every beat, a little at a time. Watch it get bigger and brighter with each beat. Also, see some little pink or green heart-shaped bubbles floating into your heart (perhaps you can even imagine angels blowing them there). As you do this, see the heart muscle get stronger and healthier. Now see the light expand out through your arteries, effortlessly dissolving any plaque or cholesterol deposits.

   You could take the visualization further if you feel that it would be good for you. Watch the light continue to expand outwards until your entire body is engulfed by it. Watch the light moving out through your body's systems. As it expands through cells, watch the cells laugh and hug each other each. They are being 'tickled pink', so to speak (if you're using pink light).

   As the light expands through your organs, watch them beat or flex in sublime health. See large smiles appear on the faces of their cells as the light from your heart is feeding health into every part of your body. Watch it move through your liver and kidneys and other organs.

   Watch the light travel to the brain and see the brain glow with the light. See the brain cells dance with delight as they are bathed in the healing light.

Returning your thoughts to the heart, watch its muscles flex and pump with the ease and effortlessness of an Olympic champion, effortlessly pumping blood around the body. It is beautiful. Hear the power too, as if you were standing right beside the beat.

Hepatitis

Hepatitis is inflammation of the liver through infection with any of the hepatitis viruses, A, B or C (D and E also exist but are less common).

Use the infections visualization or the viruses visualization. Although hepatitis is a viral infection, we often tend to think of infections as bacterial. As this is what we culturally think, it is therefore sufficient to use the infections visualization.

Additionally or alternatively, the following is a visualization that you can also use alongside, or at the end of, the infections or viruses visualization, or you can use it in place of them. It will help if you have liver damage as a result of the infection.

1. Imagine your damaged liver cells looking shrivelled-up and black. Now take an imaginary cloth and some magical green cleaning fluid and clean the cells one by one, restoring each one to perfect health.

2. Picture your liver cells as tightly inflated balloons. One by one, let the air out of them and listen to the whooshing or rasping sound as the air rushes out. See each cell, one by one, return to normal size and a healthy pink colour.

HIV

HIV is infection by human immunodeficiency virus. The relationship between HIV and AIDS is often misunderstood. AIDS (acquired immune deficiency syndrome) is the term normally used when a person's immune cell count (specifically their blood CD4 lymphocytes) drops beneath a certain level and they suffer from certain 'opportunistic' infections. Many people infected with HIV are never diagnosed with AIDS. So there isn't an AIDS virus. There is an HIV virus, which lowers the immune system to a level where opportunistic infections occur and a diagnosis of AIDS is made.

The severity of an HIV infection is down to the fact that the virus docks onto receptors on immune cells (CD4 T lymphocytes, which are often called T-cells). The immune cells are then destroyed. But before the T-cell is destroyed, more virus is replicated and released into the bloodstream. Thus the virus multiplies and the T-cell count reduces.

For HIV, use the viruses visualization. Also use the immune booster visualization. Also use the visualizations for any specific AIDS-related illness.

Alternatively, imagine the receptors that the virus docks onto on the immune cells. Imagine that they are playing a game of changing their shape so that HIV can't recognize them and therefore can't dock onto them and get into the cell. For fun, you could see the receptors disguising themselves by putting on funny wigs, large glasses or big teeth.

Imagine different ways in which the receptors could have fun preventing the HIV virus from getting into the cell. For instance, they could even turn themselves inside out or emit a sound that confuses the virus.

See the virus eventually giving up and just leaving the body.

Hypertension
See Blood Pressure.

Immune System

1. Immune cells begin their life in your bone marrow. Imagine being inside the bone marrow and see a factory that's producing immune cells. See the ingredients on conveyor belts being assembled and then eager immune cells popping out of the end. See them in any way you wish – shape, colour, etc.

There's a big dial on the wall that indicates the speed at which the immune cells are being produced. Note the setting. If it is low, then turn it up – feel yourself doing this – and watch the conveyor belt speeding up as though it's just been given a turbo boost. Watch an increased number of immune cells popping out of the end of the conveyor belt.

Watch them move out of your bone marrow, along your arteries and veins, and all around the body. See them move specifically to wherever the infection is located, neutralizing any bacteria, viruses or other pathogens.

2. Imagine teams of little construction workers constructing immune cells. See them working in a large factory, like an aircraft hanger, that's made of bone.

Imagine several of them at each table, assembling all the parts, and when each new cell is created, see it breathe with life (see it with a little smiling face), eager to get out into the body to start mopping up invaders.

See a constant stream of new immune cells leave the factory and head out into the body. See them gobbling up infection or disease.

Infections

Many diseases and conditions are caused by infections, so this visualization can be applied to any of them. It can be used for both bacterial and viral infections.

1. Use an imaginary suction hose or vacuum cleaner and suck up all of the bacteria. See the bacteria in any way you wish (e.g. as little flecks of black pepper, as brown or black sludge, as little brittle pieces of rocky substance, or as little coloured organisms). Hear the sound of your suction device as it sucks up the particles, and feel the force of the suction. Make it as real as possible. Continue until the area is free of any remaining bacteria, virus or other pathogen.

2. Switch on an imaginary power hose and direct the jet at the bacteria. Feel the force of the water rushing through the hose and hear the whooshing sound. See the bacteria fragment as they are blasted off the walls of your body parts.

   Clean up any residue or fragments of bacteria with a brush and dustpan or a vacuum cleaner, or watch globby Pac-man-like cells of the immune system jump up and swallow the pieces of bacteria. For extra smiles, when each cell has gobbled up loads of bacteria and is getting full, watch (and listen to) it burp.

3. Imagine a shower of crystal-clear healing water that pours in through the top of your head and flushes infections away.

   Imagine the feeling as the water pours through your body and out through the soles of your feet. Initially see it as dark brown as you begin to flush out the infection, but gradually see it become lighter and lighter as the infection is flushed away. Eventually only clear water flows out from the soles of the feet as all of the infection is flushed away.

4. To protect yourself from infection if people around you are sick, imagine yourself surrounded by a large bubble. If you perceive any infectious agents flying towards you, see them simply bounce off the bubble.

If you believe in angels, then you could even ask an angel to surround you with one of their bubbles of protection. This is useful if you are in a crowded place and you see someone cough or sneeze close by or if someone in your family has 'flu or something else that is infectious.

Insomnia

1. As you lie in bed, with each out-breath imagine all of your muscles sinking relaxed into the bed, and as you do this, mentally say the word 'sleep' very slowly: 'Ssssllleeeeeeeeeeeeeppp...'

2. Imagine that you have drunk a delicious natural healthy drink. It has the effect of relaxing your body with every breath you take. Its soothing effects flow into every muscle and relax it. At the same time it calms your mind and allows you to put to one side any thoughts or anxieties, so that you can drift off peacefully into a wonderfully deep sleep.

Irritable Bowel Syndrome (IBS)
IBS is often characterized by diarrhoea, abdominal pain and bloating.

Imagine your bowel and gently stroke it. Treat it the way you would treat someone who was feeling irritable. Irritable people just need some tlc, so give your bowel some tlc so that it doesn't feel irritable anymore. Give it a hug, gently stroke it and tell it that you love it. Imagine it saying it loves you too.

Strike up a conversation with it. Ask it what's wrong and if there's anything you can do to help. Maybe it'll tell you to cut out a food or drink that you regularly take, or to eat or drink something you don't normally do. Or maybe it'll suggest that you don't get so stressed about things. Listen to its advice.

Your intuitive picture of your bowel might at first appear as something with a wee angry face on it, spitting and hissing, but after some real care from you, see its face soften and then give you a big smile.

Even if this sounds silly, whoever said visualization had to be a serious thing? It's the thought that counts!

Low Self-esteem
Use the first depression visualization.

Lupus
Lupus (systemic lupus erythematosus, SLE) is an autoimmune condition. With lupus, the immune system can attack almost any organ or tissue, but it is often known for its attack on the skin – many people with lupus have a bright red rash on their face.

Use the autoimmune visualization. In addition, or alternatively, you could do specific visualizations to heal some of the areas that are affected by lupus.

Malaria
Malaria is caused by infection with the plasmodium genus of protozoa from the bite of an infected mosquito. The parasite invades and destroys red blood cells. It causes recurring (cyclic) fever and chills, sweating, fatigue and even jaundice and anaemia.

Use either the protozoa visualization or the infections visualization to neutralize the infection. You could also, or alternatively, use the immune booster visualization if you wish that as your strategy. If you use the immune booster, when the new immune cells reach the protozoa, see them eating the protozoa. And for extra smiles, imagine each immune cell letting out a loud long burp when it is full.

ME (Myalgic Encephalomyelitis) or CFS (Chronic Fatigue Syndrome)

ME is characterized by chronic mental and physical exhaustion.

Imagine a ball of light inside the brain that represents 'your power'. Notice its size and colour and how bright it appears to you. You might perceive that it isn't too bright at the moment and this would symbolize your feelings of weakness. However, your true power is much greater than this. With ME, the light has just been turned down, so you're about to turn it back up again.

Imagine turning up a dial and see the light get brighter and brighter (this is a great image for expanding your power in general). Watch the light of your power growing in intensity. You might even see a scale or meter beside it that indicates the power. Watch it go up. As it gets brighter, watch the meter reading go up. As it gets brighter, feel the light expand outwards so that it is lighting up your entire body.

See the light expand through all of the muscles and over the skin. See it light up each of the organs too so that the entire body, inside and out, is aglow with this beautiful, powerful light that represents your power. It has been suppressed but it is not suppressed any longer. It is out and you are a strong, fit, healthy and powerful person. Affirm this to yourself.

You might even imagine yourself running, jumping and laughing (lots).

Finish with an imaginary victory dance. See yourself doing your dance in celebration of your great strength. This will actually produce happy chemicals in your brain. The more regularly you do it, the more powerful the effect. You will soon be able to do a real victory dance.

Some theories of ME say that it is caused by a build-up of toxins in the body. Therefore you could also use the toxins visualization to rid the body of toxins.

Measles

Measles is caused by the measles virus, which is characterized by fever followed by a red rash.

You could use the viruses visualization for this and could also, or alternatively, do a visualization specifically for the skin rash:

1. Imagine each cell in the rash as red. Now take an imaginary cloth and some imaginary coloured cleaning fluid and get to work cleaning the cells one by one. As each is cleaned, it is restored to its normal colour.

2. Alternatively, you can take an imaginary eraser and simply erase the red colour from each cell, revealing a nice skin-coloured cell underneath.

Meningitis

Meningitis is inflammation of the meninges, which are the protective membranes covering the nerves of the central nervous system. Two main types exist – viral and bacterial. Viral is the less serious.

Use the infections visualization. The following is an additional visualization that that you could use:

Imagine kitting yourself out with a whole host of equipment – everything you can think of to completely remove the infection.

See the infection on the meninges in any way you wish. Now start shooting, blasting, sucking up, cleaning, spraying, lasering, whatever, until you have totally neutralized the infection. Put as much determination as necessary into this. And just to add a dimension of magical cleverness to this, all of your equipment can only harm infections. None of it can cause any harm to the meninges.

Spend as much time as you need to until the infected areas are totally purged of all infection. Look around you and examine your handiwork. Clear up any debris in whichever way you want (dustpan and brush, vacuum cleaner or globby Pac-man-type immune cells eating it all up).

Once it's clean, you might even give all the meninges a coat of magical 'immune paint' – a magical formula that prevents reinfection. Step back and admire the amazing clean-up job you've done. It all looks so beautiful.

Multiple Sclerosis

MS is an autoimmune disease where the immune system attacks the myelin sheath that coats axons (the arms of neurons). Therefore communication down axons is affected. Myelin is a white fatty substance.

Use the autoimmune visualization. In addition, imagine regrowing the myelin sheath as follows:

Imagine a nerve without its protective coating in any way that feels right for you. As an example, you could see it as an exposed copper wire from which the insulating plastic has worn off or as a tree with no bark. Or get a picture from a medical textbook or from the internet.

Now imagine teams of construction workers repairing the nerve, adding insulating myelin – a protective white fatty substance – all the way along the nerve. Or if you wish, add the myelin yourself.

Muscle Tears

Imagine teams of construction workers repairing the muscle tear. See them make new muscle fibres and knit them together to join the two ends of the tear. Also, see blood flowing into the area and carrying nutrients to nourish the muscle.

Imagine yourself beside the muscle tear. Imagine using magical threads to stitch it back together. With each stitch, pull the fibres together and see them fit seamlessly together.

Obesity

For obesity, you can use the same visualization as the one for weight loss or you can try one of the following. The weight visualizations will work best alongside diet and lifestyle changes.

1. Imagine fat cells melting like blocks of ice. See each cell totally melt into a pool of liquid. Melt each cell one by one. Then clean up any residue (e.g. with an imaginary mop and bucket or a suction device).

A chemical known as leptin produces an 'I'm full' signal in the brain, but there's scientific evidence to suggest that obese people are more resistant to the signal, hence they don't feel as full as others and this causes them to overeat. In some people, the OB gene (the gene that produces leptin) may actually be faulty, which might predispose them to eat more.

2. If you are told that you have a faulty OB gene and are therefore not producing enough leptin, then you could visualize OB as a little character lying on the ground as though it's been hurt. You might even see 'OB' written on its T-shirt or cloak.

Now nurse it back to life again, showing great care, compassion and attention. Give it some medicine and nutrients. See it growing stronger, giving off a glow of light.

Once it's healthy, imagine it diving into DNA. See the DNA flex with great power and a pulse of light travel its length.

Now imagine fat evaporating from the places you want it to.

If your body has become desensitized to leptin, so less able to hear the 'I'm full' call, try the following. Normally, leptin travels to the hypothalamus in the brain, where it docks onto leptin receptors. So for this visualization, we're going to assume that the leptin receptor can't hear the leptin calling.

3. Imagine a leptin molecule in any way you wish (perhaps a little brightly coloured organic shape) running about inside the hypothalamus of the brain, shouting, 'I'm full!' but not being heard. The receptor is asleep. See it on the surface of the cell in any way you wish (perhaps also a coloured shape but one that the leptin molecule could fit into).

   Imagine going over to it and giving it a shake to wake it up. It suddenly wakes, saying, 'Sorry, my alarm didn't go off' (or something of your choice that represents it waking). It stands to attention as it sees the leptin calling out, 'I'm full!' The leptin moves closer and the two hug or shake hands before the leptin disappears down the hole and into the cell.

   It's a bit of fun, but that's good.

4. Imagine yourself being the ideal weight that you want to get to. Infuse the image with fun and appreciation for all the great things about being that weight. See yourself doing some of the things that you would do and see people's reactions to you with your ideal weight and shape.

   Change the image into a light of any colour you wish and move it to the areas of fat that you want to get rid of. Imagine the fat evaporating and your body area morphing into your desired size and shape.

Pain

1. Imagine a dial indicating your pain level and slowly turn the dial down. If you feel any further waves of pain, decide where they register on your dial and turn it down again.

2. Imagine pain signals travelling up a nerve (a pain nerve) from the painful area to nerve cells in your brain (pain actually originates in the brain. It just feels as though it's at the site of any injury). Two nerves communicate with each other by sending signals across a gap between them. So imagine putting a piece of insulating polystyrene between the ends of two nerves that carry the pain signal. Imagine the pain signal travelling up the nerve like fizzles of electricity dancing along a wire and then hitting the polystyrene and just fizzling out so that no signal passes across the gap. And this is a magical piece of polystyrene because it only prevents pain signals. See signals of different colours jump through the polystyrene and affirm that it's only pain that can't get across. It allows every other type of signal in and out of your brain.

3. The following is technically not a visualization but it is quite effective for many people. Pain intensifies when we try to resist feeling it. So instead of resisting it, try to feel it. Focus completely on it. As you become aware of it, you are shifting your consciousness to an awareness that you are not the body, you are the intelligence that is aware of the body and its pain. It is a subtle shift, but a deep unconscious recognition like this can neutralize pain.

Palpitations
See Arrhythmia.

Parkinson's Disease

Parkinson's disease is characterized by muscle tremors and rigidity, mostly due to reduced production of and release of dopamine in the basal ganglia of the brain (of which the striatum is part). It's an area that connects with the movement-control area (motor area).

1. Imagine brain cells that are supposed to be producing dopamine. Picture them made of a spongy material. Now imagine giving them a squeeze and see dopamine squirt out. See the dopamine as little bubbles in any colour you wish and see them float onto the branches of nearby brain cells (like tree branches).

When each bubble touches a branch, see a pulse of electricity travel through your brain, along the nerves and into each muscle that you wish to move. Imagine moving your hands perfectly.

If you wish, you can imagine inside the area of the brain that isn't producing and releasing enough dopamine and instead of squeezing the sponge, turn up an imaginary dial and see little dopamine molecules being made and squirting out.

2. Imagine a dopamine factory inside the basal ganglia with a big sign above it saying 'Dopamine Factory'. Imagine a supervisor rushing in and saying, 'We've got a big order just come in. We need to increase production.'

Then see loads of teams of little construction workers making dopamine (imagine dopamine in any way that you wish) and loading it into big trucks where it is then taken out and released into the brain. See the little dopamine molecules swim across to the ends of the branches on a part of the brain with a big sign above it saying 'Motor Area'. The motor area is the area that controls movement.

See the dopamine molecules being absorbed into the branches of the brain cells and see electric charges pulsing along the nerves.

In addition, reread the examples of the use of mental imagery for Parkinson's and stroke rehabilitation described in Chapter 6 and do what the subjects did (for one hour, twice a week, imagine moving your muscles as if you were totally recovered. You can do more if you wish.).

Peptic Ulcer

Peptic ulcers are caused by the bacterium Helicobacter pylori and are characterized by abdominal pain, especially if fatty food is eaten.

Use the infections visualization to neutralize the Helicobacter bacteria.

In addition, or alternatively, imagine the ulcer as a small pit full of gravel in your stomach, mixed with goo. If you have ever had a mouth ulcer, imagine it's like that, but in your stomach.

Use an imaginary suction hose or vacuum cleaner to suck up all of the gravel and goo. Now imagine teams of workers filling the hole, adding new stomach-lining cells one by one. See the new cells join together perfectly, like bricks of jelly, until the hole has been filled and the stomach lining is restored to its perfect self.

Pneumonia

Pneumonia is inflammation of the lungs that is usually caused by a bacterial infection.

Use the infections visualization. You could also use the immune booster visualization.

Additionally, or alternatively, imagine being inside your lungs and notice the redness and inflammation. See the individual swollen cells. Now imagine letting the swelling out of them, like you would let air out of a balloon. Listen to the whooshing or rasping sound as the air whooshes out of the cells. See them return to normal size and a healthy pink colour.

Protozoa Infections

Protozoa are single-celled organisms that can infect the body. They act like parasites because they take over cells that they infect. For instance, the plasmodium species of protozoa that produce malaria infect and take over red blood cells.

1. Imagine surrounding your cells with a protective bubble that prevents any parasites from entering the cell. Watch them trying to get in but bouncing off the bubble. After a few attempts, watch the parasites give up and fly out of your body.

2. Imagine talking to the parasites and asking them to leave your body because they are harming you. Notice that they didn't know that they were harming you. They were just looking for food. Tell them that there is plenty of food in the world for them.

   Now see them fly out of your body. See them land in a distant forest where they can safely eat all they want.

Rheumatoid Arthritis

Rheumatoid arthritis is an autoimmune disease that causes the immune system to attack the joints.

Use the autoimmune visualization. In addition, or alternatively, use the arthritis visualization.

Scars

See the scars section of the Acne visualization.

Sciatica

Sciatica is caused by compression of the sciatic nerve.

1. To symbolize sciatic pain, imagine that the sciatic nerve is squashed underneath a boulder. Picture the nerve in any way you wish (perhaps as a taut rope).

   Now imagine rolling the boulder away and freeing up the nerve. See the tension reduce in the nerve as it returns to its normal position.

2. Imagine the sciatic nerve stretched to the right or left (away from its normal lie) and tight around a bone or muscle, like a piece of rope pulled tight around a tree or a rock.

   Now imagine gently pulling the nerve off the bone or muscle and help it to gently recoil back to its proper position. As it recoils, feel the tightness relax as you hold the nerve in your hands.

You could use the Pain visualization to neutralize the pain if you prefer that strategy.

Sinusitis

Sinusitis is caused by bacterial infection with streptococcus pneumoniae or haemophilus influenzae and leads to inflammation of the paranasal sinuses, which are air-filled spaces within the bones of the face. This can cause a blockage of the small opening from the sinus to the nose, which means that mucus can't drain freely. The resulting pressure build-up causes pain in the face or head.

1. Imagine the pressure like a highly inflated balloon. Notice how inflated it is.

   Now let the air out of it. Imagine the whooshing or rasping sound as the air rushes out. Now imagine the fluids flowing freely in the sinuses again.

2. Imagine red inflated cells that are so swollen that they are blocking a tunnel (the passage between the sinuses and the nose) and fluid can't get through.

Imagine a valve and now turn it to deflate the cells, like letting air out of a balloon. Hear the whooshing or rasping sound as the air rushes out and the cells return to normal size. And as they do, see fluid effortlessly pass through the tunnel.

You could, instead or also, use the infections visualization to tackle the infection.

Sleeping Problems
See Insomnia.

Sore Throat
See Throat.

Spinal Cord Injury
With some spinal cord injuries the spinal cord is severed, but with most injuries it remains intact but damage leads to loss of movement. The following visualizations can be done for either condition, as they are symbolic of re-establishing communication.

1. If you've ever seen a fibre optic cable, you'll know that it consists of hundreds of individual fibre optics. Imagine the spinal cord injury as a break in some of these individual 'wires' – a break in the nerves of the spinal cord.

Now imagine reconnecting the nerves, one by one, with magic thread. Tie it around one end and then thread it up to the other end of the nerve and pull the two ends together until they connect.

As each individual nerve is repaired, imagine a pulse of electricity flow across the newly repaired section in any colour you like.

Then see a pulse flow from your brain to any part of your body (whichever part that you intuitively feel is now connected). As you repair more and more nerves, imagine pulses going to every part of your body.

2. Alternatively, instead of using magic thread, you could imagine rubbing some magical fertilizer on the end of the severed nerve. Now watch the nerve grow towards the other end of the break (as if you were watching a plant or flower grow in time-lapse photography). If it only grows so far, then add some more fertilizer until the two ends connect together and the break is healed. Then see the pulse of electricity as above.

3. Imagine the inside of the bone marrow. See a room, cave or cavern full of stem cells resting. Communicate with them and ask them to become spinal cord cells. Imagine them excitedly saying, 'Yes!' They were just waiting for instructions.

See them move out of the bone marrow and travel to the site of spinal injury. Notice what the healthy spinal cord cells look like and now watch the stem cells morph into cells of that type and fit seamlessly alongside healthy cells. As the new cells take their place, see the damage to the spinal cord become fully repaired.

4. Just as with the motor imagery studies described in Chapter 6, where success was obtained for tetraplegic patients, you can also try some motor imagery. Pick a movement, for instance a finger movement. Imagine moving the finger over and over and over again. This will help to regenerate your brain maps.

Spots
See Acne.

Stress

The following visualization is one that can be done when you are feeling stressed:

1. Imagine your stress as an inflated balloon. Notice how inflated it is. Now take a deep breath, untie the balloon and let the air out. Hear the whooshing sound as the air flows out of the balloon. See it completely deflate. For extra smiles, imagine the rasping sound of the stress balloon deflating as you breathe out. You can do this as many times as you need to until you feel relaxed and calm.

   Once you feel calm, notice that your stress balloon is completely flat, symbolizing that your stress level has reduced to zero. The more you do this, the better you will get at it, until you only need to do it once to relax.

2. Imagine the stress in your mind. See it as a fizzling, sparking ball of light. Now imagine a dial with the words 'Stress Level' written above it. Note the level that the dial points to. Take a deep breath and, as you exhale, turn it down. As you do this, watch the light get smaller and smaller and smaller, until it disappears completely with a 'pop'.

3. Imagine a glass of liquid (clear or any colour you wish). It is a glass of calm. Now imagine taking a drink. See the calm liquid flow down your throat and into your body. Feel it flow into every part of your body – head, face, shoulders, arms, hands, torso, etc.

4. Imagine all of the things, people and situations that you feel stressed about. Put them all in one place and now shrink the image down smaller and smaller and smaller until it is as small as a pea. Now take it in your hands and flick it away. Imagine yourself with super strength so you can flick it right out of the village, town, city, country or planet.

Stroke

A stroke is the term used to describe a rapid loss of brain function due to a loss of blood supply. It is often accompanied by loss of use of one side of the body. The following visualizations are designed to rebuild the damaged area of the brain.

Imagine that the inside of the damaged area of the brain looks like a field of burned-out trees and bushes. It looks as though there's been a forest fire or as if an area has been deforested and all that's left is barren land.

Now imagine sowing new seeds. Place a seed in the ground and watch it grow into a tree (neuron). You can get a picture of one from a medical textbook or from the internet. Note the similarity of neural connections to the branches on a tree.

See this happen over several seconds, as if you were watching time-lapse photography of a plant or flower growing from seed to adult in a few seconds. Watch the tree grow branches.

Now sow another seed and see it also grow into a tree. And as its branches grow, see some of the branches of the two trees reach out and grow towards each other and connect.

When two branches connect, imagine a pulse of electricity flow from one to the other and then down into a part of the body where movement is impaired.

Plant more seeds, watch them grow, see the branches connect to those of nearby trees and watch the electricity pulse. Replant the entire forest.

There are two ways that you can do this. First, you could imagine planting just a bit of the forest with each visualization, maybe a few metres square, and watching the seeds grow into trees (neurons) right before your eyes. With each visualization you can plant more and more of the forest, so that after weeks or months you have regrown the entire forest and watched the new connections forged.

Second, you can sow the entire forest with seeds and imagine the trees growing gradually. Thus, you might see all of them growing over a period of weeks or months from seedlings to small plants to tall trees. You could show great care and patience as you nurture the baby trees, perhaps even talking to them as you would to a child, and showing them how to connect with one another. Eventually see the forest fully grown.

Reread the examples of stroke rehabilitation that used mental imagery (*see pages 71 and 77*). Every day, imagine moving your muscles as if you were totally recovered.

Syphilis

Syphilis is a sexually transmitted disease that's caused by infection with the treponema pallidum spirochete bacterium.

Use the infections visualization. The treponema pallidum bacterium is a spirochete (corkscrew-like) shape, so, to enhance the visualization, you could imagine the bacteria as little spirals, like pasta.

Throat (Sore Throat or Throat Infection)

You can use the visualization for infections if you wish to tackle your sore throat by neutralizing the infection or you could try the following:

Imagine spraying magical ice-cool vapour all over the red and sore area. Imagine the cool feeling. Imagine that the magical ice-cool vapour also acts like an eraser. See the redness fade to a healthy pink colour and see any swelling reduce to nothing, as if you have let air out of a balloon.

Toxins

Many substances are toxic to the body including mercury, cobalt, lead, rock dust (silica) and asbestos, also food contaminants, pesticides, and industrial solvents and chemicals.

This visualization can also be applied to any illness where you feel that there is something in your body that you want to remove. For instance, you could apply it to cancer (to remove the cancer), bacterial, viral and protozoa infections, ME or even pain.

1. Imagine crystal-clear cleansing water entering through the top of your head, flowing through your body and out through the soles of your feet. Feel it flowing through your body – through your head, shoulders, arms, torso, buttocks, legs and feet.

   At first, see it emerge from the soles of your feet as dark in colour – as dark as you feel represents the degree of toxicity in your body. But as the cleansing water continues to flow into you, see it become paler and paler as it exits your feet, until it is as crystal-clear as it was when it entered the top of your head, and there are no more toxins left in your body.

2. Imagine you have a circular net, like the ones that you use to filter dirt from stones in your garden. Imagine drawing the net from the top of your head down through your body and out of your feet, capturing toxin particles along the way. Notice the toxins in the net and dispose of each load by transporting them to the sun, where they are burned up, providing a little extra heat for the Earth.

3. Imagine the toxins as little flecks of dust or dirt sticking to tissues and organs throughout your body and use an imaginary vacuum cleaner to suck them up.

Tuberculosis (TB)

TB is caused by the mycobacterium tuberculosis bacteria, which affects the lungs. The bacteria are small rod-shaped organisms (which means that you can be quite specific with your visualizations).

1. If you imagine that some of your cells are sick because they have been hurt by the TB bacteria, you can imagine nursing them back to health one by one.

   Give them little spoonfuls of special nutrients which are made of everything that a cell could possibly need and are really tasty. See the cells smile and say, 'Mmmmmm,' as they eat each spoonful of medicine. See a healthy colour return to their faces and then see them grow stronger and stronger. See them glow with a green regenerative light, which gets brighter as their strength increases. See them regain their full strength.

2. Imagine you are inside your bone marrow. See a room, cave or cavern full of stem cells resting. Communicate with them and ask them to become whichever cells that TB has damaged. Imagine them excitedly say, 'Yes!' They were just waiting for instructions.

   See them move out of the bone marrow and travel to the area that's damaged by TB (e.g. lungs). Notice what healthy cells look like in this area (there will always be healthy ones around) and now watch the stem cells morph into cells of that type and fit seamlessly alongside healthy cells. As the new cells take their place, see the damaged area fully regenerate.

Additionally, or alternatively, use the infections visualization.

Ulcer

See Peptic Ulcer. The peptic ulcer visualization can be applied to any type of ulcer.

Varicose Veins

Varicose veins are overly dilated veins, mostly in the legs.

> Imagine a vein as overly inflated and that it has a valve on top of it. Now slowly release the air from the valve. Imagine the sound of air rushing out, as if you've let the air out of a balloon or an airbed. Imagine a balloon deflating as you do this and use this image to imagine the inflated vein shrinking back to normal. Do this for each vein.

Viruses

The following visualizations can be applied to any viral infection:

1. Imagine the receptors that the virus docks onto on the immune cells. Imagine that they are playing a game and change their shape so that the virus can't recognize them and can't dock and get into the cell. For fun, you could see the receptors disguising themselves by putting on funny wigs, large glasses or big teeth.

   Imagine different ways in which the receptors could have fun preventing the virus from getting into the cell. For instance, they could turn themselves inside out or emit a sound that confuses the virus.

   See the virus eventually giving up and just leaving the body.

2. Talk to the viruses and tell them that they are causing harm to your body. Imagine them saying that they didn't realize this. Lovingly communicate with them and ask them to leave. Then see them leaving your body with big smiles on their faces.

3. Imagine using a computer inside your body. Type the words, 'Upload universal anti-virus program [or some other title that represents a program that can cancel any virus and cannot be corrupted].' Press 'Enter.' See the words fly off the screen and turn to lights (any

colour that comes to mind). See them multiply into millions and millions of lights and move throughout your body. See them go wherever your mind takes them – into your bloodstream, to your organs, your throat, nose, etc. See your whole body glowing with the light.

Warts and Verrucas
Warts and verrucas are small areas of roughened skin caused by the human papilloma virus (HPV). They can be flat or raised.

1. Imagine taking some coloured acid and rubbing it onto the cells in the wart or verruca. Watch them dissolve. Hear the fizzling sound. As each cell is dissolved, watch as the wart or verruca gets smaller and smaller and smaller.

2. Talk to the warts and tell them that you don't need them anymore. Thank them for being a part of your life. Watch the cells leave and wave goodbye to you, while wearing big smiley faces.

Weight Loss
The following visualizations will work best along with some exercise and a healthy diet.

1. Imagine little Pac-men or piranha fish nibbling away at the fat that you want to be rid of. See them really enjoying eating the fat. Watch them get fatter and fatter. When they are really full, imagine them leaving your body with big satisfied smiles on their faces. See them replaced with new hungry Pac-men or piranhas.

2. Imagine the cells in your fatty areas. Go along the cells and imagine sucking the fat out with a hose. And as each cell is emptied of fat, imagine the skin tightening up and returning to a normal cell. Imagine each cell looking just the way you want it to.

3. Imagine that there's a little piston inside the fat on your body with a sign above it saying 'Fat Burn'. Imagine that it's going up and down really slowly. This represents the rate at which the fat is burning off you. Imagine there's a little dial on the side of the piston with speed settings. Turn it up and watch the little piston get faster and faster. Or imagine the foreman standing beside the piston. Ask him to turn the rate up and hear him enthusiastically say, 'Yes.'

Now imagine a factory chimney, only it's no ordinary chimney. It's burning your fat. Watch the smoke pour out of the top of the chimney and imagine the sound of the horn, like the one a steam train makes. Previously it was hardly visible but now there must be an inferno down below. See the smoke travel out of your body.

Alternatively, you could use either the first or third obesity visualization.

Worm Infections

Worm infections are so widespread that they infect around three billion people, especially in tropical and developing countries. Many worms live in the intestines, but some travel to other organs as they mature.

Ask to see a colour or type of light that the worms don't like so much. Now see a tiny light of this colour or type inside the body where the worms are located. Now turn up a dial and watch the light get brighter and brighter. See it get too much for the worms, without hurting them (just like we might move from the hot sun into the shade). Imagine the worms leaving the body.

Alternatively, you could lovingly communicate with them and ask them to leave.

Appendix III

DNA Visualizations

**It is the marriage of the soul with Nature that makes
the intellect fruitful, and gives birth to imagination.**
Henry David Thoreau

This section contains two visualizations. I created the first several years ago and thought it would be useful to include in the book because it can be applied to just about anything. The second visualization, which is more specific, can be applied to conditions where a person has been told that they have a faulty gene.

DNA is composed of around 25,000 genes, which I like to visualize as Christmas-tree lights, because they are constantly switching on and off. When genes switch on they produce proteins, enzymes, hormones and many other substances, so the body grows and repairs through genes being switched on and off.

The point of this visualization is to symbolically switch off some genes that produce proteins that cause or sustain an illness or disease and to switch on other genes that produce proteins that cure it. I call these sets of genes 'genetic programs'.

This is a symbolic visualization. Nervous tissue is not connected to DNA and we don't switch specific genes of our choice on and off. I believe that when we do a symbolic visualization, we give our body instructions regarding what we want to happen. The body then uses whichever biological pathways are necessary to get there. This visualization is useful for people who have an interest in the mind–DNA interface, and allows people to be more specific in their visualization in a different way from the previous visualizations.

THE FIRST VISUALIZATION

Imagine the body part where the disease/illness/condition is focused. Imagine going inside and seeing its cells. Now go inside the cells and see the DNA. If you don't know what DNA looks like, either get a picture of it from the internet or from a book or imagine it as organic intertwined strands, like two strands of spaghetti intertwined (twisted around each other like braids in hair). Now add lightbulbs to your mental picture, right along the length of the strands.

Now mentally say, 'Show me the genetic program that produces the proteins that sustain this disease/illness/condition.' Imagine some genes (one, two, or as many as you feel right with) lighting up relative to the other genes, as if your body intelligence was highlighting the exact genes that are involved.

Take a deep breath and as you exhale, imagine turning down a dial to the 'off' position and see the lights go dimmer and dimmer and dimmer until they have completely gone out as you fully exhale.

Now mentally say, 'Show me the genetic program that produces the proteins that can heal this disease/illness/condition.' Imagine some genes (one, two, or as many as you feel right with) become slightly highlighted relative to the rest. As you inhale, imagine turning the dial to the 'on' position and see the lights become

brighter and brighter and brighter until they are very bright as you fully inhale. And as you exhale, see them retain their brightness.

Now imagine coming back out of your cells, look at them and mentally say, 'Show me that it is done.' Imagine your cells breathing with new life and notice any other changes that pop into your mind's eye. Sometimes visible changes or other images spontaneously arise with visualization.

For instance, depending upon what you apply this to, imagine the diseased cells or body part returning to normal. If you have cancer, see the tumour(s) shrink down to nothing, as if they had a valve and all the air has just been drained from them.

Accept these images as confirmation that healing has taken place. Imagine your whole body now and see it move with grace and ease. See yourself in perfect health.

Say, 'Thank you. It is done. It is done. It is done.' This is how I like to finish this visualization. It adds a sense of completion and finality. The whole visualization need only take a few minutes.

The next visualization is the same as one of the visualizations listed for cancer and cystic fibrosis but I feel that it is important to reproduce it in this section too for other conditions.

Our knowledge of genetics and how genes create and cure illness, although seemingly quite advanced, is always expanding and we are constantly learning things that would have seemed impossible only a few years ago. I believe that, despite faulty genes, in many cases the body has the ability to function much better than expected. In some cases, a person may live in perfect health with few or no symptoms of an illness.

THE SECOND VISUALIZATION

Imagine the faulty gene lying on the ground as though it's been hurt. See it like a little hurt organism. Now nurse it back to life again, showing great care, compassion and attention. Give it some medicine and nutrients. See it growing stronger, giving off a glow of light. Over time, gradually see it gain its full strength. Then, once it's healthy, imagine it diving into the DNA. See the DNA flex with great power and a pulse of light travel its length. Then imagine the condition disappearing in any way that you wish.

References

CHAPTER 1

For the Mayo Clinic study of optimists and pessimists, see Toshihiko Maruta MD *et al.*, Mayo Clinic Proceedings, August 2002, or visit: www.sciencedaily.com/releases/2002/08/020813071621.htm

For the 2004 study involving 999 Dutch men, see E. J. Giltay, J. M. Geleijnse, F. G. Zitman, T. Hoekstra and E. G. Schouten, 'Dispositional optimism and all-cause and cardiovascular mortality in a prospective cohort of elderly Dutch men and women', *Archives of General Psychiatry*, 2004, 61, 1126–35.

For the nun study, see D. D. Danner, D. A. Snowdon and W. V. Friesen, 'Positive emotions in early life and longevity: findings from the nun study', *Journal of Personality and Social Psychology*, 2001, 80(5), 804–13.

For the study where volunteers were exposed to the cold or influenza viruses, see S. Cohen, C. M. Alper, W. J. Doyle, J. T. Treanor and R. B. Turner, 'Positive emotional style predicts resistance to illness after experimental exposure to rhinovirus or influenza A virus', *Psychosomatic Medicine*, 2006, 68, 809–15.

For an article containing the study of 200 telecommunications executives, see Peggy Rynk, 'The value of a healthy attitude: how faith, anger, humor, and boredom can affect your health', *Vibrant Life*, March–April 2003.

For the study of 586 people finding that attitude is the best prevention against heart disease, see D. M. Becker, 'Positive attitude is best prevention against heart disease', paper presented at the American Heart Association Annual Scientific Sessions, Anaheim, CA, 12 November 2001. To read an account of the study, visit: www. hopkinshospital.org/health_info/Heart/Reading/positive_attitude

For the study of 866 heart patients and positive attitude, see B. Brummett, 'Positive outlook linked to longer life in heart patients', paper presented at the American Psychosomatic Society, March 2003. To read an account of the study, visit: dukemednews.org/av/medminute.php?id=6511

For the emotional vitality study, see L. D. Kubzansky and R. C. Thurston, 'Emotional vitality and incident coronary heart disease: benefits of healthy psychological functioning', *Archives of General Psychiatry*, 2007, 64(12), 1393–1401.

For the Hard Marriage, Hard Heart research, see:

- T. W. Smith, C. Berg, B. N. Uchino, P. Florsheim and G. Pearce, 'Marital conflict behavior and coronary artery calcification', paper presented at the American Psychosomatic Society 64th Annual Meeting, Denver, CO, 3 March 2006.
- T. W. Smith, B. N. Uchino, C. A. Berg *et al.*, 'Hostile personality traits and coronary artery calcification in middle-aged and older married couples: different effects for self-reports versus spouse ratings', *Psychosomatic Medicine*, 2007, 69(5), 441–48.
- P. Pearsall, 'Contextual cardiology: what modern medicine can learn from ancient Hawaiian wisdom', *Cleveland Clinical Journal of Medicine*, 2007, 74(1), S99–S104.

For the 25-year hostility study, see J. C. Barefoot, W. G. Dahlstrom and R. B. Williams, 'Hostility, CHD incidence, and total mortality: A 25-year follow-up study of 255 physicians', *Psychosomatic Medicine*, 1983, 45(1), 59–63.

For the paper quoting hostility as an indicator of heart disease, see R. B. Williams, J. C. Barefoot and N. Schneiderman, 'Psychosocial risk factors for cardiovascular disease: more than one culprit at work', *Journal of the American Medical Association*, 2003, 290(16), 2190–92.

For the Finnish satisfaction study, see H. Koivumaa-Honkanen, R. Honkanen, H. Viinamäki, K. Heikkilä, J. Kaprio and M. Koskenvuo, 'Self-reported life satisfaction and 20-year mortality in healthy Finnish adults', *American Journal of Epidemiology*, 2000, 152(10), 983–91.

For the 'Money buys happiness' research, see Elizabeth Dunn, 'Money buys happiness when you spend on others: UBC and Harvard research', *University of British Columbia Media Release*, 20 March 2008. To view the media release, visit: www.publicaffairs.ubc.ca/media/releases/2008/mr-08-032.html

For the effect of attitude on ageing, see B. R. Levy, M. D. Slade, S. R. Kunkel and S. V. Kasl, 'Longevity increased by positive self-perceptions of ageing', *Journal of Personality and Social Psychology*, 2002, 83(2), 261–70.

For the study of positive attitude being good for blood pressure, see G. V. Ostir, I. M. Berges, K. S. Markides and K. J. Ottenbacher, 'Hypertension in older adults and the role of positive emotions', *Psychosomatic Medicine*, 2006, 68, 727–33.

For the study linking frailty with attitude, see G. V. Ostir, J. Ottenbacher and K. S. Markides, 'Onset of frailty in older adults and the protective role of positive affect', *Psychology and Aging*, 2004, 19(3), 402–08.

For the link between life satisfaction and longevity, see T. M. Lyyra, T. M. Törmäkangas, S. Read, T. Rantanen and S. Berg, 'Satisfaction with present life predicts survival in octogenarians', *The Journals of Gerontology Series B: Psychological Sciences and Social Sciences*, 2006, 61, 319–26.

For the Posit Science Corporation study, see:

• H. W. Mahncke, B. B. Connor, J. Appelman, O. N. Ahsanuddin, J. L. Hardy, R. A. Wood, N. M. Joyce, T. Boniske, S. M. Atkins and M. M. Merzinich, 'Memory enhancement in healthy older adults using a brain plasticity-based training program: a randomized, controlled study', *Proceedings of the National Academy of Sciences, USA*, 2006, 103(33), 12523–28.

- H. W. Mahncke, A. Bronstone and M. M. Merzinich, 'Brain plasticity and functional losses in the aged: scientific basis for a novel intervention', *Progress in Brain Research*, 2006, 157, 81–109.

For the Harvard age study going back to 1959, see Ellen J. Langer PhD, *Mindfulness* (Da Capo Press, 1990).

For information on using the brain and reducing the risk of Alzheimer's, see R. S. Wilson, C. F. Mendes de Leon, L. L. Barnes, J. A. Schneider, J. L. Bienias, D. A. Evans and D. A. Bennett, 'Participation in cognitively stimulating activities and risk of incident Alzheimer's disease', *Journal of the American Medical Association*, 2002, 287(6), 742–48.

For the priming experiments, see:

- J. A. Bargh, M. Chen and L. Burrows, 'Automaticity of social behavior: direct effects of trait construct and stereotype activation on action', *Journal of Personality and Social Psychology*, 1996, 71(2), 230–44.
- T. M. Hess, J. T. Hinson and J. A. Statham, 'Explicit and implicit stereotype activation effects on memory: do age and awareness moderate the impact of priming?', *Psychology and Aging*, 2004, 19(3), 495–505.

CHAPTER 2

The quotation from Professor Benedetti can be found in F. Benedetti, 'Mechanisms of placebo and placebo-related effects across diseases and treatments', *Annual Review of Pharmacology and Toxicology*, 2008, 46, 33–60. This is also a good review of recent research into the placebo effect.

For the release of dopamine when Parkinson's patients receive placebos, see:

- R. de la Fuente-Fernández, T. J. Ruth, V. Sossi, M. Schulzer, D. B. Calne and A. J. Stoessl, 'Expectation and dopamine release: mechanism of the placebo effect in Parkinson's disease', *Science*, 2001, 293(5532), 1164–66.
- R. de la Fuente-Fernández, A. G. Phillips, M. Zamburlini, V. Sossi, D. B. Calne, T. J. Ruth and A. J. Stoessl, 'Dopamine release in human ventral striatum and expectation of reward', *Behavioural Brain Research*, 2002, 136(2), 359–63.

The first evidence of opioid release during placebo analgesia can be found in J. D. Levine, N. C. Gordon and H. L. Fields, 'The mechanism of placebo analgesia', *Lancet*, 1978, 654–57.

For an account of placebo effects tracking closely the treatments with which they are paired, and a discussion of the similarity in brain scans while patients receive Prozac or a placebo, see F. Benedetti, H. S. Mayberg, T. D. Wager, C. S. Stohler and J.-K. Zubieta, 'Neurobiological mechanisms of the placebo effect', *Journal of Neuroscience*, 2005, 25(45), 10390–402.

For the MRI brain scans of people receiving placebos and high placebo responses, see:

- J.-K. Zubieta, J. A Bueller, L. R. Jackson, D. J. Scott, Y. Xu *et al.*, 'Placebo effects mediated by endogenous opioid activity on m-opioid receptors', *Journal of Neuroscience*, 2005, 25, 7754–62.
- T. D. Wager, D. J. Scott and J.-K. Zubieta, 'Placebo effects on human m-opioid activity during pain', *Proceedings of the National Academy of Sciences, USA*, 2007, 104(26), 11056–61.

For some clinical trial results, visit: www.clinicaltrialstoday.com/centerwatch_clinical_tria/clinical_trial_results/

For the chronic fatigue syndrome study that tested acyclovir, see S. E. Strauss, J. K. Dale, M. Tobi, T. Lawley, O. Preble, R. M. Blaese, C. Callahan and W. Henle, 'Acyclovir treatment of the chronic fatigue syndrome. Lack of efficacy in a placebo-controlled trial', *New England Journal of Medicine*, 1988, 319(26), 1692–98.

For the study using hydrocortisone, visit: www.hhs.gov/news/press/
1996pres/961013.html

For the effect of placebo on benign enlargement of the prostate, visit:
www.accessmylibrary.com/coms2/summary_0286-9308314_ITM

For the placebo studies on asthma, see:

• T. Luparello, H. A. Lyons, E. R. Bleecker and E. R. McFadden,
'Influences of suggestion on airway reactivity in asthmatic
subjects', *Psychosomatic Medicine*, 1969, XXX, 819–25.

• E. R. McFadden, T. Luparello, H. A. Lyons and E. R. Bleecker,
'The mechanism of action of suggestion in the induction of acute
asthma attacks', *Psychosomatic Medicine*, 1969, XXXI, 134–43.

For the study of performance-enhancing placebos, see F. Benedetti,
A. Pollo and L. Colloca, 'Opioid-mediated placebo responses
boost pain endurance and physical performance: is it doping in
sport competitions?', *Journal of Neuroscience*, 2007, 27(44),
11934–39.

For the study involving the hotel-room maids, visit: www.npr.org/
templates/story/story.php?storyId=17792517

For the study of women's beliefs affecting their mathematics
performance, see I. Dar-Nimrod and S. J. Heine, 'Exposure to
scientific theories affects women's math performance', *Science*,
2006, 314(5798), 435.

For information on placebo responders, as well as lots of information
on a range of placebo studies, see Daniel Moerman, *Meaning,
Medicine and the 'Placebo Effect'* (Cambridge University Press,
2002).

The 1954 bleeding ulcers study was reported in Daniel Moerman's
book (above).

For the study involving hidden arm pain, see F. Benedetti, 'The
opposite effects of the opiate antagonist naloxone and the
cholecystokinin antagonist proglumide on placebo analgesia',
Pain, 1996, 64(3), 535–43.

For the dental injections given with an 'oversell' or 'undersell' message, see S. L. Gryll and M. Katahn, 'Situational factors contributing to the placebo effect', *Psychopharmacology*, 1978, 57(3), 253–61.

For the study on the effect of positive and negative consultations, see K. B. Thomas, 'General practice consultations: is there any point in being positive?', *British Medical Journal*, 1987, 294, 1200–02.

For the studies of optimists and pessimists and how they respond in the placebo effect, see the following:

• For the pessimists study, see A. L. Geers, S. G. Helfer, K. Kosbab, P. E. Weiland and S. J. Landry, 'Reconsidering the role of personality in placebo effects: dispositional optimism, situational expectations, and the placebo response', *Journal of Psychosomatic Research*, 2005, 58(2), 212–17.

• For the optimists study, see A. L. Geers, K. Kosbab, S. G. Helfer, P. E. Weiland and J. A. Wellman, 'Further evidence for individual differences in placebo responding: an interactionist perspective', *Journal of Psychosomatic Research*, 2007, 62(5), 563–70.

For the conditioned immunosuppression using cyclosporin A, see M. U. Goebel *et al.*, 'Behavioral conditioning of immunosuppression is possible in humans', *FASEB Journal*, 2002, 16, 1869–73.

For Benedetti's conditioning of immune and growth hormone levels, see F. Benedetti, A. Pollo, L. Lopiano, M. Lanotte, S. Vighetti and I. Rainero, 'Conscious expectation and unconscious conditioning in analgesic, motor, and hormonal placebo/nocebo responses', *Journal of Neuroscience*, 2002, 23, 4315–23.

CHAPTER 3

For the 2008 antidepressants analysis that found over 80% placebo effect, see I. Kirsch, B. J. Deacon, T. B. Huedo-Medina, A. Scoboria, T. J. Moore and B. T. Johnson, 'Initial severity and antidepressant benefits: a meta-analysis of data submitted to the food and drug administration', *PLoS Medicine*, February 2008, 5(2), e45, 0260–68.

A number of the studies reported in this chapter were also cited in Daniel Moerman's excellent book, cited above. I thoroughly recommend it to anyone seeking a fuller understanding of the placebo effect and its implications.

For the quote from C. G. Helman, see his chapter entitled 'Placebos and Nocebos: The Cultural Construction of Belief' in *Understanding the Placebo Effect in Complementary Medicine: Theory, Practice and Research*, ed. D. Peters (Churchill Livingstone, 2001).

For the study of blue and pink sedatives and stimulants, see B. Blackwell, S. S. Bloomfield and C. R. Buncher, 'Demonstration to medical students of placebo responses and non-drug factors', *Lancet*, 1972, 1(7763), 1279–82.

For the study of injections versus tablets in the USA and Europe, see A. J. de Craen, J. G. Tijssen, J. de Gans and J. Kleijnen, 'Placebo effect in the acute treatment of migraine: subcutaneous placebos are better than oral placebos', *Journal of Neurology*, 2000, 247(3), 183–88.

For the study of Tagamet performed in France, see R. Lambert *et al.*, 'Treatment of duodenal and gastric ulcer with cimetidine. A multicenter double-blind trial', *Gastroenterologie Clinique et Biologique*, 1977, 1(11), 855–60. For the study in Brazil, see J. A. Salgado, C. A. de Oliveira, G. F. Lima Jr and L. de Paula Castro, 'Endoscopic findings after antacid, cimetidine and placebo for peptic ulcer – importance of staging the lesions', *Arquivos De Gastroenterologia*, 1981, 18(2), 51–3. Both studies are reported in Daniel Moerman's book, cited above.

The reduction in effectiveness of Tagamet once Zantac was available is described in Damiel Moerman's book. It is also mentioned in Herbert Benson MD's *Timeless Healing* (Scribner, 1995).

For the University of Keele aspirin study, see A. Branthwaite and P. Cooper, 'Analgesic effects of branding in treatment of headaches', *British Medical Journal*, 1981, 282, 1576–78.

For the suggestion that Viagra is enhanced by its name, see A. K. Vallance, 'Something out of nothing: the placebo effect', *Advances in Psychiatric Treatment*, 2006, 12, 287–96.

For the study of four placebos being better than two in anti-ulcer trials, see A. J. de Craen, D. E. Moerman, S. H. Heisterkamp, G. N. Tytgat, J. G. Tijssen and J. Kleijnen, 'Placebo effect in the treatment of duodenal ulcer', *British Journal of Clinical Pharmacology*, 1999, 48(6), 853–60.

For adherence in the clofibrate trial, see Coronary Drug Project Research Group, 'Influence of adherence to treatment and response of cholesterol on mortality in the coronary drug project', *New England Journal of Medicine*, 1980, 303(18), 1038–41.

For adherence in the propranolol trial, see E. J. Gallagher, C. M. Viscoli and R. I. Horwitz, 'The relationship of treatment adherence to the risk of death after myocardial infarction in women', *Journal of the American Medical Association*, 1993, 270(6), 742–44.

For adherence in the antibiotic trial, see P. A. Pizzo, K. J. Robichaud, B. K. Edwards, C. Schumaker, B. S. Kramer and A. Johnson, 'Oral antibiotic prophylaxis in patients with cancer: a double-blind randomized placebo-controlled trial', *Journal of Pediatrics*, 1983, 102(1), 125–33.

For the real versus sham mammary ligation studies, see:
- E. G. Dimond, C. F. Kittle and J. E. Crockett, 'Comparison of internal mammary artery ligation and sham operation for angina pectoris', *American Journal of Cardiology*, 1960, 5, 483–86.
- L. A. Cobb, G. I. Thomas, D. H. Dillard, K. A. Merendino and R. A. Bruce, 'An evaluation of internal-mammary-artery ligation by a double-blind technique', *New England Journal of Medicine*, 1959, 260(22), 1115–18.

For the naproxen study where patients either knew or didn't know that they were receiving it, see J. F. Bergmann, O. Chassany, J. Gandiol, P. Deblois, J. A. Kanis, J. M. Segrestaa, C. Caulin and R. Dahan, 'A randomised clinical trial of the effect of informed consent on the analgesic activity of placebo and naproxen in cancer pain', *Clinical Trials Meta-Analysis*, 1994, 29(1), 41–7.

The Benedetti quote, 'The existence of the placebo effect suggests that we must broaden our conception of the limits of... human capability,' can be found in F. Benedetti, H. S. Mayberg, T. D. Wager, C. S. Stohler and J.-K. Zubieta, 'Neurobiological mechanisms of the placebo effect', *Journal of Neuroscience*, 2005, 25(45), 10390–402.

CHAPTER 4

For the study of brain changes in symphony musicians, see V. Sluming, T. Barrick, M. Howard, E. Cezayirli, A. Mayes and N. Roberts, 'Voxel-based morphometry reveals increased gray matter density in Broca's area in male symphony orchestra musicians', *NeuroImage*, 2002, 17(3), 1613–22.

The reference to brain-map changes as blind people learn Braille can be found in Norman Doidge MD, *The Brain That Changes Itself* (Penguin, 2007).

For the study of brain changes while students were studying for exams, see B. Draganski, C. Gaser, G. Kempermann, H. G. Kuhn, J. Winkler, C. Büchel and A. May, 'Temporal and spatial dynamics of brain structure changes during extensive learning', *Journal of Neuroscience*, 2006, 26(23), 6314–17.

For the London taxi drivers study, see E. A. Maguire, K. Woollett and H. J. Spiers, 'London taxi drivers and bus drivers: a structural MRI and neuropsychological analysis', *Hippocampus*, 2006, 16, 1091–101.

For the study showing brain changes in mathematicians, see K. Aydin, A. Ucar, K. K. Oguz, O. O. Okur, A. Agayev, Z. Unal, S. Yilmaz and C. Ozturk, 'Increased gray matter density in the parietal cortex of mathematicians: a voxel-based morphometry study', *American Journal of Neuroradiology*, 2007, 28(10), 1859–64.

For the study of the effects of meditation on the brain, see S. W. Lazar, C. E. Kerr, R. H. Wasserman, J. R. Gray, D. N. Greve, M. T. Treadway, M. McGarvery, B. T. Quinn, J. A. Dusek, H. Benson, S. L. Rauch, C. I. Moore and B. Fischl, 'Meditation experience is associated with increased cortical thickness', *Neuroreport*, 2005, 16(17), 1893–97.

The Eric Kandel quote, as well as a discussion of brain changes due to psychotherapy, can be found in Norman Doidge's book, cited above.

For the study showing 15% increase in hippocampal volume due to environmental enrichment, see G. Kemperman, D. Gast and F. H. Gage, 'Neuroplasticity in old age: sustained fivefold induction of hippocampal neurogenesis by long-term environmental enrichment', *Annals of Neurology*, 2002, 52, 135–143. See also L. Lu, G. Bao, H. Chen, P. Xia, X. Fan, J. Zhang, G. Pei and L. Ma, 'Modification of hippocampal neurogenesis and neuroplasticity by social environments', *Experimental Neurology*, 2003, 183(2), 600–09.

For discovery of neurogenesis in the hippocampus, see P. S. Eriksson, E. Perfilieva, T. Björk-Eriksson, A.-M. Alborn, C. Nordborg, D. A. Peterson and F. H. Gage, 'Neurogenesis in the adult human hippocampus', *Nature Medicine*, 1998, 4(11), 1313–17.

The identification of neurogenesis right up to our final days can be found in the paper cited immediately above, on the discovery of neurogenesis in adults. The scientists received permission from terminally ill patients to inject them with a biological marker, bromodeoxyuridine (BrdU). When the patients died, neurogenesis was discovered.

For a good review of neurogenesis, see P. Taupin and F. H. Gage, 'Adult neurogenesis and neural stem cells of the central nervous system in mammals', *Journal of Neuroscience Research*, 2002, 69, 745–49.

CHAPTER 5

For a good description of the brain and how it changes with our thoughts and emotions, see Joe Dispenza, *Evolve Your Brain* (Health Communications Inc., 2007).

For the research showing that hostility slows the rate of wound healing, see J. K. Kiecolt-Glaser, T. J. Loving, J. R. Stowell, W. B. Malarkey, S. Lemeshow, S. L. Dickinson and R. Glaser, 'Hostile marital interactions, proinflammatory cytokine production, and wound healing', *Archives of General Psychiatry*, 2005, 62(12), 1377–84.

For the effects of stress on growth hormone levels and on the 'upregulation' and 'downregulation' of genes at wound sites, see S. Roy, S. Khanna, P.-E. Yeh, C. Rink, W. B. Malarkey, J. Kiecolt-Glaser, B. Laskowski, R. Glaser and C. K. Sen, 'Wound site neutrophil transcriptome in response to psychological stress in young men', *Gene Expression*, 2005, 12(4–6), 273–87.

For social support speeding up wound healing, see C. E. Detillion, T. K. S. Craft, E. R. Glaser, B. J. Prendergast and A. C. DeVries, 'Social facilitation of wound healing', *Psychoneuroendocrinology*, 2004, 29(8), 1004–11.

Trumping our genes refers to the science of epigenetics. To learn more about epigenetics, see Bruce Lipton, *The Biology of Belief* (Hay House, 2008). See also Dawson Church, *The Genie in Your Genes* (Elite Books, 2007).

For information on neurogenesis and the suggestion that the mind interacts with DNA in stem cells, see Ernest L. Rossi, *The Psychobiology of Gene Expression* (Norton, 2002).

CHAPTER 6

For the study where experimental pain was induced in fingers, see G. Montgomery and I. Kirsch, 'Mechanisms of placebo pain reduction: an empirical investigation', *Psychological Science*, 1996, 7(3), 174–76.

For the study involving capsaicin, see F. Benedetti, C. Arduino and M. Amanzio, 'Somatotopic activation of opioid systems by target-directed expectations of analgesia', *The Journal of Neuroscience*, 1999, 19(9), 3639–48.

In an email communication, I asked Fabrizio Benedetti whether a person with two different ailments would get better from one of them if he or she was given a placebo for that specific ailment (believing it to be a real drug) but not the other. Would a person with Parkinson's, say, who also had a headache, and who received an anti-Parkinson's drug (which was really a placebo) find the tremors reducing but not the headache, and vice versa? Professor Benedetti agreed that this would most likely be the case.

For the Karolinska Institute research showing that imagined movements of fingers, toes and tongue activated brain regions that governed them, see H. H. Ehrsson, S. Geyer and E. Naito, 'Imagery of voluntary movement of fingers, toes, and tongue activates corresponding body-part-specific motor representations', *Journal of Neurophysiology*, 2003, 90(5), 3304–16.

For the piano study, see A. Pascual-Leone, D. Nguyet, L. G. Cohen, J. P. Brasil-Neto, A. Cammarota and M. Hallet, 'Modulation of muscle responses evoked by transcranial magnetic stimulation during the acquisition of new fine motor skills', *Journal of Neurophysiology*, 1995, 74(3), 1037–45.

For the study where volunteers' fingers got 35% stronger through imagined training, see V. K. Ranganathan, V. Siemionow, J. Z. Liu, V. Sahgal and G. H. Yue, 'From mental power to muscle power – gaining strength by using the mind', *Neuropsychologia*, 2004, 42(7), 944–56. See also G. Yue and K. J. Cole, 'Strength increases from the motor program: comparison of training with maximal voluntary and imagined muscle contractions', *Journal of Neurophysiology*, 1992, 67(5), 1114–23.

For the study showing the differences in muscle activation depending upon the imagined weight, see A. Guillot, F. Lebon, D. Rouffet, S. Champely, J. Doyon and C. Collet, 'Muscular responses during motor imagery as a function of muscle contraction types', *International Journal of Psychophysiology*, 2007, 66(1), 18–27.

For the study where the tetraplegic person opened an email with his mind, see L. R. Hochberg, M. D. Serruya, G. M Friehs, J. A. Mukand, M. Saleh, A. H. Caplan, A. Branner, D. Chen, R. D. Penn and J. P. Donoghue, 'Neuronal ensemble control of prosthetic devices by a human with tetraplegia', *Nature*, 2006, 442, 164–71.

For research into mental walking in virtual-reality simulators, see G. Pfurtscheller, R. Leeb, C. Keinrath, D. Friedman, C. Neuper, C. Guger and M. Slater, 'Walking from thought', *Brain Research*, 2006, 1071(1), 145–52.

For mirror neurons research where volunteers watched hands, mouth or foot movements, see G. Buccino, F. Binkovski, G. R. Fink, L. Fadiga, L. Fogassi, V. Gallese, R. J. Seitz, K. Zilles, G. Rizzolatti and H.-J. Freund, 'Action observation activates premotor and parietal areas in a somatotopic manner: an fMRI study', *European Journal of Neuroscience*, 2001, 13(2), 400–04.

For the 'Bend it like Beckham' paper, see P. Bach and S. P Tipper, 'Bend it like Beckham: embodying the motor skills of famous athletes', *Quarterly Journal of Experimental Psychology*, 2006, 59(12), 2033–39.

For the study where volunteers increased finger strength through watching training, see C. A. Porro, P. Facchin, S. Fusi, G. Dri and L. Fadiga, 'Enhancement of force after action observation: behavioural and neurophysiological studies', *Neuropsychologia*, 2007, 45(13), 3114–21.

For improvements gained by stroke patients through watching people perform routine actions, see D. Ertelt, S. Small, A. Solodkin, C. Dettmers, A. McNamara, F. Binkofski and G. Buccino, 'Action observation has a positive impact on rehabilitation of motor deficits after stroke', *NeuroImage*, 2007, 36, Supplement 2, T164–73.

For activation of mirror neurons while watching someone playing a guitar, see G. Buccino, S. Vogt, A. Ritzl, G. R. Fink, K. Zilles, H.-J. Freund and G. Rizzolatti, 'Neural circuits underlying imitation learning of hand actions: an event-related fMRI study', *Neuron*, 2004, 42, 323–34.

For activation of the brain by listening to sentences describing motion, see G. Buccino, L. Riggio, G. Melli, F. Binkofski, V. Gallese and G. Rizzolati, 'Listening to action-related sentences modulates the activity of the motor system: a combined TMS and behavioral study', *Cognitive Brain Research*, 2005, 24(3), 355–63. See also M. Tettamanti, G. Buccino, M. C. Saccuman, V. Gallese, M. Danna, P. Scifo, F. Fazio, G. Rizzolatti, S. F. Cappa and D. Perani, 'Listening to action-related sentences activates fronto-parietal motor circuits', *Journal of Cognitive Neuroscience*, 2005, 17(2), 273–81.

For activation of tongue muscles by listening to speech, see L. Fadiga, L. Craighero, G. Buccino and G. Rizzolati, 'Speech listening specifically modulates the excitability of tongue muscles: a TMS study', *European Journal of Neuroscience*, 2002, 15(2), 399–402.

A good review of mirror neuron research is G. Buccino, A. Solodkin and S. L. Small, 'Functions of the mirror neuron system: implications for neurorehabilitation', *Cognitive and Behavioural Neurology*, 2006, 19(1), 55–63.

For information on increasing the sensitivity of your own body part by looking at someone else's, see P. Bach, N. A. Peatfield and S. P. Tipper, 'Focusing on body sites: the role of spatial attention in action perception', *Experimental Brain Research*, 2007, 178(4), 509–17.

For use of guided imagery for treatment of chronic obstructive pulmonary disease (COPD), see S. W.-S. Louie, 'The effects of guided imagery relaxation in people with COPD', *Occupational Therapy International*, 2004, 11(3), 145–59.

For the use of guided imagery for treatment of osteoarthritis in older women, see C. L. Baird and L. P. Sands, 'Effect of guided imagery with relaxation on health-related quality of life in older women with osteoarthritis', *Research in Nursing & Health*, 2006, 29(5), 442–51.

For the use of guided imagery for treatment of interstitial cystitis, see D. J. Carrico, K. M. Peters and A. C. Diokno, 'Guided imagery for women with interstitial cystitis: results of a prospective, randomized controlled pilot study', *Journal of Alternative and Complementary Medicine*, 2008, 14(1), 53–60.

For the effect of guided imagery on the reoccurrence of breast cancer, see L. Freeman, L. Cohen, M. Stewart, R. White, J. Link, J. L. Palmer and D. Welton, 'Imagery intervention for recovering breast cancer patients: clinical trial of safety and efficacy', *Journal of the Society of Integrative Oncology*, 2008, 6(2), 67–75.

For the use of guided imagery in wound healing after gallbladder removal surgery (cholecystectomy), see C. Holden-Lund, 'Effects of relaxation with guided imagery on surgical stress and wound healing', *Research in Nursing & Health*, 2007, 11(4), 235–44.

For the use of guided imagery for treatment of fibromyalgia pain, see E. A. Fors, H. Sexton and K. G. Götestam, 'The effect of guided imagery and amitriptyline on daily fibromyalgia pain: a prospective, randomized, controlled trial', *Journal of Psychiatric Research*, 2002, 36(3), 179–87.

For the effect of visualization ability, see:

• E. Watanabe, S. Fukuda, H. Hara, Y. Maeda, H. Ohira and T. Shirakawa, 'Differences in relaxation by means of guided imagery in a healthy community sample', *Alternative Therapies in Health and Medicine*, 2006, 12(2), 60–66.

• E. Watanabe, S. Fukuda and T. Shirakawa, 'Effects among healthy subjects of the duration of regularly practicing a guided imagery program', *BMC Complementary and Alternative Medicine*, 2005, 5, 21.

• K. Kwekkeboom, K. Huseby-Moore and S. Ward, 'Imaging ability and effective use of guided imagery', *Research in Nursing and Health*, 1998, 21(3), 189–98.

For use of mental imagery in stroke rehabilitation, see:

- S. J. Page, P. Levine and A. Leonard, 'Mental practice in chronic stroke: results of a randomized, placebo-controlled trial', *Stroke*, 2007, 38(4), 1293–97.
- S. J. Page, P. Levine and A. C. Leonard, 'Effects of mental practice on affected limb use and function in chronic stroke', *Archives of Physical Medicine and Rehabilitation*, 2005, 86(3), 399–402.

For use of mental imagery in rehabilitation after spinal cord injury, see S. C. Cramer, E. L. Orr, M. J. Cohen and M. G. Lacourse, 'Effects of imagery training after chronic, complete spinal cord injury', *Experimental Brain Research*, 2007, 177(2), 233–42.

For use of mental imagery by Parkinson's patients, see R. Tamir, R. Dickstein and M. Huberman, 'Integration of motor imagery and physical practice in group treatment applied to subjects with Parkinson's disease', *Neurorehabilitation and Neural Repair*, 2007, 21(1), 68–75.

For a summary of mental imagery research, see R. Dickstein and J. E. Deutsch, 'Motor imagery in physical therapist practice', *Physical Therapy*, 2007, 87(7), 942–53.

For use of visualization in asthma treatment, see L. W. Freeman and D. Welton, 'Effects of imagery, critical thinking, and asthma education on symptoms and mood state in adult asthma patients: a pilot study', *The Journal of Alternative and Complementary Medicine*, 2005, 11(1), 57–68.

CHAPTER 7

The reference for the 2004 meta-analysis linking stress with the immune system is S. Segerstrom and G. E. Miller, 'Psychological stress and the human immune system: a meta-analytic study of 30 years of inquiry', *Psychological Bulletin*, 2004, 130(4), 601–30.

For the effects of stress on composition of wound fluid, see E. Broadbent, K. J. Petrie, P. G. Alley and R. J. Booth, 'Psychological stress impairs early wound repair following surgery', *Psychosomatic Medicine*, 2003, 65, 865–69.

For the effects of stress on HIV and how it increases viral replication, see S.W. Cole, B. D. Naliboff, M. E. Kemeny, M. P. Griswold, J. L. Fahey and J. A. Zack, 'Impaired response to HAART in HIV-infected individuals with high autonomic nervous system activity', *Proceedings of the National Academy of Sciences, USA*, 2001, 98(22), 12695–700.

For the 18-month study linking shyness with rate of viral replication, see S. W. Cole, M. E. Kemeny, J. L. Fahey, J. A. Zack and B. D. Naliboff, 'Psychological risk factors for HIV pathogenesis: mediation by the autonomic nervous system', *Biological Psychiatry*, 2003, 54(12), 1444–56.

For the study where students wrote about traumatic experiences on four consecutive days, see J. W. Pennebaker and S. K. Beall, 'Confronting a traumatic event: toward an understanding of inhibition and disease', *Journal of Abnormal Psychology*, 1986, 95(3), 274–81.

For the effect of writing about traumatic experiences and the hepatitis B vaccination, see K. J. Petrie, R. J. Booth, J. W. Pennebaker, K. P. Davison and M. G. Thomas, 'Disclosure of trauma and immune response to hepatitis B vaccination program', *Journal of Consulting and Clinical Psychology*, 1995, 63(5), 787–92.

For the effect of writing on viral load and CD4 cell counts of HIV patients, see K. J. Petrie, I. Fontanilla, M. G. Thomas, R. J. Booth and J. W. Pennebaker, 'Effect of written emotional expression on immune function in patients with Human Immunodeficiency Virus infection: a randomized trial', *Psychosomatic Medicine*, 2004, 66, 272–5.

For effects of emotional support on the health of breast cancer patients, see B. L. Andersen, W. B. Farrar, D. Golden-Kreutz, C. F. Emery, R. Glaser, T. Crespin and W. E. Carson 3rd, 'Distress reduction from a psychological intervention contributes to improved health for cancer patients', *Brain, Behavior, and Immunity*, 2007, 21(7), 953–61.

For the effect of mindfulness-based stress reduction (MBSR) on the health of breast and prostate cancer patients, see:

- L. E. Carlson, M. Speca, P. Faris and K. D. Patel, 'One-year pre–post intervention follow-up of psychological, immune, endocrine and blood pressure outcomes of mindfulness-based stress reduction (MBSR) in breast and prostate cancer patients', *Brain, Behavior, and Immunity*, 2007, 21(8), 1038–49.

- L. E. Carlson, M. Speca, K. D. Patel and E. Goodey, 'Mindfulness-based stress reduction in relation to quality of life, mood, symptoms of stress and levels of cortisol, dehydroepiandrosterone sulfate (DHEAS) and melatonin in breast and prostate cancer outpatients', *Psychoneuroendocrinology*, 2004, 29(4), 448–74.

- M. Speca, L. E. Carlson, E. Goodey and M. Angen, 'A randomized, wait-list controlled clinical trial: the effect of a mindfulness meditation-based stress reduction program on mood and symptoms of stress in cancer outpatients', *Psychosomatic Medicine*, 2000, 62(5), 613–22.

For use of MBSR in control of glucose levels in type 2 diabetes patients, see S. Rosenzweig, D. K. Reibel, J. M. Greeson, J. S. Edman, S. A. Jasser, K. D. McMearty and B. J. Goldstein, 'Mindfulness-based stress reduction is associated with improved glycemic control in type 2 diabetes mellitus: a pilot study', *Alternative Therapies in Health and Medicine*, 2007, 13(5), 36–8.

For improvement in mood, and for reduced stress and anxiety in healthy adults using meditation, see J. D. Lane, J. E. Seskevich and C. F. Pieper, 'Brief meditation training can improve perceived stress and negative mood', *Alternative Therapies in Health and Medicine*, 2007, 13(1), 38–44.

For the effect of meditation at the genetic level, see J. A. Dusek, H. H. Otu, A. L. Wohlhueter, M. Bhasin, L. F. Zerbini, M. G. Joseph, H. Benson and T. A. Liberman, 'Genomic counter-stress changes induced by the relaxation response', *PloS ONE*, 2008, 3(7), e2576, 1–8.

NOTES

About the Author

David R. Hamilton gained a first-class honours degree in chemistry, specializing in biological and medical chemistry, and a PhD in organic chemistry before going on to be a scientist in the pharmaceutical industry in 1995. Over the next four years he also served as an athletics coach and team manager for one of the UK's top athletics clubs. He left both roles in 1999 and has since worked as a motivational speaker, co-founded an international relief charity, co-organized a nine-day, 24-event festival of peace called Spirit Aid and worked as a college lecturer in both chemistry and ecology. He has been featured on TV and radio and been the subject of national newspaper articles. He spends most of his time writing, giving talks and leading workshops.

For additional information, including details of events, lectures and workshops, see www.drdavidhamilton.com

Hay House Titles of Related Interest